# The People's Agents and the Battle to Protect the American Public

# The People's Agents and the Battle to Protect the American Public

*Special Interests, Government, and Threats to Health, Safety, and the Environment*

RENA STEINZOR AND
SIDNEY SHAPIRO

THE UNIVERSITY OF CHICAGO PRESS     CHICAGO AND LONDON

RENA STEINZOR is professor at the University of Maryland Law School and the author of *Mother Earth and Uncle Sam: How Pollution and Hollow Government Hurt Our Kids.*

SIDNEY SHAPIRO is University Chair in Law and Associate Dean for Research and Development at Wake Forest University. He is coauthor of several books, including *Sophisticated Sabotage: The Intellectual Games Used to Subvert Responsible Regulation.*

The University of Chicago Press, Chicago 60637
The University of Chicago Press, Ltd., London
© 2010 by The University of Chicago
All rights reserved. Published 2010
Printed in the United States of America
19 18 17 16 15 14 13 12 11 10     1 2 3 4 5

ISBN-13: 978-0-226-77202-8 (cloth)
ISBN-10: 0-226-77202-0 (cloth)

Library of Congress Cataloging-in-Publication Data

Steinzor, Rena.
    The people's agents and the battle to protect the American public : special interests, government, and threats to health, safety, and the environment / Rena Steinzor and Sidney Shapiro.
        p. cm.
    Includes bibliographical references and index.
    ISBN-13: 978-0-226-77202-8 (cloth : alk. paper)
    ISBN-10: 0-226-77202-0 (cloth : alk. paper) 1. Public safety—United States. 2. Public interest—United States. 3. Goverment accountability—United States. 4. Administrative agencies—United States. I. Shapiro, Sidney A., 1947– II. Title.
    HD4605.S74 2010
    363.1'060973—dc22

                                                                            2009044288

♾ The paper used in this publication meets the minimum requirements of the American National Standard for Information Sciences—Permanence of Paper for Printed Library Materials, ANSI Z39.48-1992.

# Contents

# Preface

Few envy the forty-fourth president or, for that matter, the Congress that serves with him. Confronted by a global economy in deep recession, high unemployment rates, failing industries, wars in Iraq and Afghanistan, the possibility that rogue nations like Iran and North Korea will obtain nuclear weapons, intensifying climate change, and frequent outbreaks of genocide in the developing world, their jobs appear impossibly hard. The enormous energy it will take to respond to these crises pushes more profound reform of domestic government far down on the list of foreseeable priorities. Yet our admittedly idealistic purpose in writing this book is to move such reforms—particularly in the area of protecting public health, safety, and the environment—to the head of the policy-making queue. We think our case is rock solid and our solutions are feasible, giving these issues the opportunity to compete successfully with apparently more urgent priorities.

To make our case, we will focus on the five most important agencies responsible for protecting people and natural resources from anthropogenic threats: the Consumer Product Safety Commission (CPSC), the Environmental Protection Agency (EPA), the Food and Drug Administration (FDA), the National Highway Traffic Safety Administration (NHTSA), and the Occupational Safety and Health Administration (OSHA). These agencies epitomize a pact between government and citizens that dates back to the turn of the twentieth century. The essence of this agreement, which even the harshest critics of regulation have never disowned, is that people should be able to enter the marketplace as consumers, workers, patients, and parents and use the environment's common resources (for example, ambient air, water, and public land), without fearing for their lives or suffering serious injury.

Over the last three decades, the five agencies have achieved remarkable success. During the 1960s and 1970s, rivers caught fire, cars exploded on rear impact, workers breathing benzene contracted liver cancer, and a chemical haze settled over the industrial zones of the country's cities and towns. Today, the most visible iterations of these threats are under control, and millions of people have been protected from death and debilitating injury.

But it is also true that for too many years now, the five agencies have spent a great deal of time resting on their laurels and, more recently, actively backsliding. Powerful external forces have undermined their confidence, not least the withering condemnation of meddlesome bureaucrats and oversized government by every president since Ronald Reagan. This rhetorical disrespect has taken its toll at the same time that a huge gap has developed between the statutory mandates assigned by Congress and the resources Congress and the president make available to carry out those instructions. Ideologues in the White House have second-guessed and micromanaged the judgment of career civil servants to an unprecedented extent. As the agencies shrink in fortitude and capacity, the problems they must address grow ever more complex, requiring them to be at the top of their game, not in a downward spiral.

One obvious example is the complications introduced by a globalized economy. Growing numbers of consumer products are manufactured abroad in factories that operate without any effective regulation. These trends mean that the American civil service has responsibility—but no authority—over large swaths of the marketplace. Another is the sophisticated science confirming our suspicion that we must deal with a global and not a national environment. Finding a way to get oil slicks off the Cuyahoga River was child's play compared with persuading developing and developed countries to negotiate a treaty on reducing the anthropogenic carbon emissions that cause climate change. In a sense, everything that came before was a dress rehearsal for the challenges that now confront us.

Health, safety, and environmental problems are vitally important in their own right, as we will demonstrate throughout this volume. We will also argue that these problems are corrosive to the country's well-being beyond their immediate effects. Because the American people want their government to address these issues effectively and comprehensively, when government fails to do so, its overall credibility is severely undermined.

The nation has engaged in an expansive debate about the role of government in international and domestic affairs. Which missions should we assign our military in the intensifying regional conflicts breaking out across the globe? Is it the government's job to blunt the worst effects of globalization on American workers and, if so, how? What kind of responsibility should the national government shoulder for helping millions escape poverty? What price will we pay for closing our borders to immigrants and attempting to prosecute the millions here illegally? People are divided, and politicians struggle to walk a middle line, on all of these questions.

In contrast, the public is not at all ambivalent about the government's role in policing dangerous products, drugs, and pollution. People sometimes worry about trade-offs between jobs and protecting the environment, but they also recognize that without regulation, we face serious, irreversible damage.[1] Americans are pessimistic about the state of the natural environment; 35 percent rate it as "fair," while 34 percent say it is "poor," and only 18 percent say it is "good."[2] By large majorities, Americans think that government intervention to protect the environment should be increased.[3]

If public support for a strong government role in ensuring health, safety, and environmental protection is so powerful, the converse is also likely to be true: failing to deliver on those expectations undermines people's overall confidence in government. This result occurs precisely because expectations are so high, especially with respect to the safety and purity of food, drugs, and consumer products and the maintenance of clean air and clean water. Or, to put this proposition another way, if the average American thought that she faced significant risk taking over-the-counter or prescription medicine, ordering a hamburger at a fast food chain, shopping at the local toy store, or allowing children to run around an urban playground on a hot summer day, she would blame the government, and not the dozens—even hundreds—of other entities involved in the chain reactions that create such risks. She might also wonder how the government could be so incompetent in the richest and, in its own self-concept, most powerful nation in the world.

Of course, this well-developed national consensus favoring a strong government role in protecting public health, safety, and natural resources wins only half the battle. We acknowledged earlier that to accomplish our goal of pushing the issues addressed here up the list of priorities for a new administration and Congress, pragmatic solutions must be at hand. As we see it, our job is not to write another tract explaining how serious these problems have become—the proverbial marketplace for ideas is glutted with such contributions—but rather to match our diagnosis of the reasons government is in trouble with an agenda of reasonable solutions.

In the pages that follow, we hew to one central theme: to fix government, you must rehabilitate it. We must revive the best American traditions of public service as an honorable, even noble calling. The government must recruit the best and the brightest to become civil servants, it must pay or otherwise compensate them on a par with comparable professionals in the private sector, and it must hold them accountable for their performance. Congress must get back to work, rewriting outmoded laws and adopting new tools for leveraging the best efforts from regulated industries. The courts must revert to a more traditional role, policing agencies to ensure that they stay true to their statutory mandates but not substituting judicial policy judgments for those made by civil service experts.

Grover Norquist, the influential conservative leader of the National Taxpayers Union, once said that he did not want to abolish government but rather simply hoped "to get it down to the size where we can drown it in the bathtub."[4] This visceral hostility, generally expressed in more diplomatic, opaque, and therefore confusing language, resonates throughout national politics with a power that is vastly underestimated. Just as the nation needs to move past the destructive polarization that has given its political leaders such convenient places to hide out, avoiding doing the "people's business" and embracing the most extreme wings of their respective bases, so does this attitude toward government need to change. No one has suggested an alternative to government in resolving the issues that concern us, and no one can reasonably dispute that the people want them solved.

*Rena Steinzor*
Baltimore, Maryland
*Sidney Shapiro*
Winston Salem, North Carolina

# Acknowledgments

Many people's ideas informed this work. First and foremost, we thank our friends and colleagues at the Center for Progressive Reform (CPR; http://www.progressivereform.org), a think tank of fifty-four Member Scholars who are working academics at universities across the country. The rich dialogues CPR has hosted made an important contribution to our work. We are especially grateful for the comments of Shana Jones, Matthew Freeman, Tom McGarity, Chris Schroeder, and Wendy Wagner, as well as the faculties at the University of Maryland and Wake Forest schools of law, each of which held workshops to critique the book as it was being developed.

We are also grateful to our academic institutions for their outstanding, tangible support of our work. University of Maryland research librarians Susan McCarty, Alice Johnson, and Maxine Grosshans provided exceptional cite checking, copyediting, and other research support; we could not have finished without them. Our research assistants—Joey Tsu-Yi Chen, Jay William Frantz, Shana Ginsburg, Marc Korman, Ryan Severson, and Xochitl Strohben—were enormously helpful; most of the detailed factual information in this volume is material they discovered, although they certainly bear no responsibility for the analytical mistakes we may have made. Matt Shudtz and Suzann Langrall helped us compile the budget figures in chapter 3, charting the resources in constant dollars of the five agencies that are the focus of the book, and we appreciate their careful, meticulous work very much.

We thank our families—Daniel, Hannah, Jeremy, Joyce, and Sarah—who have given us their unconditional patience and love as we argued over arcane details on the phone and in person. And we want to give special thanks to our editor at the University of Chicago Press, David Pervin, who from the beginning understood why the book was important to us and how it could become important to others.

# PART I
# Diagnosis

## CHAPTER ONE

# Public Interest Lost

## Introduction

When Barack Obama ran for president as what former secretary of state Colin Powell described as a "transformational figure,"[1] he defined the role of government as helping people when they cannot help themselves:

> Now, understand, I don't believe that government can or should try to solve all our problems. You don't believe that either. But I do believe that government should do that which we cannot do for ourselves—protect us from harm; provide a decent education for all children—invest in new roads and new bridges, in new science and technology. . . . Look, if we want [to] get through this crisis . . . we need to get beyond the old ideological debates and divides between the left and the right. We don't need bigger government or smaller government. We need better government. We need a more competent government. We need a government that upholds the values we hold in common as Americans.[2]

Without further elaboration, this fundamental principle—that government has a vital role to play in protecting people from harm—could lead to endless arguments in the arena of traditional social welfare programs over exactly when individual people cannot help themselves. But in the arena of protecting health, safety, and the environment, it is a serviceable, working proposition: when the threats are polluted urban air, dangerous drugs, and unsafe workplaces, individuals need government because control over the threat lies with someone else.

This book focuses on the five most important federal "protector agencies" created to shoulder these responsibilities—the Consumer Product

Safety Commission (CPSC), the Environmental Protection Agency (EPA), the Food and Drug Administration (FDA), the National Highway Traffic Safety Administration (NHTSA), and the Occupational Safety and Health Administration (OSHA). Each agency was established on the premise that the national government must play the primary role in protecting citizens, workers, and natural resources from the negative by-products of industrialization. Congress decided, in partnership with a long line of presidents from both political parties, that the agencies are essential because individual people, acting alone, cannot take care of these problems.

The FDA is the oldest protector, with a birth date in 1906, during the presidency of Theodore Roosevelt, a period of emerging industrialization and caveat emptor mercantilism. At the time, the marketplace was awash in products like Swaim's Panacea, a deadly combination of sarsaparilla, oil of wintergreen, and corrosive sublimate (or medical mercury), which was sold to treat everything from ulcers to venereal disease. In a series of amendments to the original law, Congress extended the FDA's mission beyond policing such dangerous frauds to an affirmative responsibility for ensuring that all drugs and food are safe and that drugs are effective. Following in those footsteps, Congress created the other four protector agencies at the height of the social reform movement spawned by the Vietnam War and the Watergate scandal in the 1960s and 1970s. The problems they were designed to address were more subtle by then, and far more ubiquitous. This period of extraordinary legislative activism marked the largest expansion of federal power since the New Deal.

Despite their idealistic origins, forty-five years later, the five agencies are in shambles. In some instances, they have proved unable to deal with highly publicized threats—consider the FDA and Vioxx or lead paint–coated toys and the CPSC. In other instances, their reputations have been shaken by lower profile yet systemic failures—consider inaction on climate change at the EPA or the dearth of controls on workplace exposure to toxic chemicals at OSHA. "Shambles" is a harsh word, and we use it advisedly. In fact, the agencies fall along a continuum of dysfunction. Two—the CPSC and OSHA—would not make it past any reasonable triage of effective institutions, just managing to stay open for limited business. At the opposite end of the spectrum lies the EPA, the poster child for the deregulatory backlash that dominated national politics for twenty years. Regardless of the negative attention lavished on it by deregulators, the EPA has managed to cut a wider and deeper swath through public affairs than the other agencies combined and has been brought to its knees only with considerable effort. In between, in less dramatic stages of disrepair, are the NHTSA and the FDA, which have clocked substantial achievements at the same time that emerging, important problems slip from their grasp.

Many of the agencies' problems are attributable to severe shortfalls in funding. They do not have nearly enough money to carry out their statutory mandates to keep air and water clean, prevent the sale of dangerous products, ensure food and drug safety, protect workers from injury and illness, and prevent traffic accidents. And yet, by any measure, the money we spend on them is extraordinarily modest, totaling about $10.3 billion, or 0.29 percent of the $3.5 trillion dollar budget Congress approved on April 2, 2009, and 0.89 percent of the $1.2 trillion deficit projected for fiscal year (FY) 2010. The five agencies also suffer from gaps in legal authority that undercut their ability to take decisive action in the face of urgent threats. Their career staffs are depleted and demoralized, repeatedly denounced for regulating too much or too little. Yet as much as they suffer from this negative attention, they are damaged much more by a chronic lack of attention from the president and Congress, except during the public crises provoked by their regulatory failures.

This chapter introduces readers to the five agencies and their missions. They are presented by the size of their workforces, from smallest to largest. With that framework established, and a clear idea of what they were intended to accomplish, we describe the symptoms that indicate they are gravely disabled. We do not attempt to present a definitive diagnosis of everything that troubles them. Not only would such a discourse bore anyone not working directly within their ambit, it would divert our attention from their cross-cutting problems and possible reforms. Rather, our explanations are intended to give the reader an accurate snapshot of today's regulatory failures. We do our best to avoid the discredited practice of cherry picking isolated examples of agency disgrace, no matter how acute and well publicized. Instead, we choose one or two issues that pose important challenges to the agencies and are illustrative of their inability to fulfill their statutory missions overall. Subsequent chapters examine the multiple causes of their paralysis as a prelude to reforms that might rescue the agencies.

Of course, each agency has its own individual problems, caused by unique historical events, the tactics of the regulated industries, the competence of the public interest groups, and the attitudes of the political appointees who lead them and the judges who sit in judgment on their decisions. Yet we hope to persuade readers that the commonality of their problems is far more meaningful. These themes, which we develop in the rest of the book, can and should be addressed holistically, renewing the rational justification for government intervention: protecting those who cannot help themselves.

## Consumer Products

*Thousands of Categories, Billions of Products*

The CPSC was created during the presidency of Richard M. Nixon in 1972, following an exhaustive study by an ad hoc entity called the National Commission on Product Safety.[3] The study estimated that as many as 20 million Americans were injured annually in their homes as a result of accidents involving consumer products, with 110,000 permanently disabled and 30,000 killed, at an annual estimated cost of $5.5 billion. In its early years, the CPSC was identified as having the potential to be the most powerful regulator in the federal constellation. It never came close to realizing that potential.

The CPSC estimates that it has jurisdiction over some 15,000 product categories including everything from backyard barbecues and electric drills to swimming pool slides and baby dolls. Or, to look at this vast jurisdiction another way, the CPSC is responsible for ensuring the safety of every consumer product except automobiles, aircraft, boats, drugs, firearms, food, and tobacco. In its heyday, circa FY 1981, the CPSC employed 891 "full-time equivalents" (FTEs) and had a budget of $41 million. Today, its resource levels are precipitously lower, coming in at approximately 420 FTEs and $80 million for FY 2008, despite a growth of 40 percent in the country's population. (Readers may notice that the budget figures we present vary by fiscal year. The government does not have a central Web site reflecting actual appropriations for all agencies and departments, leaving us dependent on individual agency Web sites that are updated erratically.)

The Consumer Product Safety Act assigns this sharply diminished workforce to "protect the public against unreasonable risks of injury" and to "assist consumers in evaluating the comparative safety" of products.[4] The CPSC is supposed to identify specific "defects" in design or construction that make a product dangerous even when it is used for its intended purpose with normal care. The statute authorizes the issuance of prospective, industry-wide standards for manufacturing safe products, but only if the manufacturers in question do not agree to develop their own "voluntary" standards that are adequate to reduce risks. As a practical matter, the CPSC staff routinely backs off issuing mandatory and enforceable standards if an industrial sector promises to come up with its own guidelines and to do its best to follow them. This approach means that only a handful of products—for example, fireworks, full-size cribs, and bike helmets—are actually covered by enforceable standards. Product-specific, after-sale "recall orders" have played a much larger role in the agency's regulatory history.

Recall orders are only applicable to products that pose a "substantial product hazard" and are typically used to require manufacturers and retailers to take products off shelves and to persuade consumers to return the items to the store.[5] To assist in the implementation of this authority, businesses must self-report instances for which they have information indicating that a product contains a defect that "could create" a substantial hazard. But because they depend heavily on free publicity and persuasion, recalls are notoriously ineffective. In FY 1997, the last year for which official figures are available, the CPSC estimated that the return rate on recalls was 16 percent.

To fulfill its missions of educating the public about hazardous products in the marketplace and highlighting areas in which enforcement action might be necessary, Congress instructed the CPSC to establish a National Electronic Injury Surveillance System. The system gets data from a representative sample of hospital emergency rooms regarding product-related injuries that come through their doors. The CPSC also gathers data from medical examiners and coroners about deaths that involve consumer products. All of this information could be used to project national injury trends and set priorities, especially in an era in which the World Wide Web makes data instantly accessible to individual consumers.

Congress anticipated that dissemination of this data could provide extraordinary disincentives to the manufacture and sale of defective products. But these businesses have worked hard to prevent such disclosures, arguing that because accidents are often caused by consumer negligence, the release of data would be deceptive, ruining the reputation of perfectly acceptable products at the same time that disclosure spotlights defects. They have clearly won this debate. Before the CPSC can release any information that identifies a specific manufacturer, it must submit the information to the company and allow a month for comment on the information's accuracy. Once these comments are received, the CPSC must investigate the manufacturer's concerns to determine whether or not they are accurate.

The CPSC initially interpreted all of these statutory restrictions to apply only to information it affirmatively wished to circulate. If the CPSC had information in its possession and a member of the public asked to see it, the agency would disclose the material without investigating accuracy. In 1980, the Supreme Court disagreed, holding that the CPSC's obligation to investigate before disclosing applied equally to information affirmatively released by the agency as well as citizen requests for information in its possession.[6] As its resources shrank in comparison with the amount of commerce it was assigned to supervise, and large manufacturers fought hard to prevent the release of such data, this burden became unsustainable. As one commentator with extensive experience as a CPSC attorney summarized it, "The Supreme Court's ruling constituted a disaster in terms of the agency's ability to release information either expeditiously or, in some cases, at all."[7]

But the CPSC's constituent industries were not quite finished with their campaign to curtail its disclosure authority. In 1981, at the outset of the first Reagan term, Congress amended the authorizing statute to circumscribe the release of the one set of data that should not have accuracy problems: notices written by the companies themselves explaining potential product defects.[8] The amendments forestalled release of manufacturer- and retailer-authored notifications that a product may cause substantial injury because, according to the Chamber of Commerce, making the information public would discourage companies from telling the government about their problems in the first place. To win authority to release the data, the CPSC must either take the company to court or engage in negotiations for a settlement with the company that would allow release of the information. The result is long delays in giving the public information about dangers the companies themselves acknowledge, including decisions by companies to voluntarily recall specific products. A report by Public Citizen found that even where the agency sued manufacturers for reporting significant defects late, the CPSC's own disclosures were delayed for long periods of time.[9] The report analyzed forty-six late notice cases that ended in product recalls and found that disclosure to consumers of the product hazard was delayed, on average, for 209 days.

As the 1981 amendments curtailing the CPSC's disclosure authority indicate, the agency came under heavy fire at the beginning of the Reagan administration, less than a decade after it was created, with some of its conservative critics proposing that Congress simply abolish it. When Congress would not agree to this radical solution, President Reagan settled for a 25 percent cut in the CPSC budget. The agency functioned in relative obscurity for many years, until 2007, when a tsunami of controversy hit it broadside.

## Poisoned Toys

Eighty percent of the toys sold in the United States are manufactured abroad, the vast majority in China. Because China has no effective regulatory structure, these imports cause a raft of new problems for the already weakened CPSC. The leading example is toys coated with lead paint, which were discovered to have flooded the U.S. market in 2007.

Ingestion of lead at very low levels can trigger poisoning serious enough to cause neurological damage in a child. The United States bans the use of lead paint in toys. But on August 14, 2007, Mattel, the world's largest toy company, announced that it was recalling some 426,000 die-cast toy cars that were coated with lead paint. The Mattel recall followed a spate of smaller recalls in 2007, the majority of which involved lead paint found in products from baby bibs to children's jewelry. Investigative reporting by the *New York Times* discovered that in China, paint with high lead levels costs one-third as much as paint with low or no lead because China is the largest producer of lead in the world and has increased its mining and processing of the toxic metal by 50 percent since 2001. Chinese executives admitted that their government does not inspect factories and that, although a national standard theoretically limits lead levels in consumer products, no one enforces it. Chinese and CPSC officials ultimately signed an agreement to ban lead in toys entirely, but it is unclear how the ban will be implemented.

Lead was not the only problem that surfaced in 2007, subsequently dubbed the "year of the recall" by consumer groups. Australian doctors found out that small beads sold as part of arts and crafts sets for children, which were also manufactured in China, released gamma hydroxybutyric acid, a powerful substance commonly referred to as the "date rape drug," when wet. Toddlers who gummed and swallowed the beads had seizures and went into comas. This discovery provoked a CPSC-ordered recall of 4.2 million Aqua Dots in early November 2007.

"If I went down the shelves of Wal-Mart and tested everything, I'm going to find serious problems," Sean McGowan, a toy industry investment expert, told the *New York Times*. "The idea that Mattel—with its high standards—has a bigger problem than everybody else is laughable. If we don't see an increase of recalls in this industry, then it's a case of denial."[10]

The Chinese toy recalls are likely to prove only the tip of the iceberg of the import problem. The value of Chinese imports in the United States marketplace is estimated to be approximately $246 billion, about 40 percent of the value of total products that the nation imports.[11] Consumer product imports from China surged to $246 billion from $62 billion between 1997 and 2007. Today, nearly 20 percent of consumer products for sale in America were made in China, compared with 5 percent in 1997.

At the time of the recalls, the CPSC had fifteen inspectors to police hundreds of billions of dollars worth of imports annually. As just one example of the mismatch between agency resources and the task at hand, Los Angeles area ports process 15 million truck-size containers annually, but only a single CPSC inspector, working two or three days a week, is available to spot-check them. None of the fifteen inspectors working nationwide have equipment capable of detecting lead in products. The only CPSC testing laboratory devoted to toys was in a cramped office in Washington, D.C. A single employee with outmoded equipment tested toys to see if they were shatterproof by dropping them in a small space behind the office door.

These embarrassing details prompted multiple congressional hearings regarding the adequacy of the CPSC's legal authority and budget. Finally, Congress passed legislation strengthening that authority and providing for significant budget increases; the Consumer Product Safety Improvement Act became law on August 14, 2008.[12] The new statute instructed the agency to issue a series of rules prohibiting the use of lead in toys, mandated that all toys have small tracking labels to aid in product recalls, and expanded protections that cover infant products like high chairs, seats, cribs, bassinets, and bathing equipment. Congress raised the CPSC's budget to $80 million, an increase of almost 30 percent, but not nearly enough to account for the increases in population, products, and complexity of its mission. In fact, Congress punted on imports, directing the CPSC to develop a "risk assessment methodology" and deliver a report to Congress for fielding inspectors at American ports and other entry points by 2011.

## Highway Safety

### The Little Agency That Stalled

> The toll of Americans killed [in crashes] since the introduction of the automobile is truly unbelievable. It is 1.5 million—more than all the combat deaths suffered in all our wars. . . . The carnage on the highways must be arrested. . . . [W]e must replace suicide with sanity and anarchy with safety — President Lyndon B. Johnson[13]

> [H]ighway safety has always been what I call a full contact sport. It's not a nice consensus-building operation. There are many fights, many disputes, especially when it centers around vehicle-related regulations or defect recalls. The issues become very acrimonious. — Brian O'Neill, President, Insurance Institute for Highway Safety[14]

Founded in 1966 in response to Ralph Nader's sensational and best-selling book, *Unsafe at Any Speed*, which revealed that American automakers knowingly manufactured cars with life-threatening defects, the NHTSA, working in partnership with the states, is charged with the ambitious mission of preventing traffic accidents.[15] The federal agency is supposed to do its best to ensure vehicle safety or "crashworthiness," while state agencies police the roads and take first-line responsibility for so-called driver errors. NHTSA is led by a single administrator, who reports to the Secretary of the Department of Transportation.

In their excellent book, *The Struggle for Auto Safety*, published in 1990, Jerry Mashaw and David Harfst explain that NHTSA was the "first of a new breed of federal regulatory agencies" created as the progeny of a "distinctive political-intellectual union" between Vietnam War–era political activism and academic critics of agency "capture."[16] By capture, the critics meant that older agencies like the Federal Trade Commission, the Federal Power Commission, and the Interstate Commerce Commission had lost the ability to focus on their central missions to protect the public interest and instead were preoccupied with serving the economic interests of the industries they were assigned to regulate. The solution to the capture problem, typified by NHTSA's central authorizing statute, the Motor Vehicle Safety Act, was to give federally employed engineers considerable authority to reduce the number of accident victims by compelling manufacturers to engineer much sturdier and less accident-prone cars.

Mashaw and Harfst describe the auto industry—especially domestic manufacturers—as caught flat-footed by this bold legislative initiative. General Motors was the most naïve and self-destructive. When Ralph Nader emerged as the charismatic leader of the 1960s consumer movement, the company had the consummate bad judgment to send a team of private investigators to discover scandal in the handsome young man's personal life. Not only did they come up empty-handed, they turned Nader into a populist hero featured on the cover of *Time* magazine and gave his allies in Congress the momentum they needed to overrun the manufacturers' objections to legislation creating NHTSA in surprisingly short order.

Despite this strong send-off, NHTSA has struggled throughout its history to overcome four powerful—at times overpowering—realities: (1) the American love affair with the automobile, the sleeker and more powerful the better; (2) the militancy of the "Big Three" domestic carmakers, which was driven by competitive reversals in the marketplace; (3) a series of unfortunate decisions by the courts that hold NHTSA to impossibly high burdens of proof in support of its regulatory decisions; and (4) the same political hostility and diminishing resources that debilitate its four sister agencies.

Given these enormous challenges, NHTSA has a "little agency that could" dimension that cannot go unremarked: the fatality rate in 2006 was 1.41 per 100 million vehicle miles traveled. Over a twelve-year period between 1994 and 2006, fatalities ranged between a high of 43,510 in 2005 and a low of 40,716 in 1994. However, "vehicle miles traveled" increased during this period from 2.358 to 3.014 billion, the number of registered vehicles went from 192 to 251 million, and the population increased from 260 to 299 million.[17] Despite this steady progress, traffic fatalities remain the leading cause of death among people ages four through thirty-four, 2,575,000 people were injured in crashes in 2006, and NHTSA has been unable to make much progress in achieving its goal of further reducing deaths by vehicle miles traveled. Critics of the agency correctly finger the advent of sport utility vehicles (SUVs) as a major cause of NHTSA's loss of momentum, as we will explain shortly.

Throughout its history, NHTSA has straddled the debate over whether the primary cause of traffic accidents is unsafe motor vehicles or driver impairment. In the past several years, its funding has tilted strongly in favor of driver impairment programs, which dominate its budget and activities by a large margin. In FY 2007, NHTSA received $599 million for "behavioral safety programs," distributed as grants to the states, $121 million for vehicle safety programs, and $107 million for behavioral safety research. NHTSA had an approved level of 616 FTEs in FY 2007, a surprisingly small workforce in comparison with its total budget. In constant dollars, its overall budget stood at roughly the same place it was in 1978.

The structure of the Motor Vehicle Safety Act was inspired by a ground-breaking analysis of accidents prepared by William Haddon, a medical doctor who became NHTSA's first administrator.[18] Haddon's methodology divided the causes of accidents into three discrete categories:

1. Precrash, when circumstances such as bad weather or sleepy or drunk drivers create the conditions precedent for a crash;
2. Crash, the stage at which equipment such as seat belts, air bags, padded dashboards, and head restraints determine injury and fatality rates; and
3. Postcrash, when the arrival (and training) of emergency personnel determine victims' fates.

From this analytical framework grew the concept that motor vehicles sold to individual consumers should be "crashworthy." The act provides NHTSA with both preventive and remedial authority. Working prospectively, NHTSA's safety engineers identify "practicable" standards for motor vehicle crashworthiness that "meet the need for motor vehicle safety" and are stated in "objective" terms.[19] Equipment meeting these standards must then be incorporated into all new cars after the new rule's effective date. Working retrospectively, NHTSA can identify defects in the design or manufacture of motor vehicles and compel manufacturers and dealers to recall and repair them.

In the first several years of its history, under presidents Johnson, Nixon, and Carter, NHTSA attempted to make aggressive use of its preventive authority to compel more crashworthy vehicle designs, only to encounter a daunting resistance by automakers and harsh scrutiny by the courts. To some extent, the agency made its own bed, insisting on prescribing highly detailed specifications for car components like windshield wipers, head and tail lamps, and rearview mirrors, rather than more general "performance standards," such as a requirement that manufacturers must ensure a good range of visibility for drivers around the perimeters of the car. Had it left manufacturers more flexibility, they might have resisted its regulatory efforts less. NHTSA's highly detailed technical specifications typically mimicked the best engineering in already available equipment, an approach that sacrificed the potential of the standards to force the development of innovative technology. This insistence on defining precise design attributes also led the NHTSA technical staff, which was grossly outmatched in numbers and laboratory resources by carmaker engineers, into a thicket of highly technical rulemaking, where the public interest groups that helped create the political momentum for NHTSA's creation soon lagged far behind the heated debates between industry and government engineers, leaving the agency's experts without an effective "left flank."

The coup de grace to this fundamentally misguided approach was delivered by the Court of Appeals for the Sixth Circuit in a 1972 case involving the Chrysler Corporation that marked the first shot fired in the inaugural battle of what would become a decades-long war to mandate "passive restraints"—in this instance, airbags.[20] The court upheld NHTSA's authority to force technology by adopting performance standards that would require the development of new, significantly better safety features. But the court required that before NHTSA issued such requirements, the agency must first develop test protocols involving crash dummies that are sufficiently precise to deliver the exact same results every time vehicles are tested.

In effect, this decision put the cart in front of the horse and then wrapped the entire procession in an enormous tangle of red tape. To force technology, NHTSA must know not only what degree of enhanced safety it wanted the new technology to deliver but must also divine how best to verify that the equipment was in fact meeting that standard. Mandating what Mashaw and Harfst characterize as "an unachievable level of scientific certainty," the court operated out of a "technological naïveté" that bore no resemblance to the way carmakers actually made decisions when they developed new products.[21]

Eventually, NHTSA abandoned plans to shift to performance-based standards from detailed specifications and then dropped prospective standard setting as the centerpiece of its regulatory efforts. Instead, NHTSA turned to recalls as its weapon of choice when vehicle crashworthiness was questioned. In 1974, Congress appeared to sanction this trend by adopting a series of reforms that made recall proceedings simpler to execute and allowed the participation of consumer groups.[22] These amendments instructed the agency to pursue a handful of specific safety standards but otherwise did not change the paralyzing dynamics of the prospective rulemaking process. Congress also responded to consumer resistance to NHTSA's efforts to compel seatbelt use, putting on hold its plans to require passive restraints; it would be almost three decades before airbags were required equipment in passenger cars.

As we saw in the context of the CPSC, the problem with recalls is that they are reactive rather than preventative, are less effective than upfront standards in driving safety technology, and, depending on the level of effort and the nature of the defect, can produce disturbingly low compliance rates. One recent example is a recall involving 10 million Ford,

Lincoln, and Mercury vehicles—a record number—with faulty cruise control switches that NHTSA has linked to 1,500 vehicle fires. After six separate recalls over a decade, the problem was corrected in only half the vehicles.

Mashaw and Harfst hypothesize that NHTSA was driven away from prospective standards and toward recalls because the latter fit into an ethos of protecting individual rights that undermines traffic safety efforts across the board. The 1966 Motor Vehicle Safety Act suggested the radical idea that people did not have the right to drive whatever vehicle and in whichever manner that they wished. Instead, it was based on the principle that society as a whole has a stake in compelling the production and use of crashworthy cars. But the 1974 amendments to the act sent a different message: consumers have no tolerance of passive restraints, so NHTSA should back off that idea. Instead, it should focus on everyone's individual right to drive defect-free—but highly disparate—cars. As we shall see in the next section, these dynamics remain very powerful to this day.

*Passenger or Target?*

The advent of the SUV realized deep-seated, intensely emotional aspirations for millions of American car lovers. As anthropologist and long-time Ford Motor Company marketing consultant Martin Goldfarb explained to reporters from the Public Broadcasting System's famed news program *Frontline*,

> [T]he whole love affair with trucks in the United States moved beyond trucks as work vehicles. . . . When they became personal use vehicles, people . . . tricked them up, they painted them, they put leather seats in them. . . . So out of the personal use of trucks grew the concept of a sport utility vehicle, higher off the ground, rugged, great visibility, because you felt you were in charge of the world. If anybody smaller than you got in front of you could kind of run them over—even though you didn't want to do that—but you had this feeling of personal power. . . . I also think these were vehicles that were uniquely American.[23]

Ironically, however, the development of the SUV was inspired as much by a loophole in the NHTSA regulatory scheme as carmakers' intuitive understanding of consumer fantasies. Motivated by the oil embargo of the 1970s, Congress instructed NHTSA to establish a corporate average fuel economy standard (CAFE) or minimum mileage-per-gallon requirements that apply fleet-wide, allowing manufacturers to average together gas guzzlers and smaller, more fuel efficient cars.[24] But the law exempted "light trucks" (motor vehicles over 8,500 pounds in total weight) from these requirements, giving the Big Three domestic automakers (General Motors, Chrysler, and Ford) a major incentive to sell more trucks as passenger vehicles. Soon, someone had the bright idea of actually converting the truck to be more passenger friendly by installing a larger, enclosed compartment on the truck bed, and the SUV was born. Critics of the SUV note that the carmakers never actually redesigned the trucks to accommodate the significantly different passenger compartments, a process that would have cost billions of dollars. Because manufacturers did not study the potential safety effects of putting a far heavier body on a frame with a relatively narrow axle that rides high off the road, manufacturers were accused of negligence in thousands of personal injury lawsuits, further raising the economic stakes for NHTSA regulation of these extremely popular vehicles. Any suggestion by the agency that the vehicles were not crashworthy would have strengthened the plaintiffs' cases.

The SUV is widely considered to be among the most treacherous type of motor vehicle ever driven, for its own occupants and for the occupants of smaller cars. The best publicized problem is rollovers; top heavy and riding high, SUVs are unstable and prone to tipping over at speeds as low as twenty-five miles per hour. The Bronco II and Ford Explorer are the two most notorious models exhibiting this problem. Needless to say, the domestic auto industry vigorously disputes these risks, claiming that SUVs are much safer for their occupants overall. Apart from rollovers, those claims are justified: SUV occupants fare far better that occupants of smaller vehicles in collisions.

"The theory that I'm going to protect myself and my family even if it costs other people's lives has been the operative incentive for the design of these new vehicles, and that's just wrong," Jeffrey Runge, a medical doctor who was NHTSA administrator during President George W. Bush's first term, told the *New York Times*. "Not to sound like a politician, but that's not compassionate conservatism."[25] Michelle White, an economist at the University of California, San Diego, has calculated that each single accident where an SUV driver remains unhurt translates into four fatalities for the smaller car's occupants, pedestrians, bicyclists, and motorcyclists: "Safety gains for those driving light trucks come at an extremely high cost to others."[26]

These problems are so prevalent that NHTSA's stalemated, fifteen-year effort to reduce traffic fatality and injury rates is often linked to growing numbers of SUVs.[27] The United States has fallen from first to ninth place in traffic safety worldwide over the last thirty years, behind Australia, Britain, and Canada, countries otherwise comparable to the United States but where SUVs never became popular with consumers. As for rollovers involving SUVs, NHTSA administrator Runge told Congress in June 2004 that this "highly lethal type of crash" accounts for 60 percent of occupant fatalities in SUVs, as compared with only one-third of such fatalities in smaller passenger vehicles.[28]

NHTSA's efforts to deal with the SUV problem can most charitably be described as conscious avoidance. Spurred by press reports about the rollover propensity of the Jeep CJ and the Ford Bronco II, Representative Tim Wirth (D-CO) petitioned NHTSA in 1986 to establish a rollover standard. NHTSA denied the Wirth petition, despite staff research showing a "pronounced and consistent pattern" connecting vehicle design, instability, and rollovers.[29]

In 1989, public interest groups asked NHTSA to consider recalling the Bronco II. NHTSA refused, noting that the Bronco II was not sufficiently more dangerous than other SUVs to warrant a recall. (*Consumer Reports* magazine warned its readers against purchasing the Bronco II at about the same time.) In 1990, NHTSA administrator Jerry Curry actively opposed tightening CAFE standards for light trucks and SUVs, basing his arguments primarily on the supposed safety advantages of the SUV in relation to smaller cars. Diane Steed, the former NHTSA administrator who had rejected the Wirth petition, led the industry coalition opposing tighter CAFE standards.

In 1994, NHTSA's resistance became bipartisan when the Clinton administration announced it would not adopt a rollover standard for new SUVs but instead would promote a "safety sticker" containing "rollover ratings" to be affixed to all new cars, light trucks, and SUVs. Even this weak effort was derailed by an "appropriations rider" cutting off any funding to support this initiative. As we explain further in chapter 5, such stealth legislative initiatives represent Congress at its worst because they are accomplished in the dead of night without any hearings or debate on the issue at hand.

## Workplace Safety and Health

### *Maligned and Disrespected*

Tyler Pipe is a gray iron foundry. Throughout the plant, molten metal is seen spilling from the cupolas, bulls and ladles. The forklift trucks transport the metal, and the ground behind the trucks often smokes with puddles of molten metal. Workers are covered with black residue from the foundry sand. Many work areas are dark, due to poor lighting and clouds of sand. Despite all the ignition and fuel sources, exit paths are not obvious. Many workers have scars or disfigurations which are noticeable from several feet away. Burns and amputations are frequent. This facility is located in a relatively small town where jobs are not plentiful. Throughout the plant, in supervisor offices and on bulletin boards, next to production charts and union memos, is posted in big orange letters: REDUCE MAN HOURS PER TON. — OSHA Inspection Report No. 300556420[30]

Founded in 1970 during President Nixon's first term, OSHA has jurisdiction over all private sector workplaces, except for the self-employed, family farms, and specific work situations governed by other agencies (for example, nuclear facilities under the jurisdiction of the Department of Energy). Led by a single administrator who reports to the Secretary of the Department of Labor, OSHA is the middle child of the five agencies we examine here, and it suffers from all the insecurity that pop psychologists attribute to that ordinal position. Unfortunately, however, the insecurity is grounded in a realistic perception of self. The agency is the most maligned and least respected of the group.

Government data show significant improvements in workplace safety in the four decades since OSHA was created. According to the Bureau of Labor Statistics (BLS), fatality rates per 100,000 workers have declined from eighteen in 1970, to thirteen in 1980, to nine in 1990, to 4.3 in 2000, and to four in 2006. Workplace injuries and illnesses numbered 4.1 million in private sector workplaces for 2006, or an average of 4.4 per 100 workers, down from 10.9 per 100 in 1972. Unfortunately, however, these figures substantially understate the true incidence of injuries and illnesses. Recent studies by independent economists suggest that actual injuries may be as much as 30–69 percent higher than BLS estimates.[31] Equally troubling, this apparent progress likely has little to do with improvements in workplace safety and instead is attributable to the loss of American jobs in heavy manufacturing and agriculture. And, although fatalities have steadily decreased, progress in the last half decade—a decrease of 0.3 in lives lost—is significantly less impressive than the safety record amassed in each of the four previous decades.

The economic costs of occupational injuries and death are daunting. According to Liberty Mutual Insurance, the nation's largest workers' compensation insurance company, 2005 data indicate that United States employers pay $48.3 billion annually in "direct costs" alone, that is, payments for medical expenses and lost wages.[32] The insurer points out that the major causes of employee injuries remained essentially the same between 1998 and 2004, even though the United States lost almost 20 percent of its manufacturing jobs and created approximately eight million service positions during this period.

The Occupational Safety and Health Act of 1970, which Congress has amended in only minor ways, gives OSHA authority to issue two kinds of rules: (1) those involving safety standards to prevent physical injuries—for example, equipment guards, automatic shutoff valves, and lighting; and (2) those involving "permissible exposure limits," which are designed to prevent exposures to toxic substances and are carried out by lowering ambient levels of these chemicals on the shop floor or requiring workers to wear such equipment as goggles, respirators, or gloves.[33] The federal OSHA implements the law in thirty-one states and territories (for example, Puerto Rico) and delegates comparable authority to twenty-four state agencies. Beginning with the Clinton administration, OSHA has placed increased emphasis on working out voluntary compliance agreements with the targets of its inspections.[34]

In 1975, OSHA was responsible for policing 3.9 million workplaces, which employed 67.8 million workers; it had 2,405 inspectors to check compliance. By 2006, the number of workplaces had grown to 8.7 million, the worker population was 133.8 million, and the number of inspectors fielded by OSHA and its state partners rarely rose above 2,000. For FY 2007, OSHA received appropriations of $487 million, an amount that in constant dollars (adjusted for inflation) was the same as what its budget was in the late 1970s.

### Phantom Enforcement

Most federal agencies depend on deterrence-based enforcement. Under a deterrence-based enforcement system, the government does not attempt to inspect every facility under its jurisdiction and confer with plant managers on compliance problems. Rather, agencies follow an approach analogous to the audit system used by the Internal Revenue Service. Inspectors visit a cross section of carefully selected, high-profile targets. They report significant violations to staff attorneys who prosecute the owners and operators of facilities. The goal of those cases is to impose fines substantial enough to recoup profits gained when management ignored the law and to punish the violators. When the government publicizes such cases, it gives similarly situated businesses adequate negative incentives to improve compliance. Such systems work well, provided that businesses believe they run a significant risk of inspection and prosecution if they misbehave.

Deterrence-based enforcement at OSHA is ineffective for three reasons. First, businesses have little reason to fear they will ever be inspected. OSHA told Congress that in FY 2009, it would try to conduct 37,000 inspections annually, employing a variety of tactics to pick the worst industries, worst workplaces, and emerging hazards. At that rate, the inspectors could visit each of the workplaces that are under its jurisdiction approximately once every 235 years. The gross mismatch between inspection resources and number of workplaces is bound to communicate a message that scofflaw employers have very little reason to fear inspection.

OSHA enforcement is also undermined by an outmoded statute, which imposes very small penalties for the most egregious violations. Penalties for "serious violation[s]," defined as circumstances where there is a "substantial probability that death or serious physical harm could result" are capped at only $7,000 per incident, while penalties for "willful violation[s]," involving situations in which an employer evinces plain indifference to the law, are capped at $70,000 per incident, even when a worker dies.[35] Compounding the gross inadequacy of these provisions, the statute does not give OSHA any authority to recoup the profits earned as a result of the lawlessness—for example, the avoided costs of forcing employees to work without safety equipment.

Third, OSHA is notorious for an unbroken history of permissive application of these pitifully weak penalty provisions. The average penalty assessed in cases involving fatalities in FY 2007 averaged just $10,133 for federal and state plans combined. Causing a worker's death through a willful violation of the law carries a maximum prison term of six months and is characterized as a misdemeanor. Between 1982 and 2002, OSHA investigated 1,242 cases in which it concluded that worker deaths were caused by willful safety violations, but it declined to seek prosecution in 93 percent of those cases. Putting these numbers into a practical context, an insightful study by Wayne Gray and John Mendeloff found that the efficacy of OSHA enforcement in motivating compliance has declined markedly.[36]

*Judicial Interference*

The federal courts have been extraordinarily tough on OSHA, narrowing its authority to issue precautionary safety standards to the point that rules, especially regarding exposures to toxic chemicals in the workplace, have slowed to a trickle. A divided Supreme Court held in *Industrial Union Department, AFL-CIO v. American Petroleum Institute*, a case involving the cancer-causing chemical benzene, that the risk of exposure must pose a "significant health risk" before OSHA could promulgate a workplace exposure limit.[37] The result was that OSHA had to withdraw its bid to lower its existing standard— ten parts per million per cubic meter of air, averaged over eight hours—to one part per million. The minority (justices Marshall, Brennan, White, and Blackmun) accused their colleagues of substituting their own policy judgments for the language used by Congress, which gave OSHA authority to promulgate standards that are "reasonably necessary or appropriate to provide safe or healthful employment."[38]

In 1987, OSHA finally gathered enough research to prove definitively that the more stringent level it had proposed a decade earlier was, in fact, the appropriate standard. Its evidence showed that in the intervening decade, workers exposed to the considerably weaker standard the Supreme Court left in effect suffered as many as ninety-five excess cancer cases per 1,000. This level of illness is unacceptably high, even tragic, under prevailing norms in health and safety policy making. As we explain in chapter 7, the case is a classic example of unjustified judicial interference in regulatory decision making that should have been left to career civil service experts.

*The Human Cost*

In December 2003, the *New York Times*, the Canadian Broadcasting Corporation program the *Fifth Estate*, and the Public Broadcasting System news program *Frontline* publicized the results of their investigation of McWane, Inc., one of the world's largest manufacturers of cast-iron sewer and water pipes.[39] The quote that opens this section is taken directly from a 1999 OSHA inspection report describing the conditions found at Tyler Pipe, a sprawling pipe foundry owned by McWane in Texas. When McWane purchased the facility in 1995, management cut the workforce by two-thirds; mandated twelve- and even sixteen-hour shifts; and eliminated quality control and safety inspectors, pollution control personnel and relief workers, and cleaning crews and maintenance workers. Turnover got so high that the company recruited inmates from local prisons who showed up for work wearing electronic monitoring bracelets. Workers who protested safety conditions were fired.

   Conditions at McWane plants were so egregious that they eventually
attracted the attention of federal and state workplace safety and environmental protection officials, but the response was phlegmatic enough that
the company began to calculate down to the penny per ton the cost of such
government fines, concluding that they were an acceptable cost of doing
business. At the time the series appeared, McWane employed 5,000 workers in a dozen American plants. The company was cited for more than four
hundred safety violations in 1995–2003, far more than its major competitors combined. Employees suffered 4,600 injuries, and nine workers were
killed at McWane, all under gruesome circumstances. OSHA concluded
that three of the deaths were a direct result of deliberate violations of
federal safety standards, while less advertent safety violations had caused
the other five fatalities. But those deaths received only cursory attention
from local authorities, who photographed the bodies and called the cor-
oner but otherwise deferred to federal investigators. OSHA ultimately
referred one death to the Department of Justice, and the case ended in a
single misdemeanor plea without any corporate executive being charged.
   Following the national media exposés, federal prosecutors at last
brought serious charges against McWane, which ended up paying millions
of dollars in fines and having several managers found guilty of multiple
felonies and sentenced to prison. Environmental statutes, which impose
dramatically tougher penalties and jail terms, played a central role in the
prosecutions. The Department of Justice set up a joint taskforce that included EPA and OSHA investigators in order to develop joint cases at
high-priority workplaces.
   The media revelations and the reaction they evoked undoubtedly made
an impression on employers, although not always a positive one. Arent Fox
LLP, one of the most prominent law firms representing major corporations
in OSHA cases, told its clients that they "would be well-served to engage
experienced counsel immediately to assist in addressing OSHA's investigation of the fatality."[40] The firm recommended that its clients do their
best to negotiate to have a "willful" violation converted to a "unclassified"
violation, noting that this "technique" was developed by defense lawyers
in the 1990s and that it has the advantage of eliminating "the stigma of
a willful violation and reduces the chances that the citation will be used
against the employer in collateral state court litigation brought by the
employee's family."[41]
   It would be reassuring to think that, despite this cynical advice, the
McWane saga made a difference in the manufacturing sector, inspiring

meaningful efforts to rectify the worst abuses. But we cannot muster much support for this hopeful view. Instead, our research indicates the opposite. At the request of Senator Edward M. Kennedy (D-MA), the Government Accountability Office (GAO) investigated conditions in the meatpacking industry, issuing its final report in 2005.[42] This workforce is dominated by young, Hispanic men. Approximately 25 percent of employees are noncitizens, and plants typically experience frequent turnover. The GAO found that although the injury and illness rate had declined from 29.5/100 in 1992 to 14.7/100 in 2001, the rate was still among the highest of any industry. It added that the many hazards present in such work suggest these data may not be valid:

> The work is physically demanding, repetitive, and often requires working in extreme temperatures—such as refrigeration units that range from below zero to 40 degrees Fahrenheit. . . . Workers often stand for long periods of time on production lines that move very quickly, wielding knives or other cutting instruments. . . . Conditions at the plant can also be loud, wet, dark, and slippery. Workers responsible for cleaning the plant must use strong chemicals and hot pressurized water to clean inside and around dangerous machinery, and may experience impaired visibility because of steam. . . . While the most common injures are cuts, strains, cumulative trauma caused by repetitive cutting motions, and injuries sustained from falls, more serious injuries, such as fractures and amputations, also occur. . . . [S]ome workers became ill because of exposure to chemicals, blood, and fecal matter, which can be exacerbated by poor ventilation and extreme temperatures.[43]

## Food and Drug Safety

### Twenty-Five Cents on the Dollar

> A strong Food and Drug Administration (FDA) is crucial for the health of our country. The benefits of a robust, progressive Agency are enormous; the risks of a debilitated, under-performing organization are incalculable. — FDA Science Board[44]

> Science at the [FDA] today is in a precarious position. In terms of both personnel and the money to support them, the agency is barely hanging on by its fingertips. . . . FDA has become a paradigmatic example of the "hollow government" syndrome— an agency with expanded responsibilities, stagnant resources, and the consequent inability to implement or enforce its statutory mandates. . . . [C]ongress must commit to a two-year appropriations program to increase the FDA employees by 50 percent and to double the FDA funding. — Peter Barton Hutt[45]

The oldest of the five protector agencies, the FDA is led by a single commissioner and is encompassed within the much larger Department of
Health and Human Services. Staffed primarily by medical doctors and
other scientific experts, its influence over public health and safety is hard
to overstate. The agency is responsible for ensuring the safety of 80 percent of the nation's food (it does not cover meat and poultry, which are
under the Department of Agriculture's jurisdiction), all over-the-counter
and prescription human and veterinary drugs, the blood supply, human
vaccines, most cosmetics, and most "medical devices" (for example, pacemakers). Together, these items total over $1 trillion in sales annually, or 25
cents of every dollar that consumers spend. In the last several years, efforts
to forestall and prepare for terrorist attacks involving the use of biological
agents such as anthrax or tampering with the food supply, as well as such
natural outbreaks as West Nile virus, SARS, and avian influenza, have
further made demands on the FDA's time and attention.

The FDA's FY 2007 appropriated budget was approximately $1.6 bil-
lion, an estimated loss of $300 million from inflation alone since its 1988
appropriation. It is literally impossible to find a single FDA constituency
willing to take the position that the agency is either adequately funded or
doing a decent job. Consumer groups have raised these alarms for many
years, but in recent years, industry groups from the Pharmaceutical Manufacturers' Association to the Grocery Manufacturers' Association have
joined their chorus.

Despite their unanimous concern about the FDA's regulatory travails,
the two sides sharply disagree on what should be done to rehabilitate the
agency. The pharmaceutical industry has long taken the position that the
FDA moves too slowly to approve new drugs. The anxiety of the drug
makers is exacerbated by their dependence on constantly turning out
"blockbusters"—the lexicon for medicines sold in large quantities for
billions of dollars to treat common problems like high blood pressure,
diabetes, and pain of all varieties. As scientific research advanced, duplicative blockbusters were marketed, intensifying cut-throat competition
among the companies without bringing significant benefits to consumers.

In contrast to these financial preoccupations, consumer groups are worried about the safety of drugs and medical devices already on the market
as well as the possibility that the new drug approval process is not stringent enough to pick up on long-term, adverse side effects. They cite a 1990
General Accounting Office (GAO, now the Government Accountability
Office) study concluding that as many as 51 percent of FDA-approved
drugs have serious adverse side effects that elude premarket studies.[46]

Writing in November 2007, the FDA Science Board issued some dire warnings about its regulatory capacity: "The demands on the FDA have soared . . . [but the] resources have not increased in proportion to the demands. . . . This imbalance is imposing a significant risk to the integrity of the food, drug, cosmetic and device regulatory system, and hence the safety of the public."[47] An Institute of Medicine panel asked to review the same issues noted that the turnover rate in FDA science staff is twice that of other agencies; the state of its information technology infrastructure is extremely disturbing; and it is poorly equipped to cope with emerging science and technologies, from human genome discoveries to nanotechnology to robotics.[48]

Recently, well-publicized and recurring incidents involving contamination of the food supply have turned up the already high heat on the agency, as we explain further below. On March 14, 2009, President Obama used his weekly radio and video address to call for an overhaul of the nation's food safety system. He announced the appointment of Margaret Hamburg as FDA commissioner and Joshua Sharfstein as deputy commissioner. These highly qualified, former big-city health commissioners will have their hands full on both sides of the FDA's jurisdiction.

*Drug Safety*

Vioxx, first approved in 1999 as a prescription painkiller for the treatment of arthritis (among other ailments), was sold by its manufacturer, Merck & Co. Inc., as a breakthrough drug that was easier on the stomach than its competitors. By the time Merck withdrew Vioxx in 2004, 20 million people had taken the drug and annual sales topped $2.5 billion. Within months after receiving the FDA's initial approval, Merck received the results of its own clinical trial, known as the VIGOR study, which showed that Vioxx nearly doubled risk of heart attack or stroke; subsequent research over the next couple of years reinforced this conclusion. Dr. David Graham, Associate Director for Science and Medicine in the FDA Office of Drug Safety, estimated that between 88,000 and 139,000 Americans suffered a heart attack or stroke as the result of taking the drug. He characterized Vioxx as "the single greatest drug safety catastrophe in the history of this country or the history of the world."[49]

What happened? The most important, systemic cause was the inherent limitations of the new drug approval process: the FDA issues approvals on the basis of clinical studies that maybe too small to identify some dangerous side effect of a drug. Consequently, these studies do not catch long-term effects that manifest themselves many months or years after patients begin taking a medication. These limitations are precisely the reason why it is so important for the FDA to monitor drugs carefully after they are approved, but this work is resource intensive and the FDA has neglected it for many years.

Critics also blame Merck's greed. The company tried to explain away the adverse studies in order to preserve Vioxx's blockbuster status, urging its sales staff to avoid talking about heart attack risks with prescribing doctors and instead to rely on a "Cardiovascular Card" containing outdated information that Vioxx might actually protect against such problems. Merck also spent $100 million in direct-to-consumer advertising. Largely based on this kind of evidence, which suggests a deliberate effort to obscure the drug's side effects, as many as 47,000 plaintiffs have filed personal injury claims against Merck. In November 2007, Merck & Co. announced that it would pay $4.85 billion to settle most of those lawsuits.

Some observers admit that Merck behaved badly but focus on the FDA's behavior as the key factor in the scandal. They argue that the FDA is the victim of agency capture, with regulators essentially being controlled by pharmaceutical industry representatives. The FDA's Graham told Congress that political appointees at the FDA tried to suppress his warnings, which were based on a computer analysis of health maintenance organization records.

Although these theories are all valid, we think that the most convincing—and often overlooked—explanation of the Vioxx crisis is a chronic and dangerous imbalance in FDA funding and priorities. In 1992, Congress passed the Prescription Drug User Fee Act of 1992 (PDUFA) with the intention of speeding up new drug approvals. From this myopic perspective, the law was an unqualified success: the median approval time for standard new drugs decreased from approximately 27 months in FY 1993 to about 13.7 months in FY 2005. But PDUFA's "gift" of additional funding turned out to be a Trojan horse: the statute said that industry fees could only be used for new drug review activities on the condition that the FDA continued to allocate the same amount of general taxpayer revenues to such approvals as it had in the year before the law was passed. These restrictions, combined with lagging congressional appropriations, meant that in the years that followed, the FDA was forced to "rob Peter to pay Paul," reallocating funds from other programs in order to keep its spending for new drug reviews high enough to meet PDUFA's perverse incentives.

Postmarket drug safety monitoring was among the areas hardest hit. Specifically, in 1992, the year the law was passed, the FDA's Center for Drug Evaluation and Research (CDER) spent about 53 percent of its budget on new drug reviews. By 2002, the amount of CDER's budget devoted to reviewing new drug applications had increased to 74 percent. In that same year, the Office of Drug Safety, the CDER unit that is responsible for monitoring the safety of drugs once they are on the market, made up only 6 percent of CDER's budget.

The result of the imbalance between the FDA's pre- and postmarket safety reviews is that the agency, and thus the public, has become increasingly reliant on industry to detect safety risks that emerge only after a drug is on the market. But, as the Vioxx episode shows, companies have overpowering incentives to keep such information from regulators. In 2005, the FDA reported that of the nearly 1,200 postmarket safety studies that drug companies committed to perform, nearly 70 percent had not yet begun.

The Institute of Medicine report mentioned earlier concluded that the FDA labors under severe resource constraints that undermine the science it applies to regulatory decisions and suffers from excessive turnover both in the ranks (scientists depart at twice the rate applicable to comparable agencies) and at the top (eight permanent commissioners and seven acting commissioners have served over the last thirty years). The report found that the FDA lacks the enforcement authority it needs to deal with the modern marketplace and that the FDA and pharmaceutical companies fail to communicate safety concerns to the public in a timely and effective fashion.

In 2007, Congress passed and the president signed a law relaxing the restrictions on how fees are used and raised the level of money collected to $392.8 million, an increase of $87 million.[50] The FDA immediately announced plans to spend $29.3 million to hire an additional eighty-two employees specifically for postmarket safety objectives. This amount is less than a third of Merck's direct-to-consumer marketing budget for Vioxx. On a brighter note, the new amendments allow the FDA to refuse approval of a new drug sponsored by any company that is in violation of agreements to conduct postmarketing studies for existing drugs, considerably strengthening the FDA's enforcement authority. It remains to be seen whether new leadership at the FDA can make better use of these improvements. But drugs are only one front in the FDA's so far losing battle to conquer public health threats.

*Food Safety*

As we mentioned earlier, the FDA is responsible for 80 percent of the food supply, covering everything but meat and poultry. The Department of Agriculture fields 8,000 inspectors who are permanently stationed at 6,300 meat and poultry processing plants across the country, at an annual cost of approximately $1 billion. But the FDA's total budget for four times the amount of food is one-half of this figure, or approximately $500 million annually, and it does not even attempt to inspect all food processing facilities under its jurisdiction.[51]

Public health officials estimate that food-borne diseases make some 76 million people sick, cause 325,000 people to be hospitalized, and kill 5,000 people annually. Such illness costs as much as $44 billion annually in medical costs and lost productivity. Ensuring the safety of food produced domestically is difficult enough. Policing imported food is difficult, if not impossible. Food imports, composed largely of produce and seafood, constituted 15 percent by volume of the U.S. food supply in 2005. Some 25,000 shipments of FDA-regulated foods arrive every day from over 100 countries, yet the agency was only able to inspect 1.3 percent of those imports in 2007, a decrease of close to 7 percent since 1992.

In 2008–2009, millions of pounds of salmonella-tainted peanut butter and peanut paste (a related product used in approximately 2,100 other products such as snack bars, desserts, and breakfast cereals) were shipped from a plant in rural Georgia that was operated by the family-owned Peanut Corporation of American. By the time the products were recalled, nine people had died and 20,000 became sick in forty-three states. The contamination was discovered months after the tainted peanuts infiltrated the food supply and then only because a team of graduate students working part-time for the Minnesota Health Department and bearing the bizarre nickname the "Diarrhea Squad" painstakingly interviewed dozens of victims, piecing together their shared consumption of products originating at the plant. This kind of "patient zero" epidemiology is extraordinarily difficult to do, is quite time-consuming, and obviously fails to prevent such incidents.

Once the source of the tainted nuts was identified, investigations by the media and the government revealed that the plant's manager had received laboratory tests showing salmonella but had shipped his products nonetheless. Company officials are now under criminal investigation. The plant had a leaking roof, water running down its walls, rodent infestation, and dysfunctional roasters. Employees, who were paid minimum wage and placed by temp firms, wore uniforms they took home with them, unnecessarily tracking contamination into the plant. In March 2008, a private inspector the company hired to comply with requirements imposed by Kellogg, one of its largest customers, inexplicably gave the plant a "superior" food safety rating after conducting a site visit that lasted less than a day. In the end, peanut producers across the country lost $1 billion as a result of the recall and attendant publicity—close to twice the FDA's entire food safety budget; amounts lost by retailers involved in the effort have not been quantified.

President Obama's pledge to overhaul food safety is still playing out as this book goes to press. Congress has held numerous hearings, and several pieces of legislation have been introduced. A March 2009 report by the Trust for America's Health pronounced that the "food safety system is in crisis" and strongly recommended realigning all of the FDA's food safety programs—now divided among four separate bureaucratic divisions—under one senior official.[52] The Government Accountability Office has praised initial plans to improve the FDA's performance proposed under the Bush II administration but called for increased resources and more drastic steps to consolidate fragmented and overlapping oversight.[53]

## Environmental Protection

*Battered Agency Syndrome*

> Man's ability to alter his environment has developed far more rapidly than his ability to foresee with certainty the effects of his alterations. It is only recently that we have begun to appreciate the danger posed by unregulated modification of the world around us, and have created watchdog agencies whose task it is to warn us, and protect us. . . . [U]nequipped with crystal balls and unable to read the future, [the agencies] are nonetheless charged with evaluating the effects of unprecedented environmental modifications, often made on a massive scale. Necessarily, they must deal with predictions and uncertainty, with developing evidence, with conflicting evidence, and, sometimes, with little or no evidence at all. — Judge Skelly Wright[54]

> The Environmental Protection Agency is now staggering under the assault of its enemies—while still gravely wounded from the gifts of its "friends." . . . [T]he image of the agency as an overweening bureaucracy is miscast. In fact, if anything, it is an *under*weening bureaucracy. Any senior EPA official will tell you that the agency has the resources to do not much more than ten percent of the things Congress has charged it to do. — William Ruckelshaus[55]

Founded during President Nixon's first term in 1970, the EPA is the largest and most powerful of the five protector agencies. It exists as a freestanding agency, as opposed to an institutional component of another department, and has a single administrator. The agency administers twelve separate laws covering a hundreds of pages, each with its own set of missions, mandates, and pollution control approaches.

Like OSHA, the EPA has the ability to delegate responsibility for implementing these laws to its counterparts at the state level. Unlike OSHA, which found only twenty-six states and territories willing to step up to the bar and run their own programs, every one of the fifty states have created "little EPAs" and have received delegations to administer most of the major national regulatory programs. Under this "cooperative federalism" approach, the EPA writes nationally applicable rules and state officials draft facility-specific permits incorporating those standards, conduct inspections, and bring enforcement actions. This partnership eases the EPA's workload considerably. But it comes with many aggravations, not the least of which is cajoling the states into line as federally crafted mandates proliferate and federal grants for program implementation decline.

The scope of EPA's jurisdiction is mind-boggling. It has the authority to control most emissions into air, water, and soil by all of the manufacturing plants in the country, including electric utilities, with the exception of plants that generate nuclear power. The EPA can compel facility owners and operators to install monitoring equipment to measure their pollution and control equipment (for example, smokestack scrubbers) to trap or clean pollution before it is released. The agency regulates the safety and purity of public drinking water; tells gas station owners what kinds of tanks to use when they store fuel underground; compels dump site owners to track the waste they receive and keep it in highly engineered landfills; orders the cleanup of hundreds of abandoned toxic waste sites across the country; controls tailpipe emissions from motor vehicles; permits large hog and chicken farms that discharge waste into nearby waterways; and compiles a national database called the Integrated Risk Information System that is used worldwide to set standards for the use and cleanup of toxic chemicals.

Congress has amended each of the eight most important environmental laws at least twice and in some cases three times. They include the (1) Clean Air Act (ambient air pollution and the sources that emit it); (2) Clean Water Act (surface water pollution and the sources that discharge it); (3) Safe Drinking Water Act (purity and security of the public water supply—that is, any drinking water system serving ten or more customers); (4) Federal Insecticide, Fungicide, and Rodenticide Act (poisons used to kill plants, insects, and other pests, generally known as "pesticides"); (5) Toxic Substances Control Act (marketing of new and existing chemicals); (6) Resource Conservation and Recovery Act (disposal of garbage and hazardous wastes); (7) Comprehensive Environmental Response, Compensation, and Liability Act (liability for responsible parties that engaged in activities that created toxic waste dumps as well as a multibillion dollar federal cleanup fund); and (8) Emergency Planning and Community Right-to- Know Act (establishment of a toxic release inventory disclosing amounts of the most common and hazardous pollutants released at facilities across the country).[56]

In the beginning, the environmental statutes were general and hortatory, like the authorizing statutes that cover the other agencies. So, for example, Congress told the EPA to make the water in the nation's lakes, rivers, and streams suitable for swimming and fishing using rulemaking and permitting no later than July 1983. As the EPA became bogged down in its efforts to implement such broad mandates, Congress began to micromanage the agency, introducing such unprecedented concepts as the "statutory deadline"—a specific date by which the EPA must perform a nondiscretionary duty, enforceable in court—and the "statutory hammer"—a legally binding instruction that if the EPA did not promulgate its own rule by a certain date, a similar rule already developed by the state of California would go into effect. (California, which encompasses one of the largest economies in the world, is consistently on the cutting edge of environmental policy making.)

Over four decades, Congress doubled and tripled the length of these laws, adding mandate upon mandate, initiating study after study, and creating ambitious new programs with little regard for the agency's capacity to get its work done.

The EPA's difficulties in keeping up with these expanding mandates were compounded by the fact that it answers to multiple congressional committees, with dozens of members anxious to establish bragging rights for the creation of new initiatives that would solve the crisis of the day. Worse, as we discuss in chapter 5, once the "authorizing committees" of Congress wrote down all their ideas, setting deadlines for each activity, the job of appropriating the resources for the EPA's work was given to a whole set of different committees, with very few overlapping members. As federal budget deficits grew, appropriations committees without any pride of authorship in the EPA's new mandates routinely cut its funding. And, in the cruelest twist of all, instead of acknowledging the dilemma created for the EPA by its need to serve such a large number of congressional masters and to do more with less, senators, representatives, and the White House blamed the agency for its growing number of regulatory failures.

Not surprisingly, given its extraordinarily broad jurisdiction, the EPA soon became the poster child for the alleged regulatory excesses of the 1980s and 1990s and has received more concerted attention from conservatives in the White House and Congress than all the other agencies combined. Efforts to bring the agency to heel have had mixed success, largely because of the strong public support for environmental protection, which is amplified by periodic revelations about the latest threat to confront us and is reflected in the robust, extraordinarily powerful presence of environmental public interest groups at the federal, state, and local levels.

Today, the EPA trudges along in a defensive posture, with about 17,000 employees spread across its Washington headquarters, ten regional offices, and a dozen labs. The agency's operating budget was $4.3 billion for its core operations in FY 2008, with an additional $3.3 billion committed to grants and loans to state and local governments for sewage treatment and drinking water infrastructure, as well as federal funding for Superfund toxic waste cleanups. This level of funding gives the agency the same purchasing power it had in the mid-1980s, before passage of a slew of new statutory mandates, including the 1990 Clean Air Act Amendments, rightly viewed as the most ambitious and expensive set of health and safety mandates on the books.

William Ruckelshaus, quoted at the outset of this section, served two tours of duty at the EPA under Republican presidents (Nixon, 1970–73; and Reagan, 1983–85) and is widely regarded as among its toughest, most loyal critics. In 1995, out of office and with the freedom to speak bluntly, he described it as suffering from "battered agency syndrome," staggering under the load of too much work, too little money, and unrelenting criticism from friend and enemy alike.[57] Ruckelshaus analogized the agency's plight to blaming pilot error for a crash when the pilot is assigned to fly from the East Coast to the West Coast but only given enough fuel to make it to Chicago.

The EPA's resource constraints are the most important cause of its many problems, but they are far from the only reason the agency struggles forward with such heavy handicaps. The agency's relationship with the courts has been fitful, at times much better than the dynamic experienced by sister agencies like OSHA and at times just as bad. The opinion by Judge Skelly Wright that we quoted at the outset of this section involved the brand-new agency's efforts to ban the use of lead as an additive in gasoline in the mid-1970s, a decision that is widely credited as saving future generations of American children from grievous brain damage. Judge Wright understood the peril of forcing health and safety agencies to wait until they could count "bodies in the street" before controlling toxic exposures. On the other hand, the Fifth Circuit Court of Appeals, writing in 1991 in *Corrosion Proof Fittings v. EPA*,[58] a case involving a ban on the use of asbestos in consumer products, took a restrictive approach, demanding that the agency make a list of all the remedies that might address a problem and select the "least burdensome" one available. The court further held that this choice must be justified by quantified benefits that outweigh costs.

We can think of many other examples of interference with the EPA by the courts, Congress, and the White House, all demonstrating its role as the top target for the powerful campaign against regulation that began in the 1990s and has dominated the new millennium. We will use them throughout this book to explain the implications of what we contend are very bad choices by those other constitutional branches. But, as we have done with the EPA's four sister agencies, we set the stage for that discussion with one overriding example of how troubled and dysfunctional the agency has become over the last decade: its paralysis with respect to climate change, the most urgent and consequential issue on its regulatory agenda. In this context, hollow government, perceived uncertainties in science, and vigorous industry opposition to affirmative action have paralyzed the agency.

## Carbon "Pollution"

> If carbon dioxide continues to increase, the study group finds no reason to doubt that climate changes will result and no reason to believe that these changes will be negligible. . . . A wait-and-see policy may mean waiting until it is too late. — National Research Council[59]

> The scientific understanding of climate change is now sufficiently clear to justify nations taking prompt action. It is vital that all nations identify cost-effective steps that they can take now, to contribute to substantial and long-term reduction in net global greenhouse gas emissions. — Joint Science Academies[60]

Producers of fossil fuels (for example, coal and oil) spent millions of dollars in the 1980s and 1990s debunking the science of climate change and convincing many Americans that we did not know the answer to three central questions: (1) whether anthropogenic (man-made) emissions had caused significant changes in the planet's climate; (2) how serious these pollution-driven changes could prove for the survival of life as we know it on the planet; and (3) what we should do in response to the problem.[61] The answers to the first and second questions are now considered indisputable by reputable scientists, as indicated by the statement of the leaders of eleven nations' premier scientific institutions that is quoted at the outset of this section. Climate change is largely driven by anthropogenic emissions and is a tremendous challenge that will have grave implications before our grandchildren are adults. While you can still find sites on the World Wide Web where diehards quibble over details, the vast majority of knowledgeable experts are growing increasingly agitated over the political gridlock that has confounded efforts to reduce these emissions.

The Intergovernmental Panel on Climate Change (IPCC) is the most exceptional effort to organize scientific expertise in history. Founded in 1988 by two organizations sponsored by the United Nations, the World Meteorological Organization and the United Nations Environment Programme, it now includes over 4,500 scientists studying every conceivable aspect of climate change, from meteorology to geology to hydrology to anthropology. The IPCC neither conducts scientific research nor monitors climate phenomena but instead reviews existing and emerging research, much of which is being conducted by its individual members. It is divided into three working groups and one taskforce, all of which operate by consensus, meaning that they achieve unanimous agreement to the text in their published reports (referred to as "assessments"). The reports are strictly limited to objective statements about the state of science, as opposed to policy issues or conclusions.[62] The IPCC has published four such assessments, in 1990 (with a supplementary report in 1992), 1995, 2001, and 2007.[63] The group shared the 2007 Nobel Peace Prize with former vice president Al Gore.

For our purposes, a few excerpts from the fourth assessment published by the IPCC, "Working Group II on Impacts, Adaptation," are sufficient to give a sense of the transcending importance of this issue for the EPA's mission:[64]

- Climate change will negatively affect the health status of millions of people through increases in malnutrition, deaths and disease due to heat waves, storms, fires, and droughts, increases in diarrhoeal disease, cardio-respiratory diseases caused by higher concentrations of ground-level ozone, and infectious diseases such as malaria;
- Many millions of people will live in areas that are flooded every year due to sea-level rise by the 2080s and perhaps sooner;

- In North America alone, water shortages in the west, wildfires in forests, and urban heat waves will increase during the course of this century; and
- Global *mean* losses in GDP could rise as high as five percent if temperatures warm by 4°C, a possibility by the end of the century.

The Clean Air Act defines "air pollutant" to include "any air pollution agent or combination of such agents, including any physical, chemical, biological, radioactive . . . substance or matter which is emitted into or otherwise enters the ambient air."[65] In 1999, environmental groups filed a petition asking the EPA to regulate tailpipe emissions from motor vehicles to lower levels of so-called greenhouse gases (carbon dioxide, methane, nitrous oxide, and fluorinated gases).[66] The EPA denied the petition in 2003, reasoning that it did not have authority to control such emissions under the act and that it would be unwise to take any action now because the science was too uncertain.[67] The groups and several states sued, and the case eventually landed in the Supreme Court.

*Massachusetts v. EPA* was resolved by a 5-4 vote.[68] The majority was clearly irritated with the EPA, giving it three options: (1) shift into gear and regulate greenhouse gas tailpipe emissions; (2) explain why it thinks these gases do not contribute to climate change—a scientific impossibility; or (3) come up with some convincing explanation of why it cannot and should not act to curtail such emissions.

The minority devoted most of its dissenting opinion to an intricate discussion of why the state of Massachusetts would not suffer enough harm from climate change in the near future to qualify it to bring a case in front of the Court. The Constitution requires that courts only hear "cases and controversies," as opposed to deciding theoretical questions. The corollary of that requirement is that the plaintiff must have sufficient "standing"—that is, injury—to bring the case before the court. Although the dissenting justices gave broad hints that they doubted the severity of climate change and whether it was worth the cost for the United States to do something about it, they did not skate out on this thin ice in their official justifications for dismissing the case, relying instead on the notion that the plaintiffs were seeking the wrong relief in the wrong forum.

Now, alert readers may remember that President George W. Bush renounced the Kyoto Protocol, a leading international agreement on climate change, soon after he took office, despite having promised to take definitive international action on climate change during the 2000 presidential campaign. Why then should we have expected "his" environmental protection agency to be proactive on these issues? As the EPA pointed out in its argument before the Supreme Court, Congress has never gotten around to writing a detailed instruction for the agency on climate change, so the agency was entitled to sit on its hands.

Yet if you asked any number of Americans what they thought was the most urgent environmental problem facing the country, they would almost certainly identify climate change, whether or not they viewed the problem as belonging in the top tier or second tier of priorities for the country. (Polling is erratic on the "saliency"—or emphasis—given the issue by the average citizen.) A 2005 poll of "opinion leaders" conducted by the Pew Center on People and the Press showed that 86 percent of scientists and engineers ranked climate change as the nation's "top long-term priority," even considering such other threats as terrorism, immigration, the spread of weapons of mass destruction, and drug trafficking. And President Obama has listed climate change and its "twin" issue, energy independence, as one of his top five or six domestic policy priorities.

In the context of this common understanding of the importance of climate change within the framework of environmental problems, what are the implications for the EPA's overall credibility that it spent close to a decade fighting any outside effort to compel it to address this overriding issue? We do not blame the agency's career civil service for these omissions. They were acting at the direction of the Bush II administration and had very little choice in the matter. Rather, our point is that the corrosive effects of sidelining the federal agency with responsibility for such a crucial problem for such a lengthy period have implications for its future performance that are only just becoming clear.

As this book goes to press, Lisa Jackson, the newly appointed EPA administrator, has pledged to forge ahead on climate change, using existing Clean Air Act authorities to do as much as she can. President Obama has pledged to push for strong action on the problem but was unable to persuade Congress to fast-track its consideration of legislation. It remains unclear how long it will take for either logjam to be broken.

## Conclusion

OSHA's experience with benzene, which caused thousands of workers to sicken and die before the agency was finally allowed to control it, is a prototype of sorts for all five protector agencies. As soon as OSHA understood the risk of exposure to this extraordinarily toxic chemical and made tentative steps toward regulatory action, it faced a veritable explosion of opposition from potential regulated industries that had the resources, financial and political, to beat the agency back. Several years later, after more scientific evidence came in, we learned that, if anything, the chemical was much worse than originally thought, and OSHA was finally allowed to take action. In fact, it is possible to count on one hand the number of times that hazards addressed by the five agencies turned out to be negligible. The overwhelming record—in food, in drugs, in the workplace, and with respect to the ambient environment—is that those hazards turn out to be worse than originally thought and delays in taking action cost us dearly. Whether regulation was stopped or curtailed in court, in Congress, or at the White House, the problems did not dissipate.

Scarce resources and the cumulative toll of years of uphill battles have left all five protectors in a frighteningly weakened state. And yet, the total amount spent on all five agencies was less than 0.29 percent of the federal budget in 2009. If history is any guide, the pendulum will swing again, and revelations regarding unaddressed threats will be pushed to center stage. The real question is how high the costs of delay will be at that point.

## CHAPTER TWO

# The People's Agents

## Introduction

Readers may well emerge from reviewing chapter 1, and think either that the future of the five protector agencies is grim or that we are exaggerating. We have spent a cumulative total of sixty years working on these matters, and we were shocked when we assembled this data in one place—a task no one else has undertaken, at least as far as we know. We assure readers that although we went looking for problems, we did not focus on small ones. Admittedly, we omitted success stories and the many pieces of routine daily work that are accomplished without fanfare. Unquestionably, the American public would be in worse shape if the five protectors, even in their hobbled form, did not exist. But if they continue to stumble along, with Congress reforming them at the margins in response to crises that periodically make front-page news, lives will be lost, people will be hurt, and natural resources will be squandered. This lament is pointless, however, unless we propose solutions. That quest depends on an accurate understanding of the reasons why the agencies have failed.

Identifying regulatory failures pales in comparison with determining which of the many possible explanations of failure are applicable to a particular issue at a specific agency. This book pushes one long and ambitious step further, searching for the cross-cutting reasons why the five protector agencies have faltered so badly. Our goal is to find reforms that will allow the five agencies to be rescued by Congress, President Barack Obama, his political appointees, and the agencies' career staff, with some discreet and finely tuned help from the courts. Our recommendations are designed to make the agencies' efforts more transparent, more efficient, and more accountable to the American people. Throughout, we use illustrations drawn from important episodes in each agency's history over the past thirty years. These case studies help us to explain the need for reform and the reasons why our proposed reforms are pragmatic solutions.

This chapter locates our pragmatic methodology within the literature of four disciplines: law, economics, political science, and public administration. We examine the theoretical explanations scholars have offered for why the agencies have strayed so far, using one central theory that runs across this literature: if the five protectors serve in the capacity of "agents" for American government's ultimate "principal"—the American people as a whole—what conflicting incentives have led them so far astray? Or, to put the problem a different way, why have the checks and balances built into our democratic republic failed to compel the agencies to stay true to the mandates they receive from Congress, the first agent that the Framers of the Constitution charged with responsibility for writing laws that would carry out the will of the people?

As these questions suggest, our analysis leads us to two general conclusions that are generally overlooked in the literature on principal-agent relationships in government. First, the five protector agencies have multiple principals—the Congress, the White House, and the courts—and each of these masters has a profound effect on their performance. Second, while agencies themselves are a source of regulatory failure, so are these principals. They contribute to regulatory failure by making it more difficult for agencies to carry out their statutory missions and failing to engage in effective oversight. To fix this broken system, each of these major institutional players needs to do business differently, beginning with the proposition that, in many instances, the protector agencies are not primarily to blame for their many problems. The ultimate solution is not to muzzle or punish the five agencies but to free them to do their jobs more vigorously.

## The Principal-Agent Framework

In general, principal-agent theory considers the reasons why one actor (the principal) will have difficulty getting another actor (the agent) to work on behalf of the first actor's preferences. Principal-agent theory was originally developed by economists analyzing the problems of large corporations. Principals who form a corporation inevitably depend on agents to achieve the gains from their collective project. Expected mutual gains are lost if an agent's self-interest diverges from a principal's goals. Agency costs are the difference between the results agents would achieve if they acted solely in the interest of the principal and the results they actually achieve.

So, for example, a midlevel manager in a manufacturing company may have the incentive to "milk the plant," ignoring necessary maintenance in order to make the plant's profitability look greater as the manager climbs the corporate ladder to a position of greater responsibility. If the plant falls into sufficient disrepair that the company ultimately must spend more to fix it than if the repairs were made in a timely manner, the additional expenses are agency costs. Or, one could argue, on a more massive and deeply troubling level, the bank managers who steered their companies into the secondary mortgage market during the last several years were elevating their own ambitions for short-term profits above the possibility that these investments would threaten the corporation's viability—and therefore shareholder equity—over the long term.

Political scientists have expended considerable effort adapting principal-agent theory to legislation and the efforts of the administrative state to implement it. The fundamental principal-agent relationships at stake in that arena are depicted in the following diagram (Figure 2.1). "Article I" and "Article II" refer to the provisions of the Constitution that create the executive and legislative branches.

An ideal model of democracy anticipates that political leaders—or political agents—who are chosen in competitive elections will assume the power and responsibility for enacting and executing policy. Voters—the principals in this context—will reward leaders who successfully create and implement public policies they favor and punish leaders who are perceived as failing in this responsibility. The model raises two threshold issues, both of long-standing interest to political scientists and other analysts. First, do American elections produce the type of accountability suggested in this idealized model? The literature examining this issue considers the imperfections that impede electoral accountability, such as whether Americans have sufficient information to judge the performance of their political agents.[1] Second, because government has grown to an extent never anticipated by the Framers of the Constitution and now depends heavily on a large workforce of unelected civil servants, political scientists ask whether this bureaucracy is sufficiently accountable to elected officials that it does not "subvert the political will and make a mockery of the democratic principle."[2] The literature examining this second question considers the imperfections that impede bureaucratic accountability, such as whether Congress can legislate specifically enough to retain its control of over public policy, especially in the domestic arena.[3]

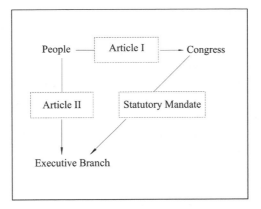

FIGURE 2.1. The people's agents.

Considerable uncertainty attends efforts to identify when agents are
acting against the interests of principals. Agents may successfully hide
their duplicity or may not realize they are being duplicitous. Agency costs
imposed by the pursuit of an agent's self-interest may not be immediately
obvious to principals or other agents. Agents can also inhabit dual roles.
So, for example, chief executive officers who make bad decisions in the
corporate context may also hold stock, serving as both principals and
agents and rendering themselves the victims of their own bad judgment.
Or, in the political context, the president, acting simultaneously as an
agent for the people and as a principal in relationship to the civil service,
may suffer an electoral backlash because the public is angry about actions
taken by an agency at his behest.

For these reasons and like any grand theory, principal-agent analysis
must be applied with humility and caution. Although we think enough
of the theory to use it throughout this book and to adopt a variation of
it as our title, we invoke it advisedly, as a helpful framework or meta-
phor for institutional failure, but not as a rigid model that can easily or
always explain the problems that plague political institutions. For us, the
theory's central value is to maintain an appropriately big picture focus on
the people most disadvantaged by agency regulatory failure—members
of the public in their individual capacities as consumers, workers, patients,
parents, eaters, or breathers. By constantly asking whether institutional
agents—the five protector agencies, Congress, the White House, and the
courts—are serving the interests of the public as a whole, we hope to
avoid becoming enmeshed in myopic analyses that overlook the influential
dynamics at play among them.

## Agents and Captors

The gap between what Congress or the president tells agencies to do and what they actually do is a kind of agency cost that is often referred to as "bureaucratic drift" or "bureaucratic slack" because it embodies the extent to which an agency has adopted policies that depart from the intent of the congressional majority that enacted the statutory mandate.[4] The possibility that bureaucrats will shirk their statutory mandates in reaction to outside pressure from regulated industries is also referred to as a manifestation of agency capture. The word "capture" is used to connote the practical reality that these departures constitute acquiescence to forces independent of, and assumed to be in conflict with, the directions of the principal.

Fear of capture animates all of the procedural law and guidance that accompanied the construction of the administrative state. Congress enacted the Administrative Procedure Act in 1947 to compel agencies and departments to employ fair and balanced procedures for considering the views of the public when they write rules and make other administrative decisions.[5] The act further specifies when and how the judiciary should oversee their decision making. These procedures create powerful incentives for the five protector agencies to listen to a wide range of views from stakeholders interested in the outcome of the regulatory process and to compile an administrative record made up of documents that provide a substantial basis—or justification—for a rule. As we shall see, however, such procedural safeguards have not always worked to prevent capture and other agency costs.

Discerning when a bureaucratic agent is captured and is acting in a way that imposes agency costs can be an extraordinarily complex undertaking. As we have explained, the principal-agent framework originated in the study of economic institutions where the prototypical transaction involves one actor (the principal) hiring or contracting with another (the agent) to accomplish a business goal of the principal. While the use of the same framework to analyze political institutions yields important insights, it is undermined by the reality that agencies answer to more than one master.

Again, under our constitutional framework, Congress, the White House, and the courts all have oversight functions with respect to agencies. The Constitution authorizes the president to appoint the senior officials who run the regulatory agencies (with the concurrence of the Senate) and to "take Care that the Laws be faithfully executed. . . ."[6] The Constitution does not explicitly mention an oversight role for the Congress with respect to the executive branch, but the Supreme Court interprets the Constitution as providing Congress with inherent powers to oversee activities by agencies and departments that may violate statutory mandates.[7] Finally, the Constitution puts the courts in an oversight role by empowering judges to act in "all Cases, in Law and Equity, arising under this Constitution [and] the Laws of the United States. . . ."[8] All three can also be regarded as principals as well as agents, and it is common to find this approach in the literature.[9] The upshot is that all three branches are responsible in different ways for ensuring that agencies comply with their statutory mandates, creating principal-agent relationships between the agency and the White House, the agency and Congress, and the agency and the courts.

A dramatic demonstration of these crosscurrents is the behavior of the ideological forces that dominated Congress between 1994, when Republicans swept control of the House of Representatives, and 2006, when Democrats recaptured that body. The conservative Republican majority spent significant time both disparaging the laws that authorized the five protector agencies and defunding their efforts to implement those mandates. Small wonder then that civil servants were confused about what their congressional principal wanted them to do.

Another aspect of the issues raised by the problem of multiple roles is that Congress shares its authority as an overseer with the president, in whom the Constitution vests all executive power. Remarkably, the extent of the president's authority under this delegation remains uncertain. This ambiguity has enabled presidents to assert that they have the authority to tell agencies how to implement the law, even though Congress has assigned final decision-making power to the agency itself; this assertion of presidential power is known as the "unitary executive theory." During the Bush II administration, the president and the vice president contended that the president should interpret the law and make final regulatory decisions so that he could carry out the policies he was elected to implement. His opponents said that his interpretations flouted clear legislative intent and that the Constitution assigns the president an overseer role rather than making him the final decision maker. Under this second view, which is our own, the president is the central principal—or people's agent—in many arenas, most notably foreign policy. But in carrying out the relatively detailed health and safety mandates conferred by Congress, he is more akin to a manager who should ensure that agency officials are faithful to congressional instructions.

In making this declaration of congressional superiority to speak as the primary principal for the people with respect to health and safety, we acknowledge that envisioning the American people as a single, monolithic principal is in and of itself an oversimplification. The people have diverse interests, which they express through collective action in a daunting variety of manifestations. For example, small business owners play a major role in the nation's politics, as do environmental groups, consumer organizations, and organized labor. Their elected representatives span the full range of views on these issues, and many disputes have regional origins.

Nevertheless, when legislation is enacted into law, the statute can be regarded as a unified expression of the people regarding the nature and scope of the policies they seek. Until and unless the law is repealed, or replaced with an alternative law, our legal system is structured to enforce it. The legislature in our constitutional system is "understood to serve—even if imperfectly and not without significant moments of contestation—as the privileged institutional expression of the capacity of the 'people' or the 'nation' to rule itself."[10] We recognize that enacted legislation may imperfectly reflect the will of the citizenry (itself another agency-cost problem), but this complication is far beyond the scope of this volume.

To make matters even more complicated, none of the three overseers is a unitary principal. Instead, each is made up of various entities, more than one of which might be involved in regulatory oversight. The president relies on the Office of Management and Budget (OMB) to oversee agency regulatory activities, but at times elements of a White House staff numbering in the hundreds also play a role in this activity. Congress fields numerous committees sharing overlapping jurisdiction over the five protector agencies. And judges appointed by different presidents review the validity of agency decisions at three levels, sometimes applying differing standards for upholding them or striking them down.

A final complication is that each of the three branches—the White House, Congress, and the courts, as well as discrete units within the three branches—can affect the capacity of the others to perform their oversight function, giving the agencies contradictory instructions, criticizing and even interrupting each other's oversight, and even seeking to rescue agencies from the influence of a competing entity within the same branch. Some analysts suggest that the relationship among agencies, the White House, Congress, and the courts is better understood as a series of network relationships,[11] with shifting combinations of actors over lengthy periods of time determining the nature and scope of agency costs.

## Antidotes to Capture

The legal literature—especially the extensive law and economics (or public choice) literature—is inordinately preoccupied with capture, to the point that some scholars view it as very difficult to have a civil service that is not dominated by special interests much of the time.[12] These scholars hypothesize that people are naturally motivated to a large extent by their personal access to money and power. In the regulatory context, among other incentives, civil servants hope to take advantage of the revolving door that will get them better paying industry jobs and therefore lean toward the views of regulated industries when making regulatory decisions.

Public choice scholars further argue that regulated industries have the clear advantage of being able to afford to be far more active during the lengthy administrative process than organizations representing the individual citizens who are the intended beneficiaries of government regulation.[13] Bureaucratic behavior is therefore more likely to generate decisions that are profitable to regulated entities, which are called "rents" in economic terminology, than decisions that benefit the general public. Or, as Professor Stephen Croley has explained it, " 'special interest' regulation denotes regulation that delivers regulatory rents to the greater detriment of society," while " '[p]ublic interested' regulation . . . denotes the alternative: regulation that improves social welfare."[14]

Empirical research confirms the greater activity of business representatives.[15] A 2005 study of registrations required by the Lobbying Disclosure Act shows that business or trade associations constituted over 94 percent of the groups whose activities on Capitol Hill required them to file reports, while only about 3 percent of the registrants were public interest groups. The study also found that 73 percent of the clients listed by lobbying firms in the reports were business interests, as compared with about 6 percent that were public interest groups. A 2009 study by the Center for Public Integrity reported that industry groups worried about climate change legislation have hired four lobbyists for each individual member of Congress, as compared with approximately 170 lobbyists who work for environmental and health groups.

This dominance on Capitol Hill is mirrored by higher rates of industry participation in rulemakings.[16] A survey of Washington-based interest groups found that individual businesses participated in over twice the number of rulemakings as other types of organizations. Business interests submitted many more comments on proposed regulations than other interests did. A study of forty rules promulgated by four agencies from 1994 to 2001 found that of the total number of comments, business interests filed 57 percent, governmental interests filed 19 percent, and nonbusiness, nongovernmental interests filed 22 percent.[17] Public interest group comments constituted only 6 percent of the total of comments submitted by nonbusiness, nongovernmental interests. Another study, examining comments filed on eleven proposed regulations at three agencies, found the same business dominance.[18] Corporations, public utilities, and trade associations filed between 66.7 and 100 percent of the comments concerning these rules, and neither the EPA nor the NHTSA received any comments from public interest groups concerning five of the eight rules.

The domination of regulatory agencies by business interests during the Bush II administration suggests that capture remains a real threat. However, the fact that business interests have more lobbyists and participate more frequently in filing rulemaking comments does not establish that they will necessarily prevail in the administrative process in the absence of sustained support from higher levels of government. The limited empirical evidence does not prove such a correlation.[19] Further, as we explain at greater length in chapter 6, some of the most notable instances of White House interference during the Bush II administration involved rebellions by civil servants against political appointees who were clearly acting on behalf of regulated industries, suggesting that an assumption of industry capture as the default position of the professional civil service is overdrawn. If civil servants are predestined to act solely in their immediate economic self-interests, what explains these important acts of resistance or, for that matter, the issuance of relatively strong rules in a variety of contexts?

Professor Croley proposes an alternative administrative process theory of regulation to account for these events. He argues that both the legislative and administrative processes present multiple opportunities for conflicting results. Special interests are certainly able to influence regulatory outcomes with greater access and superior resources for analysis. On the other hand, the instincts of career civil servants and the bright light of public attention frequently inspire outcomes more consistent with the public interest. Croley criticizes public choice theory as "oversold," "seriously incomplete and undertheorized," with "empirical predictions [that] are not supported by careful consideration of the evidence about how regulatory agencies operate or what they do."[20] He argues that career civil servants are generally motivated to pursue regulatory objectives that benefit the general public. Legal procedures assist them by protecting agencies against interest group pressures. To prove his point, Croley undertakes a series of meticulous case studies involving the regulation of ozone and fine particulate matter at the EPA, cigarettes and other tobacco products at the FDA, and limitations on roads in protected federal forest lands in order to prove his case that the regulatory process is at least as capable of producing "good" regulation as it is of being captured.

Croley's work is substantiated by other scholars, most notably professors Michael Levine and Jennifer Forrence, who argue that legislators and regulators present themselves, respectively, as public servants and civil servants to connote their commitment to the general welfare, largely because this image provides greater self-satisfaction than creating the impression that they are beholden to business interests.[21] Levine and Forrence define capture as the opposite posture, namely, "adoption by the regulator for self-regarding (private) reasons, such as enhancing electoral support or postregulatory compensation, of a policy which would not be ratified by an informed polity free of organization costs."[22] They describe the opportunity to engage in self-regarding behavior without public discovery as bureaucratic "slack" throughout their analysis. Levine and Forrence argue that so long as legislative and regulatory activity occur in public and achieve a reasonable amount of attention, capture is defeated, slack is avoided, and the public interest is served.

For many of the same reasons as Croley, Levine, and Forrence, we remain unconvinced that slack persists to the degree claimed by public choice theorists. The law requires transparency in such proceedings, providing many opportunities for exposure through the media, political competition (electoral campaigns), or scrutiny by public interest organizations and the "public policy intelligentsia."[23] Because exposure of self-regarding decisions is humiliating to bureaucrats, Levine and Forrence suggest that

> A self-interested regulator or other political actor is generally forced to make a choice between reducing or using slack: She can pursue political support by adopting—or offering to adopt—general-interest policies, and attempting at considerable expense and risk to reduce slack sufficiently for the general polity to support her because of them. Alternatively, she can solicit or accept capture, pursuing policies in return for special-interest political support, which can be substituted for (or, as in the case of political contributions, generate) general support. The principal risk in pursuing a capture strategy is that one of the slack-reducing institutions will expose the captured acts or policy to the general polity, which will then reject the regulator.[24]

Similarly, professors Kenneth Meier and Laurence O'Toole argue that the "bureaucracy itself, if infused with appropriate values, can support democratic governance."[25] They note that public administration scholars have demonstrated that institutions contain incentives—"commitment to agency values, identification with programs, satisfaction of doing difficult jobs well, solidarity benefits of associating with like-minded others"—that propel employees to fulfill an agency's mission.[26]

Earlier work by James Q. Wilson, Amitai Etzioni, and Herbert Kaufman suggests that agencies with a strong sense of their missions as safeguarding the public interest generally have a culture that influences employees to act consistently with that mission.[27] Agencies can also hire scientists, lawyers, engineers, public administrators, and other professionals who will be influenced to act according to the norms of their profession. Scientists, for example, are likely to act according to their training when it comes to the evaluation of scientific evidence, rather than follow some normative preference grounded in ideology. More broadly, Professor Gary Wamsley suggests that we can increase the influence of the previous incentives by infusing the bureaucracy with the normative responsibility of advocating for a public-interested resolution of regulatory problems, including recognizing and resisting political demands to the contrary.[28]

We will have more to say about all of the factors and institutions that are capable of enhancing or reducing slack, and how we might enhance their slack-reducing potential, in subsequent chapters. For now, we would simply submit that this carefully marshaled evidence in the literature summarized above, which explains why regulators have ample incentives to pursue policies that benefit the public interest, is considerably more convincing in its range, empiricism, and subtlety than the multiple, unproven assumptions that underlie capture theory.

## Monitoring and Accountability

In the end, the utility of the principal-agent framework is that it establishes direct links of responsibility between and among institutional players for defining a principal's goals and avoiding agency costs, including capture. By making the effort in any given situation to consider, first, the identity and goals of the principal and, second, the agent's success in achieving those goals, we have a valuable template for holding the agency accountable and, just as important, correcting the problem. Of course, identifying the relationships is only the first half of the battle. The more challenging task is to discover discrepancies between what the agencies are instructed to do and what they actually accomplish. Three large hurdles must be overcome. Another institution may sabotage the agency, undermining its ability to accomplish its mission. The mission itself may be ambiguous. The mission may depend on the development and interpretation of highly complex scientific or technical data.

## Sabotage

As we explained in chapter 1, and discuss throughout the book, Congress, the White House, and the courts have all made decisions that sabotage the five protector agencies' ability to carry out their statutory mandates. The leading example is the hollowing out of government, which we explore at length in chapter 3. A second form of sabotage occurs when institutions that compete with the agent for power undermine its performance in ways that are not visible to many of its overseers. One example is the onerous analytical requirements imposed on the five protector agencies by the OMB, which we discuss in chapter 4. Another example is intra–executive branch lobbying against stringent health and safety regulation mounted by other agencies and departments that engage in activities covered by those requirements. As we explain in chapter 6, the Department of Defense routinely opposes the EPA's pollution control proposals because it must comply in the same manner as any private business.

In a sense, the desperate funding shortfalls that undermine the five protectors are a form of agency cost because they result in grievous bureaucratic drift away from the goals set by Congress. These shortfalls could also be viewed as a modification of the original principal's goals by a subsequent Congress. Similarly, the OMB or the Department of Defense could be viewed as some kind of alternative principal that is trying to exert presidential control over the five agencies. However, these characterizations distort and misrepresent the principal-agent framework we envision. Bureaucratic drift, or slack, should be defined as actions by agents that are within the agent's control and depart from a principal's instructions. Defunding agencies without an explanation or allowing other portions of the government to distract them from the missions they were assigned by Congress are better viewed as acts of sabotage external to the principal-agent relationship.

Sabotage can be an extraordinarily difficult phenomenon to discover or define. Agencies do not acknowledge that it is occurring on any official level. Only after they have retired, and often not even then, will agency heads admit that funding shortfalls crippled the agency's performance. At that point, the admissions are no longer news, and they pass into history without garnering much attention. Interference from the OMB or other government entities similarly remains unacknowledged at the highest levels and takes place behind closed doors, although leaks by career staff have documented some of their implications and the OMB itself has publicized others. Observers often disagree about the legitimacy of this interference, raising the burden of demonstrating that it is a negative phenomenon.

*Ambiguous Goal Setting*

The potential for bureaucratic drift increases when Congress enacts ambiguous legislation that does not resolve significant issues but instead leaves them to civil servants to resolve during the administrative process, thereby delegating substantial discretion to administrators. Most of the legislation that is the subject of the book was passed in the 1960s and 1970s in reaction to public outrage over a number of highly visible environmental and safety disasters. The Cuyahoga River in Cleveland was so polluted that it caught fire; routine smog alerts afflicted Los Angeles; and a catastrophic oil spill ruined the beaches near Santa Barbara for a time. A congressional hearing revealed that General Motors hired private investigators to follow Ralph Nader in order to discredit his efforts to publicize dangerous defects in popular cars. Frequent mining catastrophes, such as the death of eighty-eight miners in Farmington, West Virginia, and the discovery of new occupational diseases, such as brown lung, focused the public on occupational safety and health risks. At about the same time, it was revealed that Frances Kelsey, an employee of the FDA, almost single-handedly prevented U.S. approval of the antinausea medication thalidomide. Dr. Kelsey acted before it became widely known that use of the drug in Great Britain had resulted in serious birth defects in children whose mothers had taken it while pregnant. That episode, among others, demonstrated that the tort system, augmented by minimal regulation, was incapable of preventing the grave injuries that result from health, safety, and environmental threats to the public.

By the end of the 1970s, Congress had passed dozens of new laws regulating business. These laws were considerably more prescriptive than the regulatory legislation that Congress passed in the Progressive Era and the New Deal, and some of the laws are more specific than others. But none of them gave sufficiently precise directives to the implementing agencies to eliminate major policy choices during the rulemaking process. In part, the lack of specificity reflected a pragmatic judgment by Congress that it would never finish its lawmaking if it spent the considerable time it would have taken to resolve every issue. Congress also recognized that health and safety regulation requires a level of scientific and technical expertise that was beyond its institutional ability.

During the Reagan and Bush I administrations, Congress amended several of the major environmental statutes in response to a widespread perception that the EPA was not acting when it should have been, was acting too slowly, or that when it did act, it did not follow the objectives of its authorizing legislation. The statutes grew in length from dozens to hundreds of pages and put the agency on strict timetables, specified a broad menu of rules and studies for it to accomplish, and even went so far in a few instances as to wade into the details of future rulemaking to an unprecedented extent. None of this effort has shielded the EPA from constant challenges to its decisions, in court and out.

While Congress can and has set reasonable limitations on what agencies can do, specifying affirmative requirements that make agency action ministerial is an unachievable goal, even if Congress wanted to try to accomplish it. The devil is in the details, and Congress lacks the expertise, the information, and the time to write the type of rules that agencies produce. However, the EPA's stature as the most effective of our five protector agencies is attributable to a large extent to ongoing congressional clarification of what it wants the agency to do, and by when. Each of the major environmental statutes has been amended twice—and some three times—since they were first enacted in the early 1970s. Congress stopped crafting these detailed mandates in 1990, and subsequent drift—or slack—was inevitable as the underfunded agency tried to grapple with new challenges in the absence of explicit statements of legislative intent. This experience indicates that a major solution to these agencies' dysfunction is for Congress to write far more detailed mandates setting priorities and resolving the most intractable political disputes before it asks agencies to implement regulatory solutions.

*Opacity*

A final factor confounding the search for agency costs is that the nature and scope of the problems addressed by the five protector agencies are extraordinarily complex from a scientific and technical perspective. At the same time, with the financial stakes of regulatory decisions very high, a multiplicity of interest groups are strongly motivated to debate the science and technology, further complicating it. The intrinsic complexity of the problems, the avid debates among interested parties, and the substantial discretion Congress grants to civil service experts make it more difficult to monitor agency performance. It is literally impossible to get very far without learning some science, knowing some technology, and having your own experts to consult when issues become impenetrable.

During the course of writing this book, and on numerous other occasions, we have each spent hundreds of hours digging into the details of high-profile decisions to determine whether they were produced by bureaucratic drift or can stand on their own merits. Paradoxically, the advent of the World Wide Web has made this work much easier, and exponentially more frustrating. Huge quantities of information are available to anyone with a click of a mouse. Yet the more one digests these data, the more apparent it becomes that the information defies easy synthesis and is chock-full of holes.

On one occasion, we attempted to discover whether the EPA was fulfilling one of its most important mandates under the 1990 Clean Air Act Amendments: the reduction of hazardous air pollution.[29] This mandate is important because hazardous air pollutants are chemicals that cause cancer, neurological damage, chronic respiratory disease and other serious, irreversible injuries and because emissions of these pollutants are also ubiquitous. Congress gave the EPA a list of 188 such pollutants, told it to figure out which industrial sources emitted the pollutants in amounts significant enough so that they should be controlled, and instructed the EPA to craft rules requiring the installation of pollution control equipment at these locations.

Anyone can go onto the World Wide Web today to discover reams of data about the EPA's efforts to implement those mandates. In fact, so much information exists that the researcher soon will have a sense of wallowing in it. This unpleasant sensation is exacerbated by the rapid escalation of complexity in these documents. A few clicks into the EPA databases and the information takes on a cast that only a person holding a doctorate in biochemistry could love.

And yet, despite this apparent surfeit of information, one can search in vain for consistent, uniform reports on the actual levels of these pollutants in the air of American cities and industrialized areas. If the researcher knew enough about the subject to understand how crucial it is to know what levels of these pollutants in the ambient air actually cause cancer or other diseases, she would not find that information on any Internet site operated by the government. Nor could she discover how much the EPA and other agencies were spending to research the impact of these pollutants on public health or to enforce these aspects of the law. This scenario is repeated over and over across the spectrum of health, safety, and environmental problems. The information is plentiful, it is extremely hard to digest, and crucial data are missing in the action. As we explain in chapter 8, the opacity of the information that is needed to monitor agency performance makes it much more difficult for other agents of the people — including mass media, public interest groups, and interested members of the public — to combat pressures on agencies from regulated industries.

## Conclusion

Our study of principals, agents, and accountability is divided into three parts. Part 1, "Diagnoses," incorporates the first, second, third, and fourth chapters and explains why the five protector agencies have failed to perform more effectively to protect Americans from safety and health hazards. These reasons include resource constraints and the imposition of additional analytical requirements on agencies that have ossified the rulemaking process. In Part 2, "Institutions," we shift to an examination of how Congress (chap. 5), the White House (chap. 6), and the courts (chap. 7) have contributed to regulatory dysfunction.

Part 3, "Solutions," that are intended to promote greater government accountability and less regulatory failure. Chapter 8 proposes performance measures that would gauge the extent to which agencies have been successful in completing their statutory mandate. The metrics would serve as an early warning that an agency's effort to implement its statutory mission is stalled or that the effectiveness of ongoing enforcement has deteriorated. Chapter 9 argues that elevating the prestige and compensation of the career civil service is an effective antidote to regulatory failure. Chapter 10 summarizes our recommendations in thematic, cross-cutting terms.

CHAPTER THREE

# Hollow Government

## Introduction

Conservative activists are cheerfully unapologetic about their enthu-
siasm for shrinking government. As Grover Norquist, the colorful
head of the conservative group Americans for Tax Reform, has explained
it, their goal is not to abolish government but to "to get it down to the
size where we can drown it in the bathtub."[1] Of course, Norquist and his
conservative allies have failed miserably in achieving this goal. During the
Bush II years, decisions to combine deep tax cuts with expensive wars
in Iraq and Afghanistan have left both federal spending and deficits at
record highs. This bad situation was rendered abysmal by a global financial recession and the decision to bail out financial institutions saddled
with bad mortgage debt. When bitter debates over the implications of the
deficit are combined with economic recession, the story line of this chapter—that the five protector agencies are starved of resources to the point
that they are "hollow"—either sinks into obscurity or, worse, is refuted
by the notion that we simply cannot afford to spend more on health and
safety protection right now.

Social spending is also in trouble because of a potent mix of deregulatory animus, a conviction that federal government spending is larded with
wasteful and unnecessary programs, and a chronic refusal to come to grips
with the entitlement spending that is by far the largest contributor to that
red ink. On the macrolevel of budget policy, the Reagan and Bush II administrations successfully forged an iron bond between the dual notions
that raising taxes is suicide for any political leader and that the federal
government is too broke to support the maintenance of existing social
welfare programs, much less add any new ones.[2] So overpowering is this

dogma that accusations about their opponents' penchant for raising taxes are the stock in trade of conservative politicians, despite the obvious fact that it will be impossible to dig out of historic deficits without collecting significantly larger revenues. Liberal politicians oblige by being cowed. To continue functioning in this polarized atmosphere, Congress developed a convoluted and opaque process to fund the government, using truncated emergency spending procedures and continuing resolutions to fund the wars in Iraq and Afghanistan, stimulus packages, the bailouts, as well as the routine operations of the government.

This contradictory, irresponsible, and angry atmosphere complicates recognition of the existence of hollow government, much less its implications. As just one recent example of the disconnect between the importance of these programs and deficit-induced budget anxiety, during the same week that a scandal erupted worldwide over Chinese milk products adulterated with melamine, a toxic chemical that causes kidney failure, Congress decided it could not afford to give the CPSC an extra $30 million in desperately needed additional funding because, according to reporting by the *Washington Post*, the bailout would deplete federal coffers.[3] Readers may remember that the CPSC is among the two most challenged of our five agencies. Growing numbers of consumer products sold in America, including 80 percent of all toys, are manufactured in China and other developing countries, which have no effective safety regulation. Yet at the time of this decision, the CPSC had a total of fifteen inspectors available nationwide to inspect such imports. The CPSC does not have jurisdiction over milk products imported from China—that difficult task is left to the similarly hollow FDA—but with thousands of Chinese babies sickened by the contamination, Congress should have made the connection that withholding desperately needed funding from any agency on the front line of protecting American consumers from hazardous imports was a bad idea. President Obama has since pledged to raise the CPSC's 2010 budget to $107 million, close to twice what it had in 2007, but not nearly enough to restore the agency's credibility.

The protector agencies are the orphans of the federal budgeting process. The budgets for the five agencies exist on the edge of the discretionary spending that is a dwindling portion of the budget in comparison with spending for Social Security, Medicare, Medicaid, and interest payments on the national debt. As deficits grow, and economic anxiety deepens, politicians on Capitol Hill and in the White House return again and again to cuts in the discretionary portion of the budget, rather than tackle entitlements.

Compounding these trends, the five agencies have had few champions among congressional appropriators, either because conservatives harbor hostility toward their missions or because sympathetic members of Congress have not made the effort to rescue them. Instead, potential agency allies have accepted the low ball budgets proposed by the last four administrations, making shortfalls in funding seem like a bipartisan and perfectly acceptable outcome.

This misplaced frugality does not make sense from a larger fiscal perspective. The total amount spent in 2008 on operating the EPA, the FDA, the CPSC, the NHTSA, and the OSHA was approximately $10.3 billion, or 0.29 percent of the $3.5 trillion budget Congress approved on April 2, 2009, and 0.89 percent of the $1.2 trillion deficit projected for FY 2010. Given the enormous leverage that catastrophic failures at these agencies can exert over public health, worker safety, and the environment, the argument that we cannot afford to increase their budgets obviously is untrue. Increasing agency budgets to realistic levels would not affect the federal deficit in any meaningful manner.

This chapter opens with an explanation of the fiscal realities the nation confronts and the dysfunctional budget process that produced them. We explore the implications of the lack of communication between the congressional committees that write the laws and the appropriations committees that fund agency efforts to implement them. We document the claim that the five agencies are starved for resources, showing their budgets in constant dollars over time and explaining how their missions have expanded as their funding has declined. We conclude with several recommendations for reforming the system with the goal of making budget trade-offs more transparent, thereby forcing Congress to either curtail the five agencies' statutory mandates or increase their budgets, or to employ some combination of both strategies.

## The Broken Budget

*Deficits, Entitlements, and "Discretionary" Spending*

As we write this chapter, economies throughout the world have gone into deep recession. The shocks to the system are sufficiently grave that predictions about the future direction of the federal government's spending are far more uncertain than usual. We therefore offer these data to give the reader some general sense of the trend lines and not because we can

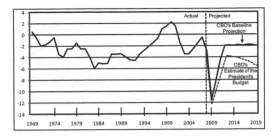

FIGURE 3.1. Total deficits or surpluses, 1969–2019 (percentage of gross domestic product). *Source*: Congressional Budget Office.

be confident that any specific aspect of its projections will prove accurate. The bottom line is that budget deficits are large and likely to grow significantly larger, unless the economy unexpectedly improves or Congress makes some very difficult choices.

Federal spending is divided into three categories. "Mandatory" spending includes benefit programs like Medicare, Medicaid, and Social Security. These funding categories are not subject to annual appropriations but rather continue from year to year, with benefits determined by eligibility criteria set periodically by Congress. Net interest is debt service on what the government owes. Discretionary spending includes funding for the operation of all federal agencies and departments and is subject to annual appropriations. The growth of entitlements and mounting public debt are gradually squeezing out all other forms of spending. As demonstrated by Figure 3.2, unless entitlements are reformed, the country will not be able to afford to maintain anything close to existing spending levels on social welfare and regulatory programs, much less defense, even after the global recession comes to an end. (This figure was published in January 2008 and was not updated in 2009.)

Even if Congress discovers the political courage to reform entitlements, or dire economic conditions force its hand, other social welfare priorities compete strenuously with existing programs for whatever money is left. Overhaul of the health care system is on the priority list, as is federal investment in combating climate change and developing clean energy sources. The straightforward "meat and potatoes" enforcement of existing law will have difficulty holding its own against those compelling alternatives, even though, as we mentioned at the outset, the combined funding of all five protector agencies is quite small.

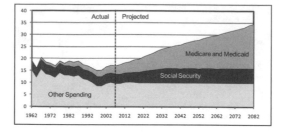

FIGURE 3.2. Projected federal spending over the long term (percentage of gross domestic product). *Source*: Congressional Budget Office.

### Indefensible Process

How did we get to the point that our national political leaders refuse to address these paralyzing fiscal circumstances? For the last thirty years, the twin mantras that the federal government must become smaller and that it has no money have collided with the strong political momentum to maintain existing programs, the fear of touching entitlements, and the powerful incentives to deliver federal spending that benefits members' states and districts. As it turns out, while the deficit-ridden, "small is better" mindset often prevails in the context of social welfare spending, including the funding of health and safety regulation, it is inexplicably neutralized with respect to the extraordinary sums we have spent prosecuting the war in Iraq.

Nobel Prize–winning economist Joseph Stiglitz and his colleague Linda Bilmes estimated in April 2008 that the war in Iraq will ultimately cost the American taxpayer three trillion dollars, in comparison with initial estimates of $50–60 billion by the Bush administration.[4] Professors Stiglitz and Bilmes used "conservative" assumptions in deriving this estimate, and they say that the ultimate total is likely to be much higher. Their projections include, in a way that the congressional budget process almost never does, the long-term costs of caring for wounded soldiers, abruptly removing from the workforce hundreds of thousands of National Guard and other reserves, and restoring the military to its prewar state.

The fact that Congress did not have any grip on these figures when it first authorized the president to embark on such a mammoth undertaking is troubling but understandable given the national state of trauma induced by the events of September 11, 2001, and the executive branch's dissembling on the subject. Congress's refusal to come to grips with these costs even after the war had been underway for many years is far harder to justify. But from a budgetary point of view, one forgotten legacy of this

tragic misadventure is congressional cooperation with the Bush II administration's strategy of requesting war funding in the form of "emergency
supplemental" legislation, in effect eliminating the traditional process of
conducting hearings that would subject such large expenditures to continuing budget estimates and force Congress to explain how such spending
would affect other national priorities. According to Stiglitz and Bilmes,
"The continued use of this emergency procedure—five years after the war
began—is budgetary sleight of hand that makes a mockery of a democratic budget process."[5]

The main reason President Bush wanted to sidestep the regular budget process is that Congress has passed a series of laws attempting to
impose accountability on itself for deficit reduction. Had these requirements applied to war funding, the impact of the war would have been front
and center in the budget process in Congress, an outcome that both a
Republican-led Congress and President Bush sought to avoid.

The cornerstone of the modern budget process is the 1974 Congressional Budget and Impoundment Control Act, which was passed to reassert
congressional hegemony over the budget after President Richard Nixon
had impounded money appropriated for specific programs.[6] The new statute created the Congressional Budget Office so that Congress would no
longer be as dependent on the White House OMB for budget estimates
and calculations. It required that Congress adopt "budget resolutions"
that establish caps on spending in twenty functional categories, including
national defense, agriculture, and transportation, for a five-year period.
The budget resolution is never sent to the president and has no independent legal standing of its own.[7] Rather, it serves as a kind of honor code for
appropriations committees, which are expected to work within the caps
it establishes. Congress often fails to adopt budget resolutions on time
and sometimes neglects to approve them altogether.[8] Nevertheless, both
houses have adopted procedural rules that allow members to object to appropriations bills that exceed such targets. Ignoring the caps is a venture
fraught with risk for any subcommittee chairman.

In 1985, with budget deficits hovering in the $200 billion range, Con-
gress and outside economists proclaimed a "budget crisis" and passed the
Gramm-Rudman-Hollings Act in an effort to bring spending under control.[9] The law took the radical approach of "sequestering" (automatically
cutting) federal spending in excess of a preordained, acceptable spending
level and was designed to compel reduction of the deficit and bring the
budget back into balanced alignment. Although the statute remains on
the books, Congress and the president made creative use of its exemptions

to circumvent the statute's prescriptions and the deficit once again rose to extraordinarily high levels.

Congress returned to the drawing board to invent a new mechanism for controlling itself one last time in 1990, passing the Budget Enforcement Act (later extended and amended by the Omnibus Budget Reconciliation Act of 1993).[10] In theory, these statutes place an overall cap on discretionary spending—spending that is subject to annual appropriations caps, including the military budget—and require a "pay-as-you-go," or PAYGO, approach to entitlements—the portion of the budget committed to benefits like Social Security, Medicare, and Medicaid. PAYGO means that before Congress increases benefits, it must ensure that they are "deficit neutral" and are either supported by new revenue or offset by spending cuts in other programs.[11] Once again, Congress has invented multiple methods for circumventing these requirements, including the drastic expansion of the definition of "emergency spending."[12] In fact, as a sign of how much congressional adherence to the law's goals has degenerated, advocates of tax cuts have long argued that they should be exempted from PAYGO, effectively placing billions of dollars of deficit-creating funding outside the process.[13]

Under traditional practice, the House of Representatives Appropriations Committee, informed by a budget resolution if one is available, reports twelve separate appropriations bills to the full body, beginning in May or June of the fiscal year preceding the expenditures and finishing by the August recess.[14] Once each is passed on the House floor, they are sent over to the Senate for consideration and amendment. Following approval on the Senate floor, the bills are sent to a conference committee for reconciliation of their differences, then returned to the two houses for final approval, and sent to the president for signature. But in half of the past ten years (FY 1998–2007), neither chamber passed all of their "regular" appropriations bills. Instead, Congress provided funding through two alternative procedures that are far less deliberative and transparent. The first is passage of "omnibus appropriations measures"—gigantic pieces of legislation that combine several individual appropriations bills in documents thousands of pages long, precluding floor debate, and depriving most members of the opportunity to understand what their votes mean. The second is temporary funding, typically extending appropriations for only a few weeks or months and enacted in legislation called a "continuing resolution."[15]

Health and safety agencies have suffered greatly under these procedures. Because statutory requirements governing the budget are routinely bypassed, their lasting legacy is not to reduce deficits but rather to provide ample justification for Congress or the executive branch to justify low-profile spending cuts regardless of their policy implications. The result is that the hollowing out of health and safety agencies continues unabated, with one year's cuts creating a lower baseline for the next year's cuts, without either authorizing or appropriations committees taking the time to evaluate the cumulative impact of those reductions.

## Authorizers versus Appropriators

### The Authorizers

What would happen to any business if one group of people determined what it would do and how it would operate and a second group, which lacked any formal mechanism for consulting with or achieving accountability between the two groups, was exclusively in charge of determining the levels of financing for such efforts? The scenario is unthinkable in a business context, but it is an accurate description of how Congress functions with respect to the five agencies and, for that matter, the rest of the federal government.

Authorizing committees in the House of Representatives and the Senate are charged with responsibility for writing the statutes that determine agencies' missions and mandates. So, for example, the Clean Air Act is the primary responsibility of the Senate Environment and Public Works Committee and the House Energy and Commerce Committee.[16] In between reauthorizing the major statutes, committees of primary jurisdiction should exert ongoing oversight of agencies' performance in order to ensure that they are fulfilling their statutory mandates. Without consistent oversight, the committees are chronically unprepared for the next reauthorization process because they lose track of what the agencies are doing.

After two periods of extraordinarily active lawmaking in the early 1970s and in the mid-1980s, congressional efforts to carry out responsibilities to reauthorize the health and safety arena withered away, to the discredit of everyone concerned. The last time the House and Senate authorizing committees convened successfully to pass a comprehensive rewrite of the Clean Air Act was during the 101st Congress (1989–90), when they engaged in a pitched and exhausting battle to craft a compromise that could gain majority support. Stories written at the time said the legislation was a "decade in the making" and was the product of "marathon closed-door talks."[17] As just one vivid example, the following describes what went on in the House of Representatives Energy and Commerce Committee at one crisis point in the proceedings:

> Staff and members horse-traded throughout the day and into the night. At 2 a.m. on April 5, according to some accounts, 30 to 35 of the committee's 43 members were still on hand. [Chaiman] Dingell had extended the committee meeting time, but only a little bit at a time, to keep members negotiating. Scores of lobbyists milled in the hallway outside the closed doors of the committee room, where a hand-lettered sign was intermittently updated by crossing out the previous meeting time and writing in a new one.
>
> Offers and counteroffers were made as late as 4:30 a.m. before members went home for a few hours, only to return to begin negotiating again. "You know the only different between being in a medium-security prison and being in Congress?" asked Rep. Bruce later that day. "There isn't any. In both facilities, .you can walk around all you want—you just can't leave."[18]

Nineteen years have passed since Congress passed the 1990 amendments, which are widely regarded as transforming the Clean Air Act into by far the most ambitious federal regulatory statute. Among other things, the amendments required the EPA to specify pollution controls over hundreds of industries that emitted any one of 188 hazardous air pollutants in significant quantities. The law also required the agency to establish an innovative new program for controlling sulfur dioxide emissions through the allocation of pollution allowances—a single allowance grants permission to emit a ton of $SO_2$ annually—to power plants that emit such pollution. These allowances can then be traded (bought and sold) among sources. The amendments updated the law's requirements for the control of smog and other common pollutants, shifting the deadlines for when many of America's largest cities had to bring emissions down to acceptable levels for public health. The 1990 amendments also demanded that the EPA and its state partners set up a rigorous new permitting program for major sources.

Over the past two decades, the EPA has struggled to implement the law's requirements. Constituencies disgruntled by those decisions have sued the EPA on numerous occasions. Changes too numerous to itemize have occurred in the way air pollution is released by industrial and other sources and how this pollution is monitored, modeled, and controlled. The catastrophic effects of unabated climate change caused by greenhouse gases have been documented by an unprecedented global scientific collaboration involving thousands of experts under the auspices of the International Panel on Climate Change. But the authorizing committees have never found the energy to revisit and update the statute. In fact, during the period when Republicans controlled both chambers, ongoing oversight of the EPA or, for that matter, the other four agencies, was for all practical purposes suspended.

## The Appropriators

Meanwhile, House and Senate appropriations committees have established funding levels for the EPA each year without the benefit of the authorizers' public advice, although we cannot, of course, account for informal consultations. Instead, the appropriators rely almost exclusively on the testimony of EPA and other agency officials, who are constrained to defend whatever the OMB has decided to approve in light of other presidential priorities. Of course, agency officials are often asked detailed questions by appropriators about what the additional resources that would be necessary to accomplish certain tasks would cost. But no official who values her professional future departs from the official bottom line for agency appropriations specified by the president.

Ironically, in 1974, Congress signaled its discomfort with this gap in communications by including a provision in the Congressional Budget Act that bound authorizing committees to provide their views on the president's budget submission to the House and Senate budget committees.[19] Despite its apparently marginal effect on final appropriations, the provision shows that Congress could do more to encourage communications between authorizers and appropriators.

If appropriators duplicated the oversight process that is—at least in theory—the responsibility of authorizing committees, the results would be wasteful, but we would have less reason to be concerned about the quality of their funding decisions. But available evidence indicates that appropriators engage in very little inquiry into an agency's performance before, during, or after making these fateful decisions.

In an insightful article on the effects of these disparities on environmental policy, Professor Richard Lazarus explained that authorizing committee staff outnumber appropriation committee staff by large margins. As a result and by design, the appropriators "do not possess the degree of focused substantive expertise and experience on substantive environmental issues."[20] Lazarus reported that in 2005, the House subcommittee with jurisdiction over the EPA's money had six staff members, who divided their attention between that agency and a slew of others, while the House Energy and Commerce Committee, again responsible for much of the EPA's authorizing legislation, had sixty-one staff members. The Energy and Commerce Committee also exerts jurisdiction over a wide variety of agencies and departments, but the suspicion that it outmatches appropriators in oversight and law-writing potential is underscored by the fact that when appropriators hold hearings in advance of developing final legislation, they typically rely upon testimony by senior agency officials, who—as explained earlier—have powerful constraints imposed both on how much they can depart from the party line presented in the president's budget and on how willing they are to be self-critical.

Professor Lazarus wrote his article to condemn the practice of legislating substantive rules during the appropriations process. Known as "appropriations riders," such provisions are typically styled as amendments that either forbid an agency from spending money to implement a policy Congress dislikes or as an outright amendment of the underlying law. The legality of the second kind of rider—those crafted as substantive amendments—was confirmed by the Supreme Court in *Robertson v. Seattle Audubon Society*, where the justices upheld a rider that allowed timber cutting in old-growth forests, taking away from environmentalists a hard-won judicial victory with the opposite result.[21] In effect, said the Court, it makes no difference from a constitutional perspective whether a piece of substantive legislation originates in the appropriations committees or in the authorizing committees; the Constitution does not compel Congress to organize itself internally in any specific respect.

Conservatives have generally made more aggressive use of appropriations riders than environmentalists, although both ends of the political spectrum, despairing of their prospects for motivating Congress to amend agency legislation in the authorizing committees, have resorted to this strategy more often in recent years. We agree with Professor Lazarus that this end run around the traditional authorizing process is unfortunate. However, the significance of these concerns pales in comparison with the overall point that the disconnect between authorizing and appropriating has produced a situation in which agencies do not get either what they want or what they really need in the process.

Grim budget realities mean that over the next few years, Congress and the president will face some extraordinarily tough budgetary choices. With too little money and too many needs, it is hard to imagine that Congress's commitment to avoiding entitlements reform will remain tenable. At the same time, continued neglect of the budgetary needs of the five protector agencies could play out as scenarios in which crises trigger intermittent remedies that do little to solve overall problems but give an illusion of reform. So, for example, dangerous imports could cause large-scale injuries and the CPSC will be given better legal authority and a small increment of a budget increase. Drugs with unacceptable side effects will go to market until an unusually high number of injured patients attract media attention and the FDA will be granted more funding for monitoring the safety of existing medications. In all instances, authorizers will make decisions about legal authority in isolation from appropriators' decisions about funding support.

Alternatively, as we suggest in the last section of this chapter, system-wide reforms could be implemented that begin the job of restoring the strength of these agencies before the next crisis. Taking a hard look at their budgets in the context of the growing demands of their missions will give us some idea of what that restoration would involve.

## Health and Safety Shortfalls

The following two figures trace the actual spending on the five agencies in constant dollars—that is, the number of dollars adjusted for inflation using the Consumer Price Index—between 1970 and 2008.[22] The CPSC, FDA, OSHA, and NHTSA are presented in one figure because their budgets are all lower than $2 billion annually. The EPA budget, which topped out at figures several times that amount, is presented in the second. The very large estimates shown for the EPA in 1972–74 were exceptional commitments of funding for state and local sewage treatment and public drinking water infrastructure.

With the exception of the FDA, which received moderate funding increases to accelerate its process for approving new drug applications, these figures show that none of the agencies have received significant increases in their budgets since roughly 1980, approximately a decade after they were created. During this time period:

- The United States population grew 34 percent, from 227 million in 1981 to 304 million in June 2008.
- In 1975, OSHA was responsible for policing 3.9 million workplaces, which employed 67.8 million workers; it had 2,405 inspectors to do the job. By 2006,

the number of workplaces had grown to 8.7 million, and worker population to 133.8 million, and the number of OSHA inspectors had fallen to 2,165.

- Between 1987 and 2006, the number of prescriptions filled in the United States came close to tripling, from 1.2 billion to 3.1 billion.

- In 1980, 155,796,000 motor vehicles were registered in the United States. By 2006, that number stood at 244,165,686.

- The EPA budget level set in 1984, which remains roughly the same amount in constant dollars as it is today, preceded passage of a series of ambitious amendments to every major environmental law, including the 1990 Clean Air Act Amendments.

If the total amount of money at stake is so limited, and the need so great, why are these agencies caught up in such powerful downward pressure on their budgets? As we have explained, the entire discretionary portion of the budget falls prey to this excruciating tension, and appropriators are sufficiently desperate about the deficit that it takes a powerful lobbying effort to compel them to separate out any agency or group of agencies for significant budget increases. Presidents can accomplish this result, and public interest groups or industry representatives might be able to do so, but none have made the necessary concerted effort in the health and safety arena.

Stakeholders at both ends of the political spectrum do not focus on budget problems, perhaps because they are convinced that this approach is a lost cause. With the country's deficit problems getting exponentially worse precisely because affirmative regulation of financial institutions was

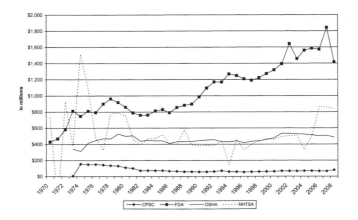

FIGURE 3.3. CPSC, FDA, OSHA, and NHTSA budgets in constant dollars, 1970–2008.

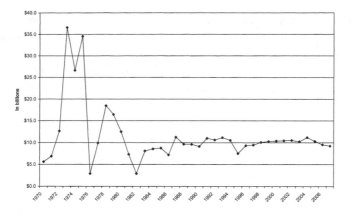

FIGURE 3.4. EPA budget in constant dollars, 1970–2007.

so seriously neglected, this pervasive atmosphere may not change. The global economic crisis should teach us that shortchanging government supervision of the marketplace is penny-wise and pound-foolish.

## Prospects for Reform

### A Clearer Vision of Government

Few politicians have acknowledged the inescapable truth that funding must increase substantially if the agencies are to regain the capacity to carry out their statutory missions. From the mantra chanted by the Clinton administration that environmental regulation could be "cleaner, cheaper, and smarter"[23] to the conservatives' attacks alleging that stringent regulation saps American competitiveness,[24] the respectable course has been to ignore these acute funding gaps. People who emphasize the need for significantly more funding are viewed as anachronistic thinkers out of touch with today's budget realities.

Given the strong trend toward blaming regulatory failures on bureaucratic inefficiency, the foundation of any effort to govern successfully in these challenging times must be a renewed vision of what government can and should do for the people. Professor Randall Strahan's observations in 1988 regarding these dynamics remain relevant today:

> The years following the Reagan Administration's 1981 tax and budget cuts may be characterized (after the fashion of the times) as the *post-liberal* era in American politics. The defining characteristics of this period include the existence of

unprecedented peacetime budget deficits together with the absence of a dominant public philosophy. Extremely large budget deficits have made clear definition of essential domestic and international responsibilities the principle task of governing at a time when the nation's political leadership is sharply divided over the role of government in society and America's role in the world.

. . .

[N]either the old liberalism nor a minimal government conservatism of the Reagan variety can provide the framework for a governing coalition in American society today. . . . [T]he prospects for effective governing in the post-liberal era will depend to a considerable extent on the development of a public philosophy that better reconciles the hard realities of the present with the historic aspirations for liberty, equality and progress that animate American political life.[25]

The fiscal and economic crises unfolding globally underscore this trenchant advice. The next generation of national political leaders would serve the public well by explaining how they would define the government's role in protecting public health, worker safety, natural resources, and the environment. If, as we think it should, their vision includes effective regulation that would avert workplace injuries and death on the job, toxic pollution, destruction of stratospheric ozone, importation of impure food and dangerous consumer products, and the approval of ineffective or harmful drugs, we must find reliable methods for figuring out how much money is really needed to support such efforts and make sure those resources are available.

As a first step, Congress and the president must revamp the arcane and often disconnected processes they use to write the budget and appropriate money to the government, restoring discipline and transparency so that their choices among national priorities become transparent and accessible to the people. President Obama has made some significant progress on budget reform by projecting expenditures out ten years rather than five, indexing the alternative minimum tax to inflation rather than assuming it will expire, estimating the costs of future military actions overseas, projecting the federal costs of disaster relief, and incorporating reimbursements to doctors serving Medicare patients rather than assuming such costs will be cut by future congresses. Republicans have responded to these efforts by accusing the new president of behaving like a "tax and spend" liberal, and we can only hope that he persists despite this well-worn rhetoric.

The other, equally daunting challenge that the president must confront is the widespread perception, again stoked by his political opponents, that the country cannot afford expensive changes in the ways health care is delivered or in how the country responds to climate change, not to mention the fearmongering that will inevitably accompany his pledge to curb entitlement spending over the long run. These dire warnings are dominating the airwaves as this book goes to press and may well provide enough friction in the momentum of budgetary reform to stall it out completely. This discouraging outcome is especially likely to happen if the global recession persists for a period of several years.

Additional funding for the protector agencies is a function of two disjointed but closely related factors: whether these issues receive enough attention from the White House to become part of the president's official agenda or, conversely, whether a coalition in Congress becomes sufficiently alarmed by high-profile regulatory failures to undertake such reforms piecemeal, on an agency-by-agency basis. The prospects for the first development depend heavily on the quality of President Obama's appointments at the five agencies and their ability to envision the severity of their funding plight. The prospects for the second development depend on the legislative skills and ideological coherence of congressional Democrats, both of which seem unstable and therefore unpredictable. Yet the two forces could meet somewhere in the middle, perhaps on an agency-by-agency basis, with worker safety, imported food, and climate change our top candidates for more money.

To prepare for that moment, some people with authority in the government—perhaps agency budget chiefs, staff of the White House OMB, or ambitious House or Senate appropriators, will need to think outside the box about matching available spending authority with agency missions, making it clear for the first time how much money it would really take to implement these mandates. Such "true-up estimates" should not consider industry compliance costs or social opportunity costs but should focus solely on the resources the government itself would need, calculated in constant dollars over a decade-long period, to do the work involved in enforcing or modifying existing rules and developing new ones. True-up estimates could be done in conjunction with the accountability metrics we introduce in chapter 8. Taken together, a list of priority accomplishments and an estimate of the cost to government of achieving those goals would make it possible, perhaps even likely, for an honest dialogue on future direction to occur.

As part of his FY 2010 budget submission to Congress, President Obama pledged to "fundamentally reconfigure" OMB's Performance Assessment Rating Tool (PART), an obscure but resource-intensive process designed by Bush II administration political appointees to evaluate the effectiveness of program management.[26] According to the Bush-era OMB,

> The [PART] was developed to assess and improve program performance so that the Federal government can achieve better results. A PART review helps identify a program's strengths and weaknesses to inform funding and management decisions aimed at making the program more effective. The PART therefore looks at all factors that affect and reflect program performance including program purpose and design; performance measurement, evaluations, and strategic planning; program management; and program results.[27]

What this euphemistic description omits is that the OMB had such a hostile relationship with the agencies that the agencies expected poor PART evaluations to result in funding cuts, undermining their incentive to cooperate with OMB auditors.

Obama administration OMB director Peter Orszag seems to understand this perverse dynamic. In testimony before the Senate Budget Committee in March 2009, Orszag pledged to revamp PART to focus on a "limited set of high priority goals" that reflect what "Americans care about and that are based on congressional intent."[28] The key to using PART, however, is to allow agencies independently to develop estimates of what they would need to fulfill their statutory missions, using a standard methodology developed by OMB, with OMB providing commentary and, if necessary, criticism, but not attempting to revise the estimates to reflect its own attitudes toward the programs.

## Conclusion

It seems beyond dispute that the country must address the difficult problems of escalating entitlement spending and the costs of the wars in Iraq and Afghanistan. Less obvious, but equally important, is the need for Congress and the president to forswear the sleight-of-hand tactics we explained earlier in order to return to a process that makes budget trade-offs more explicit.[29] These corner-cutting and dishonest techniques have allowed the nation's elected officials across the political spectrum to escape difficult choices for far too long.

Even with these reforms, as long as we keep asking how we can afford to increase spending for government, we will never get to the question of how we can afford not to. No reliable estimates have ever been prepared of the costs of regulatory failure and delay. Even with a significant effort, such estimates would be no more reliable than the exaggerated, even fanciful estimates of how much regulation costs business. Predictions regarding the monetary value of harm caused by unenforced laws and unwritten rules would be speculative at best.

Yet we have isolated, episodic glimpses of potentially avoidable costs that make the investment we have made in health and safety regulation— approximately $10.3 billion annually—look small in comparison. The peanut industry alone suffered $1 billion in losses, nine people died, and 20,000 were sickened as a result of the salmonella outbreak at a Georgia peanut processing plant during the fall and winter of 2008–2009; the recall of 2,100 types of products containing the tainted nuts must have cost much more. And, of course, from the perspectives of the families who lost loved ones, the loss was priceless. The plant was inspected and given a clean bill of health by an unqualified private-sector inspector paid by the peanut plant operator and hired under pressure from the plant owner's largest customers. The peanuts were shipped despite the owner's receipt of tests showing salmonella from an independent testing lab.

Multiply this single incident by countless episodes in the workplace, the pharmacy, the grocery store, and the playground on a code red air pollution day, and cumulative, quantifiable costs, not to mention nonquantifiable losses, are likely to dwarf the cost of making the regulatory system effective.

One final consideration is the damage inflicted on people's confidence in government by the increasingly chronic and well-publicized failure of government efforts to accomplish the fundamental protection that most people expect without really thinking about it. Or, as the GAO, bastion of an objective mind-set and an auditor's heart, producer of fact-filled narrative and dispassionate prose, expressed the problem in a recent report: "Recent events, such as lead paint in imported children's products, tainted meat, predatory mortgage lending, contract fraud, and national disasters like Hurricane Katrina and the attacks of September 11, 2001, raise questions among the American people about the capacity of the federal government to meet their most pressing needs."[30]

## CHAPTER FOUR

# Cost-Benefit Analysis

## Introduction

*T*he *Odd Couple*, a popular movie comedy released in 1968, features two men who find themselves living together by accident—the neat, precise, yet neurotic Felix Unger (played by Jack Lemmon) and the relaxed, humanitarian, yet sloppy Oscar Madison (played by Walter Matthau). The regulatory system has its own version of *The Odd Couple*. Since the 1980s, the White House has required agencies to undertake a cost-benefit analysis of rules that will impose large costs on regulated industries and result in major benefits for members of the public. The idea appears straightforward and utilitarian—after all, we need to know whether it is worth asking industry to spend money for improvements in public health and safety or the preservation of natural resources. The rub is that such analyses routinely overstate costs so significantly— and understate benefits so drastically—that they become rule killers of unwarranted proportions, thwarting the goals of the health and safety statutes.

*The Odd Couple*'s Felix runs around the apartment he shares with Oscar, berating Oscar for being such a slob and cleaning up after him. In the rule-making process, agency and White House economists seek, in Felix-like fashion, to influence the outcome of the regulatory process according to their utilitarian outlook and training, while other agency experts struggle, in Oscar-like fashion, to honor congressional instructions to minimize the number of deaths, injuries, and other harm. The clashes between these two groups are not amusing and would make a painfully dull movie. But they have gradually become more important in determining the outcomes of agency decision making than science, technology, and social values.

The Reagan administration introduced the requirement—continued by all subsequent presidents—that agencies must produce a cost-benefit analysis for every "major rule," a term of art meaning requirements imposing more than $100 million in compliance costs.[1] Cost-benefit analyses are designed to provide a quantified—or numerical—estimate of both the potential costs and benefits of a proposed rule. President Reagan and his successors also prohibited agencies from proposing or adopting rules until they are reviewed by economists at the Office of Information and Regulatory Affairs (OIRA), a division of the White House OMB.

Potential costs include whatever money regulated companies will be compelled to spend to implement the remedies proposed in the rule, such as installation of pollution-control equipment or obtaining and enforcing the use of hard hats and respirators for workers dealing with hazardous conditions or materials. The primary sources of compliance cost estimates are the industrial firms to be regulated, and those figures are routinely overstated. Agencies typically do a poor job of critically evaluating such claims.[2] Furthermore, when a rule requires the use of an emerging technology, prices fall as the market expands, lowering compliance costs, yet these dynamics are often ignored. To put these problems in perspective, everyone agrees that cost estimates are an important factor in regulatory decision making, except in specific situations, explained further below, when Congress requires agencies to develop initial standards focusing exclusively on the protection of public health.

Potential benefits of a regulatory proposal include the harm that will be avoided if the regulation is implemented. These benefits are quantified in monetary terms, an ostensibly straightforward approach that causes huge problems in practice, both because "monetizing" human suffering or the irrevocable loss of natural resources is controversial from an ethical perspective and because much of the harm addressed by health and safety regulation is very difficult to reduce to numbers.

The final problem posed by the monetization of benefits under traditional cost-benefit analysis is the economists' insistence on treating these figures as if they were any other kind of financial investments. People expect to receive a "return" on investments of money that increase the value of the initial amount over time. In essence, people get paid for allowing others—the banks or the government—to use their money. The economists argue that if someone who is exposed to a hazardous chemical today will not die of cancer for twenty-five more years, the value of the life saved by a regulatory intervention should be quantified as if it were such an investment. So the question becomes how much money would we need to invest today, at a rate of return of either 3 or 7 percent (numbers specified by OIRA economists), to come up after thirty years with $6.8 million (a common estimate of the value of saving one life). This practice is known as "discounting."

Again, to put these practices in context, we cannot overstate the vehemence of the disagreement between regulatory experts over the benefits side of the traditional cost-benefit methodology. In our view, meaningful reform of this system would eliminate altogether the monetization and discounting of benefits in favor of a balancing of factors and qualitative information by policy makers.

Because cost-benefit number-crunching deals with such uncertainty, these analyses can run to hundreds of pages of complex, dense, and highly technical data, projections, modeling, and mathematical formulas that deter any but the most determined stakeholders from challenging these analytical bottom lines. As troubling, distilling the series of arbitrary assumptions that underlie such calculations into a small set of numbers leaves a misleading impression of objectivity when, in fact, such analyses are notoriously susceptible to manipulation, making them ideal and useful political cover for decisions to weaken regulations. And, although this point is rejected by cost-benefit enthusiasts, retrospective examinations of regulatory decision making show that the primary impact of such analyses is to weaken health and safety protection, not strengthen it.

Professor David Driesen undertook a comprehensive review of studies and reports documenting the impact of OIRA review, concluding that the process slowed and reduced the stringency of environmental, safety, and health regulation in "dozens of cases."[3] He examined twenty-five rules identified by a General Accounting Office (GAO; the institution has since changed its name to the Government Accountability Office) study[4] as significantly affected by OIRA review in 2001–2002. He found that the OMB's recommended changes would have reduced regulatory protections with respect to twenty-four of the rules, while the remaining change was neutral. In a similar vein, professors Lisa Bressman and Michael Vandenbergh interviewed thirty-five top EPA political appointees during the Bush I and Clinton administrations. These respondents said that the OIRA review "regularly skews rulemaking in a deregulatory direction" and that OIRA staff use "cost-benefit analysis to impose its own normative preference for deregulation."[5] Professor Steven Croley's work substantiates these conclusions, although Croley was unable to confirm that the OIRA economists were acting in response to industry complaints when they forced such changes.[6] Lastly, professors Lisa Heinzerling and Frank Ackerman applied traditional cost-benefit analysis to three regulatory decisions made in the 1960s and 1970s that are widely regarded today as unqualified successes.[7] They concluded that the use of this methodology would have reversed all three decisions: lead would have stayed in gasoline instead of being removed; the Grand Canyon would have been dammed to generate hydroelectric power; and workers would have experienced uncontrolled exposure to vinyl chloride.

The OIRA is staffed by approximately thirty economists and technical experts who cannot possibly review every regulatory proposal thoroughly. Nevertheless, the threat of OIRA review is deeply disruptive of rulemaking. Because agencies do not know which cost-benefit analysis OIRA economists may find objectionable, they must gird up for battle over each regulation they are developing. These elaborate preparations, and the subsequent fights that do break out between OIRA and agency staff, slow rulemaking substantially.

This chapter opens with an explanation of how health and safety statutes intend for agencies to make regulatory decisions. We then explain how traditional cost-benefit analysis distorts such deliberations. We present a case study—the EPA's excessively delayed rulemaking on controlling mercury emissions from power plants—to illustrate the distinctions between the two approaches. We conclude with an evaluation of the prospects for reform.

## Pragmatic Regulatory Impact Analysis

Protective regulation proceeds in two steps.[8] An agency must first determine whether a statutory "risk trigger" is met. This trigger specifies when a threat is sufficiently serious to warrant regulation under the applicable statute. When Congress created the risk triggers, it authorized regulators to act on the basis of anticipated harm because it wanted to shift to a legal scheme that prevented injury, as opposed to one that compensated people for injuries after the fact. For example, the EPA is authorized to regulate new stationary sources of air pollution under the Clean Air Act whenever a source creates "air pollution which may reasonably be anticipated to endanger public health or welfare."[9] The FDA is authorized to regulate food color or food additives if they cause cancer in animals or humans.[10]

And OSHA is mandated to protect workers when "reasonably necessary or appropriate to provide safe or healthful employment," language that the Supreme Court has interpreted to mean that the agency must show a "significant risk" before it intervenes.[11]

Once an agency has determined that the risk trigger is met, it must then determine how strict to make the rule that will prevent or reduce that harm. This second determination is governed by "regulatory standards" set forth in the statute. These standards exist in the context of statutory provisions that define the methods to be used in selecting the appropriate remedy for the problem and run the gamut from pollution controls to information disclosure to the imposition of legal liability for failing to prevent or reduce threats. For our purposes, the regulatory standards that compel industry to take affirmative action to change industrial processes are the most relevant.

One such category of standards encompasses "health-based" statutory provisions that exclude the consideration of costs altogether. The Clean Air Act requires that the EPA protect public health with respect to criteria air pollutants (for example, smog, fine particulates, and nitrogen oxides) with an "adequate margin of safety" and without considering costs.[12] Under this standard, the EPA would consider everything that scientists and other technical experts can tell them about the release of pollutants, their "fate and transport" through ambient air, the exposure levels experienced by the population as a whole and, especially, by vulnerable populations (for example, the elderly, young children, or young wildlife), and the health effects likely to result from those exposures. Once the EPA establishes such a National Ambient Air Quality Standard, it delegates to the states the job of forcing factories and other sources to reduce emissions below that overall level.

Other regulatory standards allow agencies to consider costs. For example, OSHA's mandate to impose "feasible" remedies means that it must adopt the lowest limit on exposure that can be achieved by the best possible technology, provided that adoption of the technology will not cause significant economic disruption of an industry.[13] Across the government, the final limits on exposure produced under such "technology-based" standards are based on the availability of equipment or changes in industrial practice that prevent or reduce risks, such as process changes that eliminate a toxic chemical from the list of ingredients used to make a product, smokestack "scrubbers" that trap certain kinds of pollution before it is vented into the environment, or sewage treatment systems that filter out dissolved solids or use microorganisms to neutralize pathogens in waste-water. Numerical limits are extrapolated from levels produced when those technologies are fully operational.

Costs are a factor in the selection of technologies because these standards generally do not mandate the selection of experimental, extraordinarily expensive pieces of equipment. Modifying adjectives are added to the statutory standard to connote how rare and how expensive equipment must be before it is considered out of regulatory bounds. So, for example, depending on the extent of air pollution in a given geographical area, the Clean Air Act requires the use of Reasonably Available Control Technology, Best Demonstrated Available Technology, Best Available Control Technology, Maximum Achievable Control Technology, and Lowest Achievable Emissions Reduction.[14] The Clean Water Act has a similar list of standards.

Because health-based and technology-based standards are both expressed as limits on the amount of pollution present in the air or water, newcomers to the area often have difficulty telling them apart without-examining their statutory origins. But they could not be more different in their analytical derivation. A health-based standard is a level of pollution that—at least in theory—is not unsafe for most people. A technology-based standard is the level of pollution reductions we can achieve using the best equipment available. This level may or may not be unsafe to people and natural resources.

Implementation of health-based and technology-based standards requires a full-blown regulatory investigation of both the harm and the solution that can take years to complete. Yet three decades of experience with the major environmental statutes provides convincing evidence that the development of technology-based standards offers significantly less opportunity for delay because the selection of the right pollution-control equipment is considerably more straightforward than a determination of how much pollution is actually unsafe.[15]

That track record was dealt a body blow by the Supreme Court's 2009 decision in *Entergy v. Riverkeeper*.[16] The case involved a challenge brought by environmentalists to a weak rule issued by the Bush II Administration's EPA that was supposed to address the environmental problems caused by power plants that suck hundreds of billions of gallons of cooling water out of rivers and streams annually, in the process destroying as many as three billion aquatic organisms annually. The agency had already adopted a requirement that new power plants install technology that does not involve the intake of huge quantities of cooling water, but the electric utilities opposed the use of such advanced equipment on existing plants. The EPA sided with industry but in order to justify its decision, it decided to apply traditional cost-benefit analysis to restrict its experts' determination regarding which pollution control technologies would satisfy the relevant statutory standard. Justice Scalia, writing for the 5-3-1 majority (Justice Breyer agreed with the result but not the reasoning), endorsed the agency's discretion to go beyond a straightforward evaluation of technology costs to predict and quantify the benefits of avoiding massive aquatic kills. From our perspective, the decision is very unfortunate because, although it does not require the EPA to use cost-benefit analysis in technology-based decision making, it could give economists at the EPA and the OMB license to at least slow down and most probably diminish future efforts to protect the environment.

Sometimes, Congress employs a mixture of health-based and technology-based standards, instructing agencies to engage in "open-ended balancing" that evaluates a variety of factors but gives the agency discretion regarding how much weight to give each one. The EPA regulates pesticides under the Federal Insecticide, Fungicide, and Rodenticide Act by imposing conditions on the use of a pesticide to the extent necessary to avoid "unreasonable adverse effects on the environment" that pose "any unreasonable risk to man or the environment, taking into account the economic, social, and environmental costs and benefits" of a pesticide's use.[17] In deciding whether a pesticide use is unreasonable (obviously, the key adjective here), the agency considers what kinds of problems might arise if people or nature are exposed to high levels of the pesticide; whether those problems are reversible or long lasting; how important the pesticide is to the preservation of the food supply or the control of pests that cause a threat (for example, vector-borne disease); and the availability of alternative pesticides that might do a worse or better job for more or less risk. The agency also considers whether the remedies it has available—placement of warning labels on pesticide containers and special training for people who apply pesticides in large quantities—could reduce these risks to reasonable levels. The standard requires multifactor balancing, but the tool is a series of performance-based requirements.

One other point about the application of standards should be obvious by now and is absolutely crucial: people from a broad range of disciplines must collaborate to get the final decision right. Biologists, toxicologists, epidemiologists, neurologists, pharmacologists (to estimate dose), pediatricians, and similar experts must participate to predict the effect of a pollutant or other safety threat on people and natural resources. Meteorologists, climatologists, chemists, statisticians, modelers, and engineers must participate to estimate what happens to a pollutant as it travels through the environment at stake (workplace, ambient air, surface and ground water, soil). Engineers with different specialties (pollution-control equipment design, heavy machinery design, motor vehicle design, pollution monitoring) must participate to evaluate both threats and potential remedies. Enforcement and administrative law experts must participate to help gauge whether remedies will work in practice. And lawyers must participate to evaluate whether the final rule conforms to statutory requirements. The need for collaboration among all these disciplines is the reason why rules take a long time to develop. It is also the reason why narrowing power over the final decision to a small group of economists who take the rich, granular detail of those collaborations and reduce them to a set of numbers makes little sense.

In sum, all of the laws require agencies to assemble as much information as they can find about the sources of health, safety, and environmental threats. Considerable uncertainty is inevitable when gauging the nature and scope of these risks. The statutes anticipate that human beings in positions of authority will make their best judgment, tolerating not just imprecision but controversy over the choices that are made. For the remainder of this chapter and this book, we will refer to this process as "pragmatic regulatory impact analysis" or "PRIA" for short.[18] PRIA demands that regulators explain their reasons in narrative form rather than in obscure calculations. Often described as "discursive," this format requires analysts to come up with reasons for choosing one policy option over another. In a cost-benefit approach, by comparison, the analyst is expected to produce calculations that demonstrate which option is preferable. While PRIA would fully consider available numerical data on the magnitude and impact of risks, it would not convert that information into monetary estimates of the value of regulatory benefits and would instead describe such benefits in a qualitative manner. Thus, PRIA does not assume, as practitioners of cost-benefit do, that a quantitative framework is essential, when in fact available data are simply insufficient to monetize regulatory benefits accurately and without bias.

If designed and implemented as the statutes intended, draft PRIAs would be published early in the regulatory decision-making process. Their purpose would be to outline the issues that must be resolved in promulgating a new regulation and to describe the relevant factors that must be considered in resolving these issues. A regulatory agency would then invite input from relevant stakeholders on how to resolve the necessary issues for reaching a regulatory decision. The agency would take this input into account as it moves toward a tentative regulatory decision, which it would announce in the Notice of Proposed Rulemaking, again taking public comments on its proposed regulatory approaches. The final rule would be announced at the same time that the final PRIA was issued. Notably, the individual regulatory agencies would conduct and make decisions to finalize their own PRIAs rather than submitting cost-benefit analyses of individual rules to an office like OIRA for centralized review.

Critics of this approach argue that without attaching some numbers to regulatory benefits, however unreliable those numbers may be, the analytical process will not provide sufficient guidance to agencies. Rather than discarding monetization, they propose more careful use of monetary estimates in light of those uncertainties.[19] However, as a practical matter, agencies have moved in the opposite direction, becoming ever more inventive in their efforts to quantify—or simply ignore—benefits, and we are dubious that things will change. As Professor Laurence Tribe has explained, even when numbers are accompanied by full disclosure of the uncertainties at issue, their superficial appearance of precision takes on a power of their own, misleading users of the information.[20]

Written by economists for economists, traditional cost-benefit analyses are laden with jargon, elaborate formulas, and dense graphs and charts. We doubt that these reports are ever read carefully by agency decision makers, and we are even more certain that they are not read, and certainly not understood, by members of the public. Indeed, we have asked our students to read them—and our students are not only among the best and brightest young minds in the country but are clearly motivated to follow our instructions—only to be met with frustration and confusion over the assumptions that are so deeply embedded in their text. Our ultimate argument for a return to the PRIA anticipated by the statutes is the deep need to make regulatory decisions more transparent, and understandable, to all the participants in the process, not just the economists themselves.

## Cost-Benefit Analysis in Practice

*Fragile Foundations*

Defenders of cost-benefit analysis justify its use on the basis that the decisions by Congress to maximize protection have resulted in excessively expensive regulations. But they offer little persuasive evidence to substantiate this complaint. The assertion that in the absence of cost-benefit analysis, health and safety regulations would be grossly inefficient is based on the work of three analysts: John Morrall, a staff economist at OIRA; John Graham, who served as administrator of OIRA for most of the Bush II administration; and Robert Hahn, a senior economist at the conservative think tank, the American Enterprise Institute.

Morrall analyzed the cost-effectiveness of forty-four proposed, final, and rejected rules on the basis of data that agencies had submitted to the OIRA in an extraordinarily influential article published in 1986.[21] He took the relatively simplistic approach of dividing the compliance costs by the estimated number of deaths that the rule was expected to prevent in order to derive the cost per life saved of each rule that he covered. The most expensive rule had a cost of $72 billion per life saved, while the least expensive rule had an average cost of only $100,000. Twenty-four rules had a cost of more than $7.0 million/life, and another seventeen had an average cost of over $50 million/life. Morrall's results have been cited time and again for three propositions. First, in light of the considerable disparity in the cost of saving a life, regulatory priorities are not established in any rational manner. Second, the nation could achieve more safety and health protection if it focused on risks that cost less to prevent. Third, because a life saved is really only worth about $6.1 million, regulations costing more than $7.0 million are, by definition, inefficient.

In an article with the apt title "Regulatory Costs of Mythical Proportions," Professor Lisa Heinzerling discredits Morrall's entire body of work by unpacking the assumptions embedded in his superficially straightforward table.[22] She notes that Morrall included a large number of proposed and withdrawn rules in his study. The assertion that government regulation is inefficient on the basis of calculations that involve rules the government never adopted is a mistake of major—if not mythical—proportions. Morrall also altered agency estimates of the number of lives saved. In some cases, he simply rejected the agency's estimate of how many lives would be saved and substituted his own lower estimate without explaining his reasoning. He discounted the number of lives that would be saved using a 10 percent discount rate. Or, in other words, preventing a single death twenty years from now was not counted as saving an entire life but only as saving 0.123 of a life. Ironically, when Heinzerling redid Morrall's calculations without discounting, the cost of all but two of the rules was less than $5.0 million per avoided death, putting them well within the range of "acceptable" expenditures even from Morrall's point of view. Morrall's case for economic inefficiency, then, depends almost entirely on his decision to count a death prevented in the future as saving a fraction of a life. Despite this devastating critique, Morrall's work lives on and is still cited by cost-benefit proponents.

John Graham, with coauthors, completed two studies using methodology analogous to Morrall's but with the goal of exploring whether the country could regulate differently and get more bang for its buck.[23] Graham estimated the average cost of preventing one premature death for 587 life-saving interventions, finding a wide disparity in the average cost of preventing a premature death. A second study estimated the opportunity costs of pursuing more expensive live-saving interventions instead of less expensive ones. The study calculated that we could save an additional 60,200 lives if resources were redirected toward inventions costing $7.57 million or less. Graham concluded that the country was committing "statistical murder" by missing the opportunity to save lives because of the high costs of some interventions, particularly the regulation of toxic chemicals.

This superheated charge depends on the assumption that all of the money needed to pay for life-saving interventions comes out of the same bank account. But this argument, taken to its logical conclusion, reduces congressionally imposed statutory priorities to nonsense, suggesting instead that economic analysis be given free rein to reject some protections in favor of others on the basis of an imaginary, finite regulatory budget that no elected body of the people's agents has ever approved. Further, as Professor Heinzerling has pointed out, even assuming the validity of commentators making such trade-offs in the context of a policy debate, Graham's charges reflect a highly selective, politicized agenda because

> [He does] not ask, for example, whether the billions of dollars in subsidies to the mining, logging, ranching, and farming industries might be better spent on, for instance, smoking cessation and childhood immunizations. [Graham and his co-author] do not even ask whether money spent subsidizing tobacco itself might better be spent on smoking cessation programs.[24]

Professor Richard Parker subjected the details of Graham's work to the same intense scrutiny as Heinzerling did with Morrall.[25] He discovered that, like Morrall, Graham discounts with abandon: a life saved in the future does not count as a life saved but as a fraction of a life saved. Also like Morrall, Graham considers regulations that were never adopted.

He calculates the cost of ninety EPA rules, but the agency only finalized eleven. Graham also uses the number of years that an intervention prolongs a life as the measure of effectiveness of the regulation. Or, in other words, an intervention that saves the life of an older person is less worthy than one that would save a younger person or, to put it more bluntly, society benefits less when it saves the life of a middle-aged or elderly person. This assumption biases Graham's study against regulations that reduce the likelihood of cancer because the disease occurs decades after the exposure to carcinogens, when, for example, workers in petrochemical plants have grown into middle age.

Robert Hahn's 1999 study was based on data that agencies had submitted to OMB on 106 final regulations adopted between 1981 and mid-1991.[26] He found that only 57 percent of the regulations had positive benefits. Hahn and five prominent colleagues then concluded on the basis of this study that "[b]alancing the incremental benefits and costs could help reduce waste and inefficiency and improve economic welfare."[27] The other economists presumably accepted the accuracy of Hahn's results, but, once again, a thorough analysis by Professor Parker, who gained access to Hahn's underlying data, casts substantial doubt on his and their conclusions.[28]

For example, Hahn assigned a zero benefit to forty-one of the 106 regulations because the agency did not quantify and monetize the benefits. The agencies failed to take this step because they did not have adequate risk information to estimate exactly how many lives might be saved if the regulation were adopted, but their honesty does not indicate that these benefits have no value. When evaluating the validity of Hahn's decision to ignore benefits in cases in which they were not quantified because the science was too uncertain, we should also keep in mind the one, overriding historical lesson of toxic chemical regulation in the United States: the vast majority of interventions taken with respect to toxic chemicals over the last thirty years have turned out to be prescient because the more we learn, the more we realize that the chemicals are even more hazardous than we first imagine. It is literally possible to count on one hand the instances in which a chemical was "exonerated" in comparison with our initial assessments when subsequent testing found it less hazardous (the two most prominent examples of this very small second group are saccharin and asbestos fibers dissolved in water).

In sum, the case made by cost-benefit enthusiasts that the methodology is essential to prevent the waste of millions of dollars on excessive regulation has been largely discredited by its critics at the same time that the case against the methodology as a killer of protective rules has been strengthened. We move now to a more detailed examination of the methodology's flaws in practice to support our charge that it produces unreliable results that are subject to easy manipulation in the service of blatantly ideological goals.

*Methodological Flaws*

As practiced in the field, traditional cost-benefit analysis is plagued by two fundamental flaws that undermine its credibility: it crunches numbers on the basis of outdated and unsubstantiated assumptions, and it incorporates moral judgments that many people would find troubling if these judgments were ever disclosed. We would be the first to admit that our alternative—the statutorily based pragmatic regulatory impact analysis— also has methodological problems, most of which are caused by scientific uncertainty. But this uncertainty comes with the territory in any regulatory regime that tries to prevent harm as opposed to waiting until injury or death has happened and tracing the causes of that harm back to the industrial activity. In contrast, the problems with traditional cost-benefit analysis are rarely acknowledged by its proponents, much less subject to field corrections that would make these analyses less damaging to the core statutory missions of the agencies that must carry them out. We cover the three central flaws we mentioned at the outset of this chapter here: overstated costs, understated benefits, and discounting.

OVERSTATED COSTS.    When projecting future compliance costs, government economists typically rely on estimates submitted by the firms that are going to be regulated. The firms have strong incentives to overstate costs in order to discourage strict regulation, yet the government has spent far more time attempting to monetize uncertain benefits than studying how to avoid overstated costs. Consider NHTSA's experience with airbags. Before the agency required that automobile manufacturers provide automatic occupant protection in cars, the industry claimed that the cost per car for a single, driver-side airbag would be $1,000. To test this claim, the agency took apart an airbag, identified all of its parts, and determined what each part would cost if it was purchased in the open market by a car company. It then put the airbag back together, calculated the time, and multiplied that by industry wage standards. When the agency added up the individual costs of the components, the labor costs to assemble the bag, and a reasonable profit, it estimated the cost of an airbag to be $300.[29]

UNDERSTATED BENEFITS.    On the benefits side of the equation, economists multiply the estimated number of statistical lives saved against the estimated value of a single life. So, for example, if experts predict that a respirator will save one worker from getting cancer, economists translate that "statistical life" into money. The going rate for a single life at the five protector agencies ranges from $1 million to $10 million. On the other hand, if exposures to hazardous conditions cause subtle neurological damage, reduce fertility, produce birth defects, or exacerbate chronic but nonfatal diseases, these economic calculations become even more convoluted. The suffering caused by health effects that can be overcome by medical treatment often gets dropped from the number-crunching and consigned to "qualitative" narratives that are easily obscured by the deceiving precision of numbers.

How did the economists arrive at these figures for a statistical life saved, and why is there such a large range between them? One logical way to derive such a number would be to count the wages lost when a person dies prematurely. This approach is applied without too many problems by the courts in civil wrongful death suits when juries can focus on one or, at the most, a few specific lives. It does not work with respect to decisions designed to prevent harm because we would have a hard time averaging the wide range of wages earned by people exposed to anticipated hazards. Unfortunately, the supposedly better alternative that economists have selected is just as arbitrary: they calculate the monetary value of preventing a premature death by using data on wage premiums.

Wage premiums are the amount of additional compensation that workers are theoretically paid in exchange for accepting the risks that accompany a dangerous job. In theory, a wage premium indicates how much a worker is willing to pay for a safer work environment because if the worker moves to a safer job, he or she has to give up the wage premium. Because companies do not quantify and disclose these amounts, the differences are extrapolated by economists from average wages in a nondangerous occupation (for example, office worker) and a more risky occupation (for example, production line worker in a petrochemical plant). Economists then extrapolate from these extrapolations, concluding that individuals are willing to pay between $1 million and $10 million to prevent one fatal accident.[30]

The flaws in this series of assumptions are obvious. To bargain for full compensation, workers must be able to calculate precisely the value of the risks presented by the more dangerous job. Advocates of cost-benefit analysis have never demonstrated that this kind of bargaining occurs in the real world. Moreover, considerable evidence in the psychological literature demonstrates that people misunderstand risk information even when it is available to them.[31] It is well-known, for example, that young people engage in risky behavior because they believe that they are invincible.

In similar fashion, the value that individuals assign to reductions in nonfatal risks is determined from how much money consumers pay for safer products or, in one particularly strange example, the monetary value of how much time mothers spend buckling their children into car seats correctly.[32] In that study, economists watched women putting infants into car seats and calculated the difference in the larger amount of time spent by mothers who did it correctly compared with mothers who did it incorrectly. They then assumed that the women who spent less time were willing to accept a greater risk that their children would be injured in a crash and translated this saved time into dollars on the basis of the wages paid for the typical blue-collar jobs. Once again, like the assumption that workers bargain over—or even are cognizant of—the wage premiums they will get paid for dangerous jobs, this approach assumes a conscious calculation of risk as opposed to simple ignorance of how to place the car seat correctly.

In addition to the problems inherent in these threshold calculations of regulatory benefits, several additional sources of bias are routinely incorporated into the process. First, the risk assessments used to estimate benefits are themselves grounded in a series of assumptions that confound accurate economic evaluation. Analysts have techniques to address the uncertainty and omissions in risk data, but they are not capable of producing the accurate pinpoint estimates of actual risks necessary to monetize regulatory benefits in a useful way. For example, no one wears a monitor around during normal work and leisure activities in and out of doors. Estimates of how much pollution people inhale or ingest are therefore fraught with error. The magnitude of health risks is also very difficult to gauge because few toxic materials have been subject to full-scale toxicological testing in laboratory animals, and even fewer have been assessed in statistically valid epidemiological studies. As a result, estimates of the benefits of regulatory interventions are often stated in ranges so large as to undermine any conviction that they are accurate. In one study, the benefits in human health protection that would be achieved by the EPA rule controlling arsenic in drinking water ranged from a low of $10 million to a high of $1.2 billion.[33]

The estimation of safety risks—for example, the consequences of a car crash between a small car and an SUV—are generally more accurate because we have better evidence about the number of people injured in such incidents. Nevertheless, agencies must struggle to obtain such data from local authorities, analyze the reasons for the crash to determine which were caused by vehicle defects and which resulted from driver error, and develop estimates of what a broken pelvis is worth to a person beyond the hospital bills incurred to treat the injury.

A second problem is that economists use estimates of how much workers pay to avoid safety risks to estimate the benefits of reducing health risks, such as dying prematurely from cancer as a result of exposure to carcinogens in the air, water, or workplace. But they do not offer any persuasive evidence that individuals treat safety and health risks similarly. If anything, individuals appear to be willing to pay more to avoid health risks, particularly cancer.[34] Further, although available evidence reflects how much money men are paid for risky work, academic studies indicate that women are much more risk averse than men.[35] Data about workplace risks also ignore people who live outside the workplace, including vulnerable populations such as the elderly, the disabled, children, and pregnant and nursing mothers.

As difficult as they are from a scientific perspective, the problems of monetizing human injury pale in comparison with the complexity of quantifying adverse consequences for nature. In one recent, high-profile case decided by the Supreme Court, the issue was cooling water intakes at power plants across the country.[36] Existing power plants, many of which were built over thirty years ago using antiquated pollution-control technology, suck up an estimated 214 billion gallons of water per day to cool down overheated equipment. In the process they pull as many as 3.4 billion aquatic organisms into their mechanical systems. The effect of these huge aquatic kills on natural ecosystems is unknown. Yet the traditional cost-benefit analysis conducted by the EPA counted only the 1.8 percent of dead organisms because it focused exclusively on fish that were large enough for humans to eat for dinner. We can have little confidence that ignoring the effects of these aquatic kills down the food chain of such ecosystems will produce a decision that allows water quality to improve and the systems to sustain themselves. In fact, scientists tell us, ecosystem webs are notoriously sensitive to disruptions at any level. Consider, for example, worldwide alarm about the sudden decrease in the population of the honeybee, a crucial part of ecosystems that allows fruit trees and other edible plants to thrive. No one eats honeybees for dinner.

DISCOUNTING.    The final flaw arises because of economists' insistence on discounting benefits. This practice rests on the idea that a regulation is like an investment in the sense that it will produce future results that have a monetary value and the value of those results is worth less today than in the future because of the time value of money. The time value of money recognizes that a dollar invested today is worth more in the future because interest payments will increase its value. By this logic, regulatory benefits worth $10,000 in ten years have a present value of $4,751 using a 7 percent discount rate. Current OMB guidelines recommend that agencies apply both a 3 percent and 7 percent discount rate when conducting cost-benefit analysis.[37] So, for example, a life worth $6.1 million in twenty-five years, at a 7 percent discount rate, would be worth only $1.1 million today. Discounting discourages regulatory action to prevent cancer because the costs of the regulation occur in the near future while the benefits occur in twenty or thirty years. The benefits are delayed because the onset of cancer generally does not occur until later in a person's life.

Surprisingly, economic analysts even use discounting when they are attempting to determine how many lives a regulation will save in the near future. For example, if one hundred people are exposed to a toxic chemical today that will cause them to develop cancer in thirty years, discounting at a 7 percent rate would result in the assumption that only 11.474 lives would actually be saved. At a 3 percent discount rate, this calculation would result in an estimate of 38.834 lives saved. But as Professor Richard Parker has explained,

> [D]eath does not recognize human accounting conventions and death does not discount. As a result, if 1,000,000 people are exposed to a toxic chemical that produces a 1:10,000 probability of fatal cancer among those exposed, then the odds are quite high that approximately 100 people (not 37 . . .) will lose their lives to cancer. . . . [W]hatever the interior logic to some economists of discounting monetary values for risk to life, the average reader . . . (and, I suspect, the majority of senior policymakers) are unlikely to understand that the physical reality of 100 lives saved in 20 years is, in fact, being treated as 37 . . . lives saved today.[38]

If the discount rate is applied for a long enough time horizon, then any regulatory benefit disappears. The result is that little or no regulatory action is justified at the present time, no matter how significant the benefit—for example, preserving the planet for future generations—might be in noneconomic terms. Scientists estimate that as many as 40 percent of animal species could disappear within fifty years if the anthropogenic releases of carbon that are causing climate change are not reduced. These warnings mean that the present generation must undertake costly greenhouse gas reductions now in order to avoid potentially catastrophic consequences for the benefit of the children of our children and their children. Once the value of those benefits is discounted, action to prevent global climate change appears to lack any economic justification.

## Mercury

*PRIA*

One recent and high-profile example of decision making by the EPA illustrates the difference between the interdisciplinary process of PRIA and economist-driven, traditional cost-benefit analysis. Congress decided in 1990 that it wanted the EPA to consider controlling mercury emissions from power plants that burn coal.[39] Mercury is extraordinarily toxic, even in small amounts. It poses the greatest dangers to public health when transformed by the interaction between elemental mercury and aquatic organisms into a bioavailable form known as methylmercury. This substance is then taken up through the aquatic food chain into large fish that are part of the human food chain. Using the most reliable tests, we have discovered that as many as 15 percent of women of childbearing age have elevated, potentially dangerous levels of mercury in their blood.

Congress told the EPA to begin by characterizing the public health problems caused by methylmercury exposure and evaluating the contribution electric utility plants made to those risks. If the harm would not be addressed by pollution controls designed to eliminate other pollutants from power plant smokestack emissions, the EPA was to craft specific technology-based requirements for mercury alone. All of this work was to be completed by 1994. But, to its everlasting discredit, the Clinton administration EPA did not produce a final finding on these questions until late 2000, shortly before President Clinton left office.

The EPA reported that relatively low doses of methylmercury cause neurological damage in infants and babies in utero. This step sounds simple but involves a complex analysis of scientific evidence that ranges from studies on rats and other animals to epidemiological studies involving actual human populations. This "reference dose" was confirmed in 2003 by a peer review at the National Research Council (a branch of the National Academies of Science and Engineering), the "gold standard" for scientific bodies throughout the world.[40] The EPA discovered that as many as 8 percent of women of childbearing age have mercury blood levels higher than the reference dose. Scientists also found that these already alarming levels are even higher for low-income women of Native American and Asian descent living in the areas near the Great Lakes who eat large quantities of contaminated fish caught there by their families; as many as one-third of these women had elevated blood levels of mercury.

The EPA also considered how much mercury is emitted by power plants, what happens to those emissions as they travel through the atmosphere, whether a significant amount of them are transformed into methylmercury, and when technology that could control such emissions would be available. Congress told the EPA to require that new and existing power plants install a "maximum achievable control technology" to reduce the emissions. With respect to existing plants, that technology is defined as the best one used by the top 12 percent of the cleanest plants in the country; new plants must install the highest performing control technology that is used by the single best controlled similar source. Once the technology was selected, the EPA would have nothing left to do but check whether plants were installing it.

*Cost-Benefit Analysis*

Soon after the Clinton administration left office, the Bush II administration decided to change course radically. Instead of requiring the installation of pollution-control equipment by 2007, the EPA announced that it would adopt a "cap and trade" approach that assigned "allowances" (permission to emit specific amounts of mercury annually) to each coal-fired power plant in the country. This new system would not begin to operate until 2018 and would generally impose far less stringent restrictions on mercury emissions. Between the time the change of course was proposed and a final rule adopting cap and trade was adopted—a period of a little over one year, the agency produced a 570-page cost-benefit analysis.[41]

The centerpiece of this analysis was the determination that, depending on the analytical approach, a child of freshwater fishers lost approximately 0.06–0.07 IQ points from mercury exposure in 2001. The economists calculated benefits based on an association between IQ points and earning capacity. The average present value of net earnings losses associated with a one-point decrease in IQ was $7,765 in 1992 dollars. The analysis corrected this amount for inflation. The economists then reduced the total value per point by $943, ostensibly in recognition of the fact that people with lower IQs go to school for shorter time periods, saving the costs of educating them more completely and allowing them to produce additional income as they work in lower paying jobs.

This analysis appears precise if you ignore the values implicated by a decision to award only $8,800 for the loss of an IQ point by a young child—after all, would any of us accept that amount of money in exchange for such an injury to one of our children? But it obscures a crucial point about this particular rule. Asian and Native Americans suffer greater exposure to methylmercury because they eat tainted fish as a significantly larger part of their diet than the average American. Because large portions of these two populations are also poor, they are far more likely to depend on subsistence fishing—eating what they are able to catch in nearby bodies of water—for survival. EPA data indicate that Native American women who eat fish caught in the heavily polluted Great Lakes are exposed to mercury at levels ten times higher than a safe dose. Rather than obscuring these realities in mathematical calculations of average numbers, a pragmatic analysis would consider the health and cultural significance of fishing in the Native American communities near the Great Lakes, as well as the government's treaty and trust responsibilities to tribes.

The primary argument made in defense of the EPA's approach to mercury power plant emissions is that other countries are the real culprits because they tolerate the operation of dirty plants that make far larger contributions to the global mercury cycle. According to this reasoning, we should wait for China and Brazil to clean up their acts before we impose any further costs on the utility industry. A corollary argument is that tuna fish, caught in international oceans, is the leading culprit in elevated blood methylmercury levels among American women and that control of U.S. plants will do little to eliminate that contamination. Lastly, the utility industry argues that increases in electricity prices prompted by a stricter rule will hurt the poor, defeating the purpose of protecting the poor Native Americans and Asians most affected by mercury contamination. None of these arguments were reflected in the cost-benefit analysis done with respect to the rule, but the decision to act on U.S. mercury emissions without regard to what other countries do was resolved in 1990 by Congress, and the other arguments were considered in the PRIA conducted by the EPA multidisciplinary staff.

As a postscript, a panel of judges on the U.S. Court of Appeals for the District of Columbia Circuit overturned the EPA's cap-and-trade rule in 2008, shortly before this book went to press, on the basis that it did not conform to the statute.[42]

## Conclusion

President Obama appears ready to follow in his predecessors' footsteps and continue the use of cost-benefit analysis. He has chosen Professor Cass Sunstein, a strong supporter of the methodology, to lead the OIRA. The popularity of cost-benefit analysis with conservative Republican presidents is not difficult to understand; it offers a justification to oppose strong regulation. It is less obvious why Democratic presidents have chosen to employ this flawed tool.

We suspect that President Clinton continued and endorsed the use of cost-benefit analysis in order to demonstrate his commitment to rein in "big government," thereby shoring up his credentials as a new and different type of Democrat rather than one who reflexively endorsed big government. During the Clinton administration, cost-benefit analysis was practiced in a version that admittedly was far less aggressive and destructive than the versions applied under Republican presidents, especially during the Reagan and Bush II administrations. The former Clinton OIRA director under Clinton, Sally Katzen, has advanced the spirited argument that the methodology, like internal medicine, is not intrinsically bad but can be quite useful in the hands of trained professionals. Katzen and others— most notably, Professor Richard Revesz—have argued for reforms that would modulate its impact, such as lowering the discount rate required for benefit calculations or abandoning discounting altogether for regulatory issues such as climate change that deal with the impact that the activities of current generations will have on their children.[43]

In moments of fatigue, we are tempted to accept the inevitability that cost-benefit analysis will continue for the foreseeable future and to join the growing camp of those trying to improve it at the margins. But the methodology suffers from so many intrinsic flaws and represents such an elevation of false economic predictions over well-informed human judgment that we cannot bring ourselves to do it. After all, any approach so susceptible to manipulation that it can encompass the aspirations of such different electoral mandates seems to us to be as potentially corrupt as it is facile.

We cannot really improve on Professor Thomas McGarity's final verdict on cost-benefit analysis: "[O]ne is left with a pressing need to know why [anyone] would conclude that all of this occasionally comprehensible, but frequently preposterous and always manipulable number spinning, could possibly lead to better decisionmaking in the real world."[44] The answer may be a willingness to believe that making the protection of people a statutory priority is horribly inefficient, although there is no good support for that conclusion. Or the answer may be the belief that, despite its many problems, the methodology is better than having no systematic way to study the potential impacts of a regulation before it is adopted. Although genuine, this belief is mistaken. We have presented a pragmatic alternative based in the statutes and derived from a substantial social science literature that would forge improvements in both the substance and transparency of regulatory policy.

The requirement to undertake cost-benefit analysis is a serious drag on an agency's capacity to fulfill its statutory mandate. It offers little or no assistance to the agency in assessing the difficult policy issues that it must resolve under its statutory mandates, while at the same time it deflects agency time and resources into an activity that produces little worthwhile information. Worse, it embroils the agency in fights with the OIRA over data, which in reality are not about the data but about the agency's attempts to fulfill its statutory mission. The OIRA's economists may well distrust those mandates, but the agency has no legal authority to override statutory commitments to protect people and the environment.

It is time for Felix Unger to stop harassing Oscar Madison and move out of the apartment.

# PART II

# Institutions

## CHAPTER FIVE

# Congress

## Introduction

> Not only does Congress have an approval rating below bubonic plague and head lice, I saw a recent poll that as many as 40 percent of people still believe that Congress is in Republican hands. I wish we could get a little accuracy out there about who is in charge—and let those ratings fall where they may. — Representative Jeb Hensarling (R-TX)[1]

In addition to his penchant for characterizing political realities in vivid language, Representative Hensarling is right that Congress's approval rating dropped steadily during the last dozen years. He is wrong to claim that these declines are attributable to Democratic leadership, which controlled the House of Representatives for less than a third of this period. Public disillusionment with the performance of the "first branch"—so called because the Framers of the Constitution established Congress in Article I of that document—was growing steadily throughout the Bush II administration. Polls show approval ratings in the 50–60 percent range in 1998, dropping down through the 40s during the first four years of Bush II, and falling into the 30s, 20s, and even the low teens (a historic low) in 2005–2008.[2] President Barack Obama's election and congressional action in response to the global economic crisis lifted these ratings to numbers in the mid-30s as this book goes to press.

When asked why they hold Congress in such low esteem, voters say that they perceive that members are entrenched in their jobs, care more about themselves than the country, are often untruthful, and seem to be in perpetual stalemate, unable to get anything done.[3] The public's perception that Congress is not "earning its keep" is undoubtedly exacerbated

by the fact that the domestic policy agenda has been severely constricted during much of this period by foreign wars, budget deficits, and a
rhetorical commitment to "small government." Even President Clinton,
who presided over several years of budget surpluses, aligned himself with
this rhetoric, famously declaring that "the era of big government is over"
in his 1996 State of the Union address.[4] In a more scholarly and empirical
vein, a study by Professor Paul Light found that presidents have been
"dreaming smaller since the Great Society," advocating fewer and far
more constricted changes in the federal government's mission.[5] With a
few notable exceptions—the prescription drug benefit, the occasional
stimulus package, and the widely disparaged No Child Left Behind law,
Congress has done little to impress the public with its relevance to their
daily lives in quite a long time.

Why does the public have such a harsh opinion of Congress if it also
agrees that a small national government is desirable? One likely answer
is that, given spectacular increases in deficits, especially under the Bush
II administration, the small government rationale seems blatantly hypo-
critical. A second, even more intriguing possibility is that the public has
embraced the attack on the "Washington insiders" who have served as
conservative scapegoats for many years and now views Congress itself as
a gathering point for such people. A third possibility is that the public is
deeply concerned about the failure of the social safety net and the fragility
of global financial markets and wants the national government to define a
proactive role for itself in solving these problems.

After years of cannibalizing the national government's role in ensuring
equal opportunity and a good quality of life, congressional conservatives
have ensured that the House and Senate are seen as central contributors
to the drift, ennui, and downright hard times that afflict the country. Progressive Democrats have not done very well in articulating an alternative message and, in any event, have not had the votes needed to deliver
an affirmative vision of government's role, even if they manage to develop one. But by far the most serious implication of the stalemate that
has persisted between the two sides is the erosion of Congress's capacity
to legislate should one party or one ideology succeed in gaining the upper
hand.

In their excellent book, *The Broken Branch: How Congress Is Failing America and How to Get It Back on Track,* self-confessed Congress
lovers Norman Ornstein, a scholar at the conservative-leaning American
Enterprise Institute, and Thomas Mann, a scholar at the liberal Brookings

Institute, portray Congress's scant output as symptomatic of a far more damaging erosion of its internal structure and culture.[6] They characterize the younger generation of members who will soon dominate both chambers as having lost any sense of institutional pride or loyalty. Instead, a seat in Congress is viewed more as a bully pulpit for ideological agendas than as a job that demands a gift for compromise and the hard study of policy alternatives. From its roots in the 1994 "Gingrich Revolution" when Republicans took back control of the House after forty years of Democratic leadership, Mann and Ornstein chart trajectories of centralization and partisanship, which have become sufficiently serious to deprive the House and—to a lesser extent—the Senate of fundamental due process in lawmaking.

Congressional relations have been fraught with ill feeling at many junctures over the nation's history. Ornstein and Mann report that in the nineteenth century, duels between members of Congress were held frequently, some with fatal outcomes. Members punched and threatened each other on the floor of the House and the Senate. During the debate over the abolition of slavery in 1856, a Democratic representative from South Carolina beat a Republican senator from Massachusetts over the head with a cane on the Senate floor, injuring him severely.

Of course, periodic outbursts of anger and even a little pushing and shoving aside, the modern Congress is significantly more genteel.[7] Yet contemporary anger and bitterness are in many ways no less serious because they have spawned fundamental changes in the rules that govern both bodies and produced a chronic, deep-seated inability to cooperate across party lines. These changes—extraordinarily short work weeks, abandonment of the "regular order" for considering bills, neglect of oversight, exclusion of the minority from legislative drafting, and indefinite extensions of roll call votes—have undermined the productivity of Congress to the point that it can no longer exercise its authority to oversee existing programs, much less craft new ones.

The Constitution's brilliance is its tripartite structure—legislative, executive, and judicial branches—and its intention that each branch of government provide checks and balances on the others. In an ideal world, bright ideas originate in the White House, the Senate, or the House of Representatives; are vetted thoroughly by congressional committees, travel across the floor of both bodies, and are sent to conference, with congressional staff in constant consultations with executive branch officials. They are modified to attract a critical mass of bipartisan supporters before they are sent to the president for signature. For two decades, partisan rancor has disrupted this process to the point that important bills are routinely pulled onto the floor without committee hearings, minority members do not see a copy of legislation until right before they are required to vote and are excluded from conference committees, and the Senate assumes the role of burial ground for most initiatives that emerge from the House.

Congressional weakness creates a vacuum for executive branch excess, as the country has learned to its great detriment over the past decade. As harmful as this imbalance has been for foreign relations, the integrity of the military, and the nation's economy, the weakness of the first branch has taken a huge toll on the administrative system in general and on health and safety agencies in particular. As we explained in chapter 2 and bring into sharper focus in this chapter, Congress must be the leading "people's agent" of our title, providing the authority and the money that animate the regulatory process. After a period of extraordinary activism in the 1970s and 1980s, Congress has sat dormant, willfully ignoring the decay of these institutions. Reviving its interest in these five agencies and pushing it back into the driver's seat of setting health and safety policies in broad terms are essential steps.

As this book goes to press, Democrats dominate both chambers and promise profound and immediate changes in their institutions' productivity. Confronted by a global economic crisis, Congress has managed to eke out major pieces of legislation to cope with the crisis, but it now faces a complex legislative agenda on health care, climate change, and other issues. It remains to be seen whether Democratic leaders can push any of these initiatives across the floor, and we certainly hope for the best. But we will be very surprised if Congress can repair the dysfunctional legislative process we describe in this chapter in the immediate future. Slow repair is possible, especially if the electorate continues to repudiate the polarized politics that have eroded Congress's effectiveness. However slowly they come, these reforms are crucial because passing ambitious legislation in areas like climate change is only the first step; someone has to be home at the agencies to implement it.

This chapter begins with a brief history of the roots of contemporary partisanship. We discuss the changes in the rules documented by Ornstein and Mann, updating their statistics to include the 110th Congress, which was led by Democrats. We use a case study involving the Superfund toxic waste cleanup program to illustrate why congressional gridlock is so harmful to the protection of human health and the environment.

## Brink of the Abyss

Democrats were in the majority of the House of Representatives between 1954 and 1994, longer than a generation, and had become complacent in their control of the body's agenda, possession of the lion's share of its staff and other resources, and domination of the media limelight. Bipartisan alliances were frequent and shifting, arising along ideological lines, with fiscal conservatives organizing to fight spending and probusiness members joining to reform tax laws. To be sure, it was not nearly as satisfying to be a Republican as a Democrat, especially in the ranks of junior members, and seemingly permanent minority status rankled. But the House managed to legislate and to work out its differences with the Senate, whose members attracted at least as much animosity from House members as they shared among themselves.

It took a firebrand named Newt Gingrich to end this period of stolid complacency. Gingrich was first elected to his seat representing Georgia's sixth congressional district (stretching from the southern Atlanta suburbs to the Alabama border) in 1978. He came to Washington not to rise through the power structure but to foment rebellion from the proverbial back bench. In a strange, long-latency embrace of the most conservative instincts of the Reagan era, he managed to engineer the historic Republican takeover of the House in 1994, six years after the president left office, mounting what seemed at the time like a stealth attack on the liberal-to-moderate Democratic leadership. Gingrich served as Speaker of the House in the 104th and 105th congresses. His agenda was extreme enough, his rhetoric heated enough, and his miscalculations in dealing with President Clinton sufficiently acute that he faced a rebellion among his own troops that drove him from the post in 1998, right before the House impeached the president. He also resigned from Congress, leaving behind a cadre of loyalists who have continued the guerilla warfare he began.

Most of the proposals of Gingrich's "Contract with America" never became law, usually because they were blocked in the Senate. But the revolution's influence on House internal governance and the atmosphere on Capitol Hill was extensive and persists to this day. Gingrich was not as extreme on health and safety issues as some of his most important allies—most notably, Tom DeLay, a former exterminator from Texas, who compared the EPA to the Nazi Gestapo in a speech on the House floor.[8] But Gingrich's overarching legacy of demeaning government as an enemy of the people blew the smoldering embers of Reaganism back into flames, and it is possible to draw a direct line between the short-lived Gingrich Revolution and the longer lived Bush II administration.

The institutional implications of the Gingrich era are vital. Gingrich positioned his coalition not as an influential voice in determining how to run the government it was were elected to lead, but rather as a crusading army determined to curtail a government viewed as an outside enemy. Gingrich and his allies saw the havoc that might erupt in response to their initiatives as necessary to the success of the crusade and not as a breach of a fiduciary duty to take their leadership responsibilities seriously. Two poorly chosen epic battles, both of which they lost, showcase these implications.

The first fight involved a showdown with President Clinton over a continuing resolution necessary to keep the government operating in the short term. The House was far behind in passing regular appropriations bills, and Gingrich decided to load the already bloated spending measure down with proposals that President Clinton opposed, including deep cuts in Medicare. His explicit intent was a winner-take-all confrontation with the president: "He can run the parts of government that are left [after the cuts], or he can run no government," Gingrich announced. "Which of the two of us do you think worries more about the government not showing up?"[9] When Clinton vetoed the bill, triggering a government shutdown, Gingrich and his allies were shocked to discover that the crisis did not play well with the public, which felt apprehensive about the disruption of services and pinned the blame on the House renegades. Republicans lost five seats in the next election, and a backlash built against Gingrich among his own members that ultimately cost him the speakership.

The second lost battle was a significantly more serious threat to government stability. In late 1998, right before the Christmas holiday, the House majority initiated impeachment proceedings in response to special prosecutor Kenneth Starr's report on Clinton's sexual relations with Monica Lewinsky, a White House intern.[10] Embroiled in what many of his closest allies described as an "obsession" with Clinton's moral failings and determined to drive him from office, Gingrich laid the groundwork for the president's destruction with care, only to face a second backlash from the public.[11] By this time, Gingrich was on his way out of Washington, consumed in a vicious challenge to his leadership by his closest lieutenants. Ironically, Robert Livingston of Louisiana, the leader of that revolt, was nominated as Gingrich's replacement, only to resign in disgrace on the eve of impeachment, after confessing on the House floor to his own extramarital dalliances.

On December 19, 1998, in party-line votes, the House sent three of four original articles of impeachment to the Senate, where they evolved into a censure resolution. The process took an enormous toll on the House, which degenerated into a "viper's nest" according to no less a mainstream media source than *Time* magazine.[12] Referring to President Clinton's decision that same week to bomb Iraq in retaliation for its refusal to cooperate with international nuclear weapons inspectors, the reporters wrote,

> [T]he air over Baghdad exploded. So did the air over Washington, where the constant outcry over sex, lies, desperation and hypocrisy had created an atmosphere of venom and mayhem. All around the city there was a feeling that brutal, lasting damage had been done to an already threadbare culture of political accommodation, that impeachment would be not the end of something but the beginning. And that it would be something bad.
>
> . . .
>
> It was [Minority Leader Dick] Gephardt who made the Democrats' pre-Christmas offer of peace ring across the Capitol. "We need to start healing; we need to start binding up our wounds; we need to end this downward spiral that will end with the death of our representative democracy." . . . "Our Founding Fathers created a system of government of men, not of angels. We are on the brink of the abyss. The only way we stop this insanity is through the force of our own will."[13]

To be fair, and as the reporters also pointed out, the impeachment marked an "intensification of congressional partisanship" that had roots in earlier battles—for example, the decision by the Democratic Senate to block the nomination of Robert Bork for the Supreme Court. As in a bad marriage, neither side was blameless in the conflagration over impeachment, least of all President Clinton, who came close to squandering his legacy over behavior that was as inexplicable as it was sordid. At this point, however, it does not matter who threw the first or the most stones. Congress, and especially the House, have never recovered from the downward spiral described by Gephardt. As Democratic representative and political scientist David Price has written:

> Within the House, the experience had few of the cathartic or sobering effects some had hoped for. On the contrary: in both its procedural precedents and its polarizing political impact, impeachment shaped the atmosphere and the tactics of partisanship in the House for years to come. Not even the September

11, 2001, terrorist attacks could induce more than a temporary and partial de-escalation.[14]

Of course, as Representative Price also explained, President George W. Bush's decision to govern from the " 'right in' rather than the 'center out' " reinforced partisan tendencies, and Congress might well be a much different place had a different president come into power. Instead, Gingrich's Republican successors did not make much effort to recruit Democrats to their cause, relying instead on party-line votes to deliver the Bush II agenda on budget and tax cuts. In addition to squeezing moderate Republicans out of the party, these trends took their toll on the regular order of the House and Senate, undermining the foundation of rules and traditions that have shaped the House and Senate for two hundred years.

## Institutionalization of Congress

In a seminal 1968 article published in the *American Political Science Review*, Professor Nelson Polsby proposes several criteria for determining whether a political organization is sufficiently "institutionalized" to perform "tasks of authoritative resource allocation, problem solving, conflict settlement, and so on, in behalf of a population of any substantial size."[15] The entity must be "well-bounded," meaning that it has a distinct identity and is not confused with other, similar institutions. Its members should be easily identifiable, chosen through a rigorous process, and should select their leaders from among their own ranks. The organization must be "complex," meaning, first, that its parts are "internally separated" on a "regular and explicit basis" and yet are internally interdependent and, second, that the entity embraces a division of labor that also involves carefully differentiated roles. The entity should use "universalistic rather than particularistic criteria, and automatic rather than discretionary methods for conducting its internal business. Precedents and rules are followed; merit systems replace favoritism and nepotism; and impersonal codes supplant personal preferences as prescriptions for behavior."[16]

Reviewing the House of Representatives' history from colonial times, Polsby concluded that the body is well on its way to being institutionalized. Its members are a distinct group of easily identifiable people who undergo the grueling process of standing for election. The large majority achieve safe seats as individually popular incumbents, lending stability to the institution. Committees are the vehicle for a division of labor and, over time, become efficient at both exercising and guarding their jurisdictions, although their power waxes and wanes in relationship to the influence of the House leadership (speaker, majority and minority leaders, and whips). Polsby noted approvingly that the significant increases in resources committed to internal management also boded well for the institutional coming-of-age of the House. He argued that strict use of seniority to choose committee chairs and ranking minority members combats uncertainty and preserves a level playing field.

Both the House and the Senate took huge strides forward under all three criteria two years after Polsby published his article. The Legislative Reorganization Act of 1970 requires that (1) members' votes go on the record; (2) hearings and markups (voting sessions) occur in public; (3) minimum time periods be allocated for debate on amendments; and (4) three days elapse between the reporting of a bill out of a committee and the time it is brought up on the floor.[17] The law also allows members to bring "discharge petitions" to dislodge bills from committee over the chairperson's objections. These changes remind us that, as recently as four decades ago, Congress functioned in a considerably less organized, open, and democratic manner than it does today.

Nevertheless, open procedures have eroded in the last fifteen years, even in comparison with Congress's earlier history. When these recent trends are considered in the context of the 1970 reforms, it is clear that, overall, Congress has taken two steps forward and two and a half steps back. As damaging, in the age of the World Wide Web, a twenty-four-hour news cycle, and the installation of cameras on the House and Senate floors, these deficiencies are on full display, not just to Washington insiders but to the general public.

## Irregular Disorder

Mann and Ornstein cite three overarching trends that have diminished congressional effectiveness. First, the quantity and quality of deliberation in Congress has eroded. The hours Congress spends on the people's business have shrunk precipitously at the same time that the majority has increased the use of procedural tactics to exclude the minority. Second, Congress has abandoned its historical role as the Constitution's counterweight to the president by decreasing executive oversight and tolerating executive branch secrecy. Third, loose campaign finance laws, the unprec-edented mobilization of Washington lobbyists, and an astonishing lack of ethical accountability have led to the impression that Congress is domi-nated by special interests with the power to block lawmaking that might cause them financial hardship.

*Time at Work*

Readers will remember that each Congress sits for a two-year period, bro-ken into two annual sessions, or, to put it another way, a bill introduced in the first session survives to the end of the second but must be reintro-duced when a new Congress starts. During the 1960s and 1970s, the aver-age Congress met to transact business for a total of 323 legislative days. By the 1980s and 1990s, this average declined to 278. During the first six years of the Bush administration, the average declined even further, to ap-proximately 250 days. The 109th Congress (2005–2006), widely regarded as among the most fractious in memory, established a new low: 140 days in legislative session for the House and 159 for the Senate.[18] Time spent in committees also diminished. During the 1960s and 1970s, the average Con-gress held 5,372 House committee and subcommittee meetings, including hearings, markups, and other sessions. During the 1980s and 1990s, this average shrank to 4,793. During the 108th Congress (2003–2004), House committees and subcommittees met just 2,135 times.

*Exclusionary Tactics*

Sensing rightly that much of the public's disgust with Congress is based on endless partisan backbiting, which often seems to be its members' fa-vorite activity, both candidates for president in the 2008 election pledged to work across party lines, reach across the aisle, and make government accountable again. These pledges sound commendable, but the primary pressure on the winner of the election—President Barack Obama—will be to get things done. Depending on the margins of votes on any given issue, bipartisanship might not be necessary to pass legislation in either house. The dynamics between the House and the Senate, which often transcend party, are also crucial to legislative outcomes. For example, consider how quickly the rebellious House caucus of conservative Republicans reversed course to vote in favor of the financial bailout package crafted by House and Senate Democratic leaders and the Bush administration in the fall of 2008, after the Senate voted across party lines to approve the legislation.

But if Democratic leaders in the White House, Senate, and House decide to flip the Bush II administration model of governing from the "right in" to governing from the "left in," they will have a harder time reversing the perception that backbiting, especially in the House, is the dominant mode of doing business. Because the rhetoric employed by the embittered minority—whether the Democratic left or the Republican right—has been constantly stoked by what Mann and Ornstein call the "demise of regular order," members shut out from the process have little incentive to do anything but obstruct routine business in both chambers.[19]

The concept of the "regular order" includes the key reforms made in the 1970 Reorganization Act: bills should be considered in public sessions in committee and on the floor, with votes recorded for posterity. Members should have adequate opportunity to review the text of bills and offer amendments. Debate should be as complete as possible, with both majority and minority members having an opportunity to justify their votes. The minority should have an unfettered opportunity to participate in committee deliberations, floor debates, and—most crucial of all—the conference committees that meet to craft final legislation. Actual voting should follow prescribed procedures, including the time period that is allowed members to cast their final votes.

Breaches of the regular order have plagued Congress throughout its history. Democratic majorities were by no means blameless, and such high-handed tactics were on the rise in the 1980s, causing considerable outrage among Republicans. As soon as Republicans came to power in 1994, however, the new majority took these procedures to new levels. From the 103d Congress (the last controlled by Democrats until 2007) to the 108th Congress, the percentage of open or modified open rules, which allow members to offer amendments to legislation that is brought to the House floor, dropped from 44 to 26 percent, while the percentage of closed or modified closed rules jumped from 18 to 49 percent. The House Rules Committee created 60 percent of these rules during "emergency meetings," called with little warning and at odd hours, to prevent minority Democrats from participating. This approach made it virtually impossible to discover the content of a final piece of legislation, or whether amendments would be permitted, before members were asked to vote on these provisions. In a few notable instances, the actual voting process, which routinely is limited to fifteen minutes, was extended for hours to allow the House leadership time to twist enough arms to pass the president's package.

These changes at the back end of the legislative process were exacerbated by changes at the front end. Because committees and subcommittees

spent considerably less time meeting in public, any legislation up for serious consideration was typically drafted behind closed doors, often by
leadership staff, and presented as a fait accompli to minority members.
When important bills went to conference committees, minority members
were often shut out of the deliberations.

In one particularly egregious example, the final 850-page conference
report on the Medicare prescription drug bill—arguably the most important domestic policy initiative of the Bush II administration—was filed
with the clerk of the House at 1:17 A.M. on November 21, 2003. Voting
commenced at 3:00 A.M. on November 22, 2003, and the final legislation
was approved by a narrow margin at 6:00 A.M. on November 22, 2003. During another embarrassing incident, a 3,000-page omnibus appropriations
bill, assembled by congressional staff and sent to the floor in the early
morning hours, turned out to include a provision that gave appropriators
and their aides the right to access individual tax returns on file at the Internal Revenue Service. Writing for *Roll Call*, the newspaper that covers
Congress on a daily basis, former appropriations staff member Scott Lilly
condemned the process:

> While the flawed language should have been spotted, the circumstances in
> which it was added make such mistakes almost inevitable.
>
> Why do we conduct the people's business this way? . . .
>
> The reason the old system of legislating no longer works is that the current
> leadership has not only assumed the role of passing the legislation required of
> Congress, but has also taken on the responsibility of insuring that the content of
> that legislation is consistent with a specific ideological criteria that is often not
> the will of a majority in the House.
>
> . . .
>
> The House was intended to be the centerpiece of our democracy. It can again
> function as a democratic institution if we return to the "regular order." When
> even subcommittee chairmen don't know the content of the legislation bearing
> their own name, the role of elected representatives has been diminished to the
> point that ordinary citizens can have little confidence that their views have any
> weight in decisions made by Congress.[20]

## Sixty Plus

The Senate has not figured much in our story so far, in part because the
House was ground zero for the 1994 Gingrich Revolution and in part be-

cause, with one hundred members rather than 435, the Senate has operated under looser procedures that indulge minority views and allocate considerably more time for floor debate. It takes unanimous consent to get legislation to the floor of the Senate for a vote. Such consent is usually granted by the minority leader, on behalf of minority members, to the majority leader, who is responsible for doing the scheduling. Once debate has opened, senators can—at least in theory—talk as long as they like. In normal and healthy practice, the two leaders generally agree to limit debate to a certain number of hours and allocate the time among members concerned enough about the legislation to come to the floor to speak.

From time to time, however, a proposal is sufficiently offensive to one or more senators that it may trigger a filibuster threat—that is, members threaten to keep talking continuously until the legislation is pulled down from the calendar and efforts to pass it are abandoned. In 1917, at the urging of President Woodrow Wilson, the Democratic Senate adopted a "cloture rule" providing that a two-thirds majority of the Senate could cut off debate and move to a vote; the Senate changed this number to sixty votes in 1949. The last period when filibusters actually occurred with any regularity was during the civil rights debates of the 1950s and 1960s. Over the last several decades, the mere threat of a filibuster is enough to dissuade the leadership from bringing a bill to the floor.

In 2005, during the ill-fated and exceptionally contentious 109th Congress, Senate Republican Majority Leader William Frist launched an attack on his Democratic colleagues over judicial appointments, charging that they were sitting on the nominations of conservative jurists and flouting the prerogatives of President Bush to appoint jurists who shared his beliefs. The merits of this fight—which party has historically blocked more judicial nominations and what criteria the opposition party should employ in thwarting the president's wishes—are too complex to discuss here. Suffice it to say that Frist, confident that he could win the battle for public opinion, provoked a political crisis that cast in sharp relief the developing partisan breakdown in the supposedly more dignified and moderate Senate.

Frist announced his intention to use a simple majority vote to cut off debate on judicial nominations, in effect terminating the minority's filibuster rights. Dubbed the "nuclear option" by Senator Trent Lott (R-MS), this threat became the cause célèbre for liberal groups across the country until an eclectic group of senators known as the "gang of fourteen" (seven moderate Republicans and seven conservative Democrats) signed an agreement to oppose both filibusters of judicial nominations and employment of the nuclear option during that Congress. The Senate backed off the proverbial window ledge, and the immediate crisis was averted, although that agreement has expired, and it is conceivable that the nuclear option could be resurrected by either party.

The long-term effects of this episode for the institutional tone and reputation of the Senate are as serious as the corner cutting we just described in the House. If a piece of legislation has stirred up any significant controversy among Senate members, majority and minority leaders immediately assume that it will take sixty votes to pass it, as opposed to a simple majority. This thought process is so automatic that members who might oppose the legislation, or who hope to exact concessions from its sponsors, have a significantly lighter burden to sustain. They no longer need to be ready to stand up and filibuster the proposal in order to threaten that outcome; they merely need to make their displeasure known. If the leader of the party in power is unsure he can muster sixty votes, he will do everything possible to resolve such objections. The sixty-vote bar, far higher than the old majority vote procedure, encourages those with views outside the mainstream to use their potential to disrupt the body as much as they can.

At a meeting of state officials and congressional staff that one of the authors (Steinzor) attended in March 2009, Joseph Goffman, senior counsel for Senate Environment and Public Works Chairwoman Barbara Boxer (D-CA), told the group that the substance of upcoming climate change legislation would be determined by the preferences of the forty-first senator who could be found to support a theoretical cloture motion allowing the bill to come to the floor. What is startling about this statement is that Senator Boxer had not even begun to craft legislation. Instead of articulating the substance of what she hoped to achieve and embracing the process of providing leadership in persuading her colleagues to endorse those approaches, the senator's senior staff and perhaps the senator herself have already lowered their sights considerably, as they strained to win the vote of the Senate's forty-first least conservative member, as opposed to its fiftieth least liberal member.

Democrats hold a sizeable majority in the Senate as we finish this volume, especially with the party switch of the moderate Republican Senator from Pennsylvania, Arlen Specter, to their ranks and the victory of Democratic candidate Al Franken in the hotly contested Minnesota Senate race. However, the Senate is not, if it ever was, well disciplined along party lines, and Specter is known for his independence from party leadership, except when he perceives that his own political interests are directly threatened.

We foresee the continuation of serious problems in producing legislation to carry out President Obama's agenda, although the Specter defection undoubtedly brought Democrats closer to that goal.

The "sixty votes without filibuster" problem is exacerbated by the opportunity for individual members to place "holds" on legislation, often without disclosing their identity. The consequence of a hold is that Senate leaders will have difficulty bringing the bill to the floor without mollifying that member because the dissenter has an opportunity to object to consideration of the legislation and even launch a filibuster of it. One particularly notorious example involved legislation to keep guns out of the hands of the mentally ill, which was passed unanimously (!) by the House in the wake of the shootings that killed thirty-two people at Virginia Tech University in April 2008. Although it was supported by an unusual coalition that included the National Rifle Association and the Brady Campaign to Prevent Gun Violence,[21] the legislation was held up in the Senate for months by Senator Tom Coburn, Republican of Oklahoma and a charter member of the Gingrich Revolution's 1994 entering class, who was nicknamed "Dr. No" by his resentful colleagues.[22]

In the face of filibuster threats, holds, and other symptoms of a poisoned atmosphere that discourages normal legislative negotiation, Democratic leaders have begun to file cloture motions asking for a vote to end an anticipated filibuster as a routine matter. In the first session of the 110th Congress, seventy-eight such motions were filed, a record number that was nearly 50 percent higher than the previous record in 2002. By comparison, forty-two were filed in 1995 and twenty-seven in 2005. Most of the 2007 motions were filed to stop filibusters on the Iraq War, but some were filed on routine issues such as the reauthorization of Amtrak funding.

Acknowledging the time-honored traditions of the Senate and the concomitant difficulty of taking away such procedures as filibusters and holds without erring too far in the opposite direction of riding roughshod over minority rights, Ornstein advances moderate, interim proposals. The Senate could change the rules to require that at least five objections be filed before blocking a bill from coming to the floor, reducing the influence of "one crank to bring the whole institution to a halt."[23] Or it could compel disclosure of the identity of senators who place holds so that they could be subject to normal lobbying by interest groups that favor legislation or appointments. But in the end, he concludes ruefully, "the problems here are less the rules and more the culture. And that is not going to change anytime soon."[24]

*Ethical Self-Regulation*

Congress has been awash in ethical scandals for the last two decades. These episodes are nothing new, of course. Democratic Speaker Jim Wright's ethical troubles, involving money, not sex, are often cited as a contributing factor to the 1994 Gingrich Revolution, and Gingrich himself had similar ethical problems that made him more vulnerable to efforts to depose him following the 1998 midterm elections. Indeed, it is tempting to speculate that these incidents, especially those that involve money, serve as a kind of safety valve that allow Congress as a whole to avoid more troubling and deep-seated questions about campaign finance reform.

Ethical problems unquestionably contribute to Congress's credibility crisis for three related reasons. First, the cumulative effect of these scandals fuels the public's disgust with Congress, exacerbating the perceptions not only that members are not focusing on the people's business but, far worse, that elections do not screen out the most troubled and unsuitable individuals from assuming office. Second, scandals affect elections. Third, recent episodes suggest that Congress has great difficulty investigating these problems.

The shocking story of Mark Foley (R-FL), who sexually harassed young male pages for many years before the press ran stories on his exploits, was a significant factor in the Republicans' loss of the House in 2006. Foley was another member of the 1994 Gingrich Revolution entering class and was identified early on as a sexual predator by his staff.[25] Yet he managed to rise in Republican ranks, including (embarrassingly enough) serving as the chair of the House Caucus on Missing and Exploited Children. Foley's propensities became public when he sent pornographic text messages and e-mails to young men enrolled in the page program, an externship program for high school students from around the country who live in publicly sponsored dormitories near the Capitol and work on the House and Senate floor. One recipient sent copies of the messages to the press. One week after his resignation on the House floor, a *CNN/Newsweek* poll showed that half of those surveyed thought that the Republican leadership had engaged in a "deliberate cover-up" of the scandal.[26] Although the Foley affair had far-reaching political ramifications when it erupted, from an institutional perspective, the fact that his problems had long been known among Republican staff and members influenced public opinion as much as Foley's behavior did.

The Republican leadership was also discredited when Speaker Dennis

Hastert (R-IL) attempted to protect Minority Whip Tom DeLay (the man who had compared the EPA to the Gestapo, as mentioned earlier in this chapter) from the normal ethics process. Speaker Dennis Hastert removed Committee on Standards of Official Conduct chairman Joel Hefley and two other GOP committee members from their posts following completion of the DeLay investigation. The move was unprecedented retaliation against members who followed traditional, bipartisan ethics procedures. The new chair, Representative Doc Hastings (R-WA), sought to staff the committee with people from his personal office, a clear violation of the historical practice of employing bipartisan staff. Democrats boycotted committee business for several months, but the episode crippled the House ethics process until Democrats took over in 2006. As Ornstein and Mann write,

> The actions taken by the Speaker—in effect firing those Republican members who had done their job and upheld the ethical standards of the House—were unprecedented.
>
> . . .
>
> The signals sent by the Speaker could not have been more clear: take your responsibilities as guardians of House ethics seriously and you will be the ones stigmatized; play the game and make sure that no ethics issues are raised about your party colleagues or are downplayed and diluted, and career enhancement awaits.[27]

### The New Democratic Majority

Republican leadership of the House came to an end in 2006, and Democrats most recently took back the Senate in 2007. Neither change arrested the steady erosion of public opinion regarding Congress, although leaders of the Democrat-led 110th Congress (2007–2008) were painfully aware of this slide and took office promising reform. Constrained by narrow margins in both bodies, Democrats made limited but measurable progress in some areas, picking up the pace of legislative activity and putting more time into their legislative work.

On the other hand, the Democratic leadership in the House has continued the practice of bringing controversial bills to the floor under closed rules. "It sounds like we're not going what we said we would do—I understand that," House Majority Leader Steny H. Hoyer (D-MD) told the *Washington Post*. "Here, however, we believe we are very justified in one of the most important issues confronting the country, which clearly was a huge issue in the election and which got bottled up in the Senate."[28] He was referring to the Iraq War.

Although they clearly have a long distance to go in reversing the worst abridgments of the regular order, Democrats have revived among the most important activities of an independent Congress—oversight. In an article for *Foreign Affairs*, Mann and Ornstein characterize the congressional oversight process during the Bush II administrations as "virtually collapsed."[29] Noting the absence of oversight on everything from the government's response to Hurricane Katrina to the wars in Iraq and Afghanistan, they are adamant in their evaluation of its importance:

> One of Congress' key roles is oversight: making sure that the laws it writes are faithfully executed and vetting the military and diplomatic activities of the executive. Congressional oversight is meant to keep mistakes from happening or from spiraling out of control; it helps draw out lessons from catastrophes in order to prevent them, or others like them, from recurring. Good oversight cuts waste, punishes fraud or scandal, and keeps policymakers on their toes. The task is not easy. Examining a department of agency, its personnel, and it implementation policies is time-consuming. Investigating possible scandals can easily lapse into a partisan exercise that ignores broad policy issues for the sake of cheap publicity.[30]

The statistics fully document their concerns. During the Republican-led 109th Congress (2005–2006), the House held 521 oversight hearings and sixty-eight hearings on the war in Iraq; the Democrat-led 110th Congress increased that number to 844 and 166 on Iraq.

## Eroding Identity

The foregoing analysis shows that both parties have played important roles in the decline of Congress as a partner with the president in governing the country. This decline was accelerated by the destructively partisan approaches of the Bush II administration and especially by the election of members of the House and Senate who owed first loyalty to their ideological beliefs rather than their duty to serve the public interest. Mann and Ornstein conclude that this erosion of "strong institutional identity" among members is the root cause of Congress's problems, dating its emergence to the 1994 Gingrich Revolution. "Members of the majority [Republican] party, including congressional leaders, act as field lieutenants in the president's army rather than as members of an independent branch of government," they explain, basing their conclusions on "comments we have heard from many members of Congress."[31]

Mann and Ornstein spend a great deal of time with members of Congress and are well respected not just as scholars but as active participants in efforts to reform its institutional rules and traditions.[32] But how much credence can we accord their reports of what people tell them when those people are never named? Admittedly, they have little choice but to use anonymous quotes because very few sitting or former members of this select group ever speak about such sensitive issues for public attribution. However, the few available retirement statements, especially from House Republicans whose careers spanned this troubling period, confirm their reporting.

In early October 2008, the *New York Times* ran a truly exceptional profile of one of the many senior Republican House members who have decided to retire. Tom Davis, who has represented Virginia's 11th District (encompassing the Washington, D.C., suburbs in the north of the state) since 1995, was a well-respected, senior member of the Republican caucus. Asked why he had decided not to run again, Davis said,

> [I]f we were a dog food, they would take us off the shelf.
> . . .
> You know, the Cubs fans used to put the bags over their heads. . . . That's what I feel when you say you're from Congress, because there are just so many things we're not doing.
> . . .
> "When you get the majority, the leadership team sits around the table, and the first question the winners ask, sitting in this ornate room, is "How do we stay in the majority?" . . . Now the members, a lot of them, are willing to tackle these issues, but they elect leaders, and the leaders' report card is: Do they get their members re-elected? You see what I'm saying? And the minority, by the way, sits in a little less ornate room, a little smaller room in the Capitol, and they say, "How do we get it back?" And so for every issue it's "Do we cooperate or do we try to embarrass them?" Very few times they cooperate.[33]

A cynic might conclude that Davis retired primarily because he is in the minority after years as an influential member of the majority. And it is certainly true that being in the minority these days can be an unpleasant experience. The manipulation of the rules, ethics scandals, exclusionary decision making, and a high tolerance for disruption of the regular order became routine in the House and Senate and, as we have seen, can just as easily be used to make the Republican minority's life miserable as they were used to plague the Democrats. But it is rare indeed to hear a man whose highest achievement was serving as a senior member of the House of Representative speak with such candid disillusionment about the core competency of the institution. Davis is angry and frustrated because he thinks he has let the people of his district down. He believes that he can no longer rationalize this outcome—if he ever could—by reference to a higher ideology.

In chapter 3, we explained how the erosion of the regular order in the context of congressional budgeting and appropriations caused the "hollowing out" of the five health and safety agencies that are at the heart of this book. The five are hardly unique; many other functions and programs are similarly shortchanged. Yet the implications of a dysfunctional Congress reach even further than the considerable problems caused by hollow government. In this final section, we explore how congressional neglect mangled the implementation of an environmental law that affects millions of Americans, costing taxpayers much more when, according to the original congressional intent, it should have cost them much less.

## The Toll of Superfund Neglect

Passed by a Democratic Congress in a rare lame duck session held on the eve of Ronald Reagan's first term, the Comprehensive Environmental Response, Compensation, and Liability Act (CERCLA, or Superfund)[34] established two sources of funding—and two distinct strategies—for accomplishing the cleanup of thousands of toxic waste sites around the country. The government may either sue the entities responsible for creating the sites in the first place to get a court order forcing them to clean up ("lawyers first, shovels later"), or it may use money from a multibillion-dollar fund to pay for cleanup and then recover those expenses from liable parties ("shovels first, lawyers later"). The two strategies were integrally related to one another—without the resources provided by the trust fund, the government could not investigate sites, prosecute responsible parties, or use government-funded cleanup to abate immediate threats to public health. Conversely, enforcement actions replenished the trust fund.

Although Congress never anticipated that the program would become self-supporting, given the costs of administering the program and the likelihood that some sites would prove to be "orphans" with no responsible parties to pay the bills, the two tracks ensured that thousands of identifiable polluters would end up either paying now or paying later.

The trust fund was primarily supported by industry taxes in the form of a broad-based corporate income tax, as well as "feedstock taxes" targeted at the oil and petrochemical industries. The statute required the EPA to compile a list of the worst hazardous waste dump sites in the country and begin working its way through them. Because the law was drafted very broadly, however, and applied to both the legacy of past and future dumping, regardless of its legality at the time, its stringent liability provisions served as a powerful deterrent to generators of toxic substances, including every entity from a Fortune 100 chemical plant to a small garage using solvents to a local government that collected and arranged for the disposal of their residents' ordinary household garbage.

Superfund sites come in many guises. Many are located in heavily populated urban or suburban neighborhoods and contain a toxic soup of harmful chemicals with direct routes of exposure—for example, contaminated water, soil, or air—for the people who live in surrounding communities. The sites were used by manufacturers to dispose of liquid and solid toxic wastes for many decades. Some sites date back as far as the turn of the last century. Among the most heavily polluted are sites owned by companies that used extremely toxic chemicals, some of which (for example, creosote and lead) are now banned for most purposes. Over decades, excess chemicals and metals spilled or dropped onto the bare ground, where they seeped into underground aquifers or were washed by rain into adjacent storm sewers, rivers, or creeks. Other sites served as dumping grounds for multiple companies, many of which have changed their names, metamorphosing into other businesses or simply disappearing. A large number of sites span hundreds of acres where ordinary household garbage served as the foundation for disposal of millions of gallons of liquid industrial waste.

Congress has actually gotten around to reauthorizing the 1980 law only once, in 1986, after Superfund-related scandals had forced the resignation of President Reagan's first EPA administrator, Ann Gorsuch Burford, and sent the political appointee directly responsible for the program, Rita Lavelle, to jail following her conviction on perjury charges. The Superfund Amendments and Reauthorization Act of 1986 increased the funding for the program from approximately $1.6 billion over a five-year period to approximately $1.7 billion annually and also greatly expanded the law's detailed statutory mandates. For example, the 1986 amendments (1) required the EPA to pick up the pace of cleanup at "shovels first" sites; (2) gave the agency new authority in "lawyers first" enforcement cases; (3) increased the number of sites included on its National Priorities List (NPL); (4) told the agency to supervise cleanups at federally owned facilities such as military bases; and (5) established uniform standards for when a site would be considered sufficiently safe that cleanup could be deemed completed.

The Superfund program has always generated controversy. Citizens living near NPL sites were frustrated that cleanup could take so long. Large corporations were angered by the statute's liability scheme, which they perceived as draconian. In addition to imposing liability without regard to fault—that is, it did not matter if disposal of toxics in an unlined pit in the ground was perfectly legal at the time—the statute made everyone who sent or transported waste to the site, along with site owners and operators, "strictly, jointly and severally" liable for cleanup costs. This standard means that the federal government could sue a few large companies for all of the costs and they would be compelled to pay but could seek "contributions" from smaller, jointly liable entities at their own expense. Large manufacturing firms soon took advantage of the statute's broad scope, bringing small businesses and local governments into court. Compounding the complexity of the litigation, court decisions in many states held that standard property and casualty insurance policies covered the insured company's liabilities under Superfund, even though the insurers thought they had excluded everything but the expenses of remediating sudden, accidental toxic spills.

Despite the problems generated by the statute's liability scheme, when it came time to reauthorize the program again in the early 1990s, Superfund's diverse stakeholders could not agree on an alternative. Estimates of cleanup costs ran into the billions of dollars, and the only alternative to the statute's so-called polluter pays liability scheme was some kind of taxpayer-financed "public works program," an approach opposed by environmentalists and, interestingly enough, the vast majority of manufacturing sector companies that had already paid millions to settle individual Superfund cases in the first few years of the program. Anxious to play a central role in negotiations to chart its future, a group known as the National Commission on Superfund was convened to develop a consensus proposal.[35] The commission included the chief executive officers—or their functional equivalents—of organizations and companies that represented every major, nonfederal stakeholder, including Fortune 100 petrochemical companies, small businesses, insurers, national environmental groups, grassroots community activists, and state and municipal officials.

By the fall of 1993, using the group's negotiated blueprint as a starting point, the Clinton administration, along with a surprisingly broad coalition that ran the gamut from Monsanto to the Sierra Club, lobbied Congress to pass legislation modeled on the deal. The compromise retained liability but provided for streamlined settlement procedures to cut the costs of litigation. It also specified more detailed standards to control cleanup costs. The only group of stakeholders opposed to these terms was the insurance industry, and the Clinton administration was trying to develop a settlement fund that would assuage its concerns. Unfortunately, however, the 103d Congress (1993–94) ran out of time to enact the compromise. Rather than resurrect it in the 104th (1995–96), the newly elected Republican leadership in the House tabled further consideration of reauthorization legislation.

In 1995, the industry taxes supporting the trust fund expired, and the only sources for annual appropriations were either unspent amounts left in the trust fund or general taxpayer revenues. At the time of their expiration, Superfund corporate income and feedstock taxes raised revenues of approximately $1.5 billion annually (or $4 million daily), an amount that clearly is not burdensome on industry, amounting to approximately 1.8 percent of the 2006 profits of just six of the nation's largest oil and petrochemical companies in 2007.[36]

The full impact of this development did not become obvious in the short term because hundreds of millions of dollars remained in the fund and the EPA slowed the pace of spending. By 2001, however, the number of "construction completions" at sites on the Superfund NPL had fallen from eighty-seven in 2000 to forty-seven; in 2007, the number had fallen to twenty-one.[37] In 1999, the think tank Resources for the Future (RFF) conducted a study of the funding requirements of the Superfund program.[38] The results of the study suggested that the missing taxes and diminishing congressional appropriations had left a funding gap of billions of dollars. An author of the RFF report recently observed, "Hundreds of sites across the country have been remediated, but there's not enough money to finish work on the sites already designated, never mind the new ones that are still being added."[39]

As for the larger consequences of these failures, a report cosponsored by the Center for Progressive Reform and the Center for American Progress examined the impact of inadequate funding by studying five of the worst Superfund sites in each of the ten most populous states.[40] This analysis revealed that many of the 1,244 sites now on the Superfund NPL have languished there for more than two decades. Between 205,000 and 803,000 people live within one mile of these sites, including 34,000 children and 14,000 elderly persons; a disproportionate percentage of these persons are low income and people of color.

Subsequent congresses never did reauthorize Superfund, leaving the program with exactly the same substantive provisions as it had twenty-two years ago. Had Congress made a principled decision to terminate the taxes, it certainly could have articulated reasons for the decision, including the tacit assumption that has become a practical reality in the thirteen years after the taxes expired: the general taxpayer and not industry should pay to finish the cleanup job. In addition, Congress either could have sanctioned the Bush II administration's slowdown in cleanup or it could have curtailed the scope and requirements of the program to make its demands more achievable for an EPA program with significantly less money. Or it could have chided the Bush administration publicly for allowing such an important environmental program to fall into disrepair.

But Congress did none of these things. It held only a handful of oversight hearings in the twenty-two years since the statute was last reauthorized, never seriously considered statutory amendments, and ignored the entreaties of community and environmental groups. Unlike the self-inflicted wounds of sex scandals, financial corruption, and partisan bickering, however, the institution that paid the price for this negligence was not Congress but the EPA.

After taking office, President Obama proposed reinstatement of the tax and committed $600 million in general taxpayer revenues from the stimulus package to fund lagging cleanup. His FY 2010 budget assumes that the additional revenue from reinstating the tax will be added to the federal budget. It remains to be seen whether Congress will approve these proposals.

## Conclusion

"Unfortunately," Mann and Ornstein conclude in *The Broken Branch*, "there is no quick fix for a dysfunctional institution."[41] They suggest a series of moderate reforms, including an independent and professionally staffed entity to investigate ethics violations. They call for a return to the regular order: guaranteeing members three days to read legislation before it reaches the floor of either house, banning the practice of eliminating minority member participation in conference committees, and similar proposals. They mention various efforts to toughen campaign finance laws, including the elimination of leadership political action committees that give senior members incentives to dangle before members with less secure seats. They urge the courts to curtail the most egregious practices of political gerrymandering—redrawing congressional districts in bizarre ways to create safe Democratic or Republican seats. And they suggest various ways to lengthen the congressional work week, giving members an incentive to move their families to Washington, D.C., rather than leaving them at home in the states, a development that Mann and Ornstein believe would reestablish a network of personal relationships across the aisle, restoring some sense of institutional loyalty.

To this list, we would add the importance of rethinking the Senate leadership's posture toward filibusters and holds. Rather than automatically assume that the opposition to even the most popular proposals will generate a filibuster, and therefore setting a bar for themselves of achieving sixty votes, Senate leaders should allow a few well-chosen pieces of legislation to go onto the floor and be filibustered until the pressure of public scrutiny forces a workable compromise between minority opponents and the majority. An individual senator's placement of a hold on a policy matter or an appointment should be made public so that voters understand the importance and implications of such backroom dealing.

Although we think these changes could have a constructive effect on Congress, in the end we agree with Mann and Ornstein that it will take consistent electoral expressions of public disgust to give leaders in both houses, on both sides of the aisle, adequate incentives to reform Congress to the point that it begins to function again as a responsible and effective institution, as the Framers intended. As we hope we have illustrated, the future of health, safety, and environmental protections in this country depends a great deal on that result.

## CHAPTER SIX

# The White House

## Introduction

Surveying the vast government that appears to be spread at their feet on Inauguration Day, presidents must feel as daunted as they are elated. To be sure, they will bear the harsh, often frustrating judgments of the Congress that stands behind them—535 voices raising criticism, sowing doubt, constantly importuning, and only occasionally doing what they are told. They must confront the scrutiny of the Supreme Court one block away, which exists in large measure to ensure that they do not overstep their constitutional boundaries. But even those challenges are dwarfed by the arduous demands of managing fifteen departments and sixty-five agencies, which together employ some 2.7 million civilian employees, 1.1 million active-duty military, 935,000 civilian military, and 1.5 million members of the military reserve and National Guard.

Most presidents come into office worried about winning the loyalty of the bureaucracy left behind by their predecessors, especially predecessors who have served two terms. Instinctively, they are reluctant to trust the career civil service. Franklin Roosevelt, commonly perceived as the president who created the modern American government by dramatically expanding its jurisdiction during the New Deal, was sufficiently suspicious of civil servants that he created a slew of new entities, with handpicked staff, to launch those initiatives. His successor, Harry Truman, famously joked about the bureaucracy's perceived intransigence shortly before his successor, General Dwight Eisenhower, took office, "He'll sit here, and he'll say, 'Do this! Do that!' *And nothing will happen.* Poor Ike—it won't be a bit like the Army. He'll find it very frustrating."[1] Richard Nixon warned his cabinet to move quickly to replace holdover bureaucrats with people who believed in the goals of his administration so that the career civil servants would not have an opportunity to sabotage new initiatives from within.

Presidents have found it much easier to quash civil servants when they try to do things the president dislikes than to inspire them to act aggressively in the public interest. This simple reality does not pose as many problems for conservative presidents, who see their primary role as limiting government's intrusiveness, as it does for liberal or progressive presidents, who need a talented, committed, hardworking civil service to implement their signature domestic programs successfully.

Over the past thirty years, presidents have used three closely related but distinct strategies to master the bureaucracy. First, they have centralized power within the White House by expanding the number of hand-picked and loyal staffers who work to save the president from surprise and embarrassment. When George W. Bush left office, 2,000 people worked for a series of White House "councils," appointed to help the president ride herd on the civil service. In addition to ensuring that career employees report up a long chain before taking significant action, White House centralization offers multiple opportunities for regulated industries to plead their case, appealing defeats they may have suffered at the agency level.

Second, and at least as important, presidents have done their best to deploy political appointees to the bureaucratic front lines at the agencies in order to ensure that career civil servants remain under control. The number of senior and midlevel managers serving at the pleasure of the president has expanded steadily. As the Bush II administration came to an end, 3,000 appointees served throughout the government, and this number may well increase under the Obama administration. Professor David Lewis has conducted an empirical analysis of historical data and reports that the number of political appointees expands by an average of three hundred when a different political party takes back the White House.[2]

Third, presidents have used executive orders imposing "analytical requirements" before rules are promulgated to restrict regulatory agencies. These requirements are sufficiently arduous that they often delay or chill the initiation of regulation because they require agencies to rewrite regulatory impact statements, engage in lengthy negotiations with White House staff, and attempt to mollify other federal agencies and departments that object to their policy choices.

All three strategies have been criticized as the "politicization" of regulatory government, meaning that presidents use them to deflect administrators from outcomes recommended by agency staff and to push instead for results that will please constituencies on the right end of the political spectrum (regulated industries) or on the left (public interest groups). We oppose constituent-based decision making not only because it results in the "capture" of the agencies, but because it introduces factors never mentioned in their authorizing statutes. But agencies are given discretion to make decisions for "policy" reasons, and we recognize the challenge of drawing clear lines between decisions based on policy analysis and decisions that reflect purely political considerations. Indeed, to believe that such line drawing is easy would mean that, in theory, agencies could function the same way under presidents from different parties with different ideologies, a proposition that is naïve to the point of being nonsensical. For these reasons, we think using the term "politicization" paints with too broad a brush and confuses the debate as often as it provides enlightenment.

On the most profound level, politics are the backbone of American democracy, encompassing the process by which the people select their agents in Congress, the president, and the vice president. Electoral politics, in the small "d" sense of the word, combines the very good qualities of democracy—open debates, appearances before voters, scrutiny by the free press, and voters' choices on the issues of the day—with some of its unfortunate qualities—the corrupting influence of campaign contributions by well-heeled special interests or a myopic focus on sex scandals rather than issues. Critics also use the term "politics" to mean the practice of basing decisions on a stagnant bath of shortsighted calculations about which choices would anger or please the constituencies that elected leaders most want to keep happy, regardless of the merits of the issue at hand. We may lament the influence of these negative characteristics but believe it is not just unwise, but untenable, to tar the entire process by turning "politics" into a dirty word.

Often, the alternative to politicization offered by regulatory critics is to base decisions on "sound science." While science should provide the foundation of regulatory policy, the problem with this argument, as we discuss shortly, is that the very nature of science makes it impossible for science to produce reliable final decisions, either because the science is too uncertain or because the science is affected by policy choices. In any event, while our legal system emphasizes the centrality of science, it does not in any way anticipate that scientists can provide final answers.

The bottom line is that politics do not end at the edge of the property occupied by Congress on Capitol Hill, shutting off like a light switch as soon as a piece of legislation is sent over to an agency for implementation. Agencies, especially the civil service, must do their best to interpret their authorizing statutes honestly and to clarify the scientific and technical foundations that should inform any decision. In the end, however, agencies cannot avoid acting with politics in mind, in both the good and bad senses of that term. Agencies have discretion to choose regulatory policies, and those with an interest in the outcome, including the president, members of Congress, corporate interests, and public interest groups, all work to pressure the agency to favor their preferences.

To avoid the many problems caused by indiscriminate use of the term "politicization," we will instead use the terms "good politics," mixed politics," and "bad politics." A decision involves good politics when an agency acts on the basis of policy choices that are consistent with its statute. So, for example, an EPA decision to protect low-income children in the inner city more aggressively than upper class children in the exurbs would be good politics if the EPA reasoned that the first group has little if any health care, a larger pollution burden in their immediate ambient environment, and a worse diet, making them significantly more vulnerable to pollution-caused diseases. On the other hand, the same decision would be bad politics if the sole reason the EPA chose more protective policies was a threat from an inner-city congressman to cut off its funding. The EPA's decision would reflect mixed politics if the agency acted in response to both motivations.

We hope this illustration shows that the job of distinguishing between policy-based and political-based decision making is much easier said than done. We are confident, however, that the effort to draw these distinctions, rather than painting with the overly broad brush of denouncing politicization per se, will be worthwhile for us and for the reader.

This chapter argues that presidents can no longer afford—if they ever could—to approach the civil service with suspicion and disdain. Progressive presidents are especially ill served by these dynamics because they are a major factor in demoralizing the civil service, slowing regulation, and making agencies dysfunctional. We explain why the trends toward centralization and politicization cause dysfunction by conflicting with the statutory structure of laws to protect the public health, worker safety, and the environment and by jeopardizing the integrity of policy making in those arenas. We conclude with a critique of the "unitary executive" theory, which is often invoked to justify centralization.

## Bureaucracy Bashing

> Americans distrust government's powers and motives. They immediately get
> the joke that has a federal inspector or a state administrator fatuously saying,
> "We're from the government and here to help." Such suspicion is a healthy
> instinct—but one that is being carried to destructive and demagogic lengths.
> — Jim Hoagland, *Washington Post* columnist[3]

Political scientists and public administration scholars date the worst of what
is commonly referred to as "bureaucracy bashing" to Ronald Reagan's
two terms as president, although they acknowledge that Jimmy Carter was
no great friend of the bureaucracy. According to Professor Larry Hubbell,
President Reagan used "four categories" to portray federal bureaucrats as
"loafers, incompetent buffoons, good ole boys, or tyrants" (these words are
Hubbell's own), with tyrants being the worst category because it describes
officials who extend the "long hand of the federal government" into citizens' private lives.[4] Hubbell suggested that these characterizations played
well with the American people because federal workers are better paid
and more educated than the average American, triggering "many people's
latent anti-intellectualism. So, many people perceive federal bureaucrats
as being quite out of touch with reality. In these people's and their leaders'
minds, many federal bureaucrats are head-in-the clouds intellectuals—
incapable of clear thought and effective management."[5]

In the years since Reagan left office, Republican conservatives have
certainly been the most vehement public critics of government and its
workers, but they have encountered little meaningful resistance from
Democrats. One notable exception came in the aftermath of the bomb-
ing of the Murrah Office Building in Oklahoma City, when President Bill
Clinton told the 1995 graduating class at Michigan State University that
"there is nothing patriotic about hating your country or pretending that
you can love your country but despise your Government."[6] The president specifically mentioned local militias as perpetrators of violence that
threatened the rule of law, although at least one scholar—Professor Thad
Hall—has interpreted the speech to also apply to congressional conservatives, arguing that Clinton was drawing a link between elected leaders'
participation in bureaucracy bashing and this stunning act of violence.[7]

Exacerbating the effects of bureaucracy bashing is the common practice of modern presidents to come into office promising ambitious reform
or "reinvention" of government. The announced goals of these efforts are

to reduce the size of government and to make government workers more efficient. Such promises are always justified by the assertion that the bureaucracy is inefficient because its employees are incompetent or, at the very least, uninspired and lazy.

Ronald Reagan, for example, urged the Grace Commission, a group of 2,000 businesspeople deployed throughout the government to identify opportunities for cost reductions, "We want your team to work like tireless bloodhounds. Don't leave any stone unturned in your search to root out inefficiency."[8] He told the story of California state workers who tried to fit oversize state forms into standard-size manila folders until a member of a similar commission he had convened when he was governor of the state picked up the phone and ordered that the print shop change the size of the forms. Reagan claimed that this brilliant insight, so obvious to executives from the private sector and yet so elusive to the small-minded bureaucrats, allowed the state to buy 4,200 fewer file cabinets each year. The brand of reinvention favored by President Clinton and Vice President Al Gore, who assumed control of the National Performance Review initiative, used similarly harsh rhetoric, although its intentions were less hostile: "Our goal is to make the entire federal government both less expensive and more efficient, and to change the culture of our national bureaucracy away from complacency and entitlement toward initiative and empowerment."[9]

The two Bush presidencies eschewed formal campaigns to reinvent government and instead adopted a stance of benign neglect, with the notable exception of using the White House to micromanage the bureaucracy on a selective basis. The senior President Bush convened a so-called Competitiveness Council to hear appeals on rules industry found excessive, chaired by Vice President Daniel Quayle. The council was widely known as a burial ground for controversial regulations; the EPA was its most frequent target. Under George W. Bush, the leading proponent of regulatory micromanagement was Vice President Richard Cheney, who earned great notoriety by delving deeply into the bureaucracy to affect administrative decisions without attracting much attention. In a prize-winning series on the vice president, *Washington Post* reporters Jo Becker and Barton Gellman report on one such foray:

Sue Ellen Wooldridge, the 19th-ranking Interior Department official, arrived at her desk in Room 6140 a few months after Inauguration Day 2001. A phone message awaited her.

"This is Dick Cheney," said the man on her voice mail, Wooldridge recalled in an interview. "I understand you are the person handling this Klamath situation. Please call me at—hmm, I guess I don't know my own number. I'm over at the White House."[10]

The call was the first step in Cheney's successful campaign to reverse a civil service decision to protect endangered species by cutting off water to farmers in Oregon's Klamath Basin.

A second incident involved EPA regulations controlling emissions from power plants under the Clean Air Act, a subject that interested Cheney from the moment he convened his secret White House "energy taskforce" composed of high-level utility executives and energy producers. As newly minted EPA administrator Christine Todd Whitman, the former governor of New Jersey and by no means a political novice, explained the situation to the *Washington Post,*

Sitting through Cheney's task force meetings, Whitman had been stunned by what she viewed as an unquestioned belief that EPA's regulations were primarily to blame for keeping companies from building new power plants. "I was upset, mad, offended that there seemed to be so much head-nodding around the table," she said.

Whitman said she had to fight "tooth and nail" to prevent Cheney's task force from handing over the job of reforming the [rules] to the Energy Department.

. . .

Cheney listened to her arguments, and as usual didn't say much. Whitman said she also met with the president to "explain my concerns" and to offer an alternative.[11]

In the end, the rules were written at the White House and Whitman resigned, ostensibly to spend more time with her family. We will have more to say about her predicament later in this chapter.

Experiences like these can prove as influential as the launch of grandiose programs like the Grace Commission and the National Performance Review. Spread by word of mouth and instilling more than a small increment of fear, anecdotes about the White House's ruthlessness not only discourage professional civil servants from speaking their minds but cause them to lower their expectations regarding policy recommendations that might fly in a rearranged political landscape.

Not surprisingly, members of Congress have also succumbed to the temptation to blame bureaucrats for the nation's ills. Professor Hall conducted a study that considered the use of the relatively positive term "public servant" and the clearly disparaging label "bureaucrat" during the 103d (1993–94) and 104th (1995–96) congresses. Readers will remember that this period was momentous for Congress, marking the Democrats' loss of control over the House of Representatives for the first time since 1954 and the ascension to power of Speaker of the House Newt Gingrich and Majority Whip Tom DeLay. Hall's study documented a dramatic increase in the use of the derisive term "bureaucrat" by Republican members, especially after the Clinton administration succeeded the Bush I administration. Hall added that the bureaucrats so excoriated were never identified as working at any particular agency but rather "are everywhere but nowhere."[12]

In 2006, a group of public administration and political science scholars convened focus groups of Senior Executive Service personnel to discuss the effects of bureaucrat bashing. Several participants in the study characterized the effects of such criticism as destructive, even devastating, and acknowledged that they hesitated to admit they were civil servants in some social situations: "[Y]ou really felt uneasy about being federal employees. People would look at you as if you had cancer."[13] The authors of the study noted that "[s]enior managers repeatedly said that bashing creates permanent and overwhelming negative mental frames and political symbols for career bureaucrats, which affects morale, recruitment, training, and overall work environment."[14]

## Centralization

Distrust of the career civil service has motivated presidents since Eisenhower to centralize authority to approve regulatory proposals in the White House. Paradoxically, the statutes that created the five protector agencies delegate authority to make such decisions directly to the highest officials at each agency: (1) the Consumer Product Safety Act instructs "the commission" to take action; (2) the environmental laws command the EPA "administrator" to undertake specific work; (3) the Food, Drug, and Cosmetic Act confers mandates on the "secretary" of the Department of Health and Human Services; (4) the Occupational Safety and Health Act requires regulation by the "secretary" of the Department of Labor; and (5) the National Highway Traffic Safety Act charges the "secretary" of the Department of Transportation with responsibility for preventing traffic accidents.[15] Had Congress intended the White House to exert such extensive control over regulatory policy making, it could and would have drafted very different language.

These explicit delegations do not mean that presidential directives are illegal or even inappropriate, assuming they fall within the boundaries set by the statutes. They do mean that, as we explained in chapter 2 and chapter 5, the five protector agencies are directly accountable to—and therefore the agents who act on behalf of—the Congress. Congress intends the agencies to make decisions based on science, technology, and policy analysis. The criteria it directs them to consider in determining these outcomes never mention achieving the approval of specific political constituencies, which constitutes bad politics in the lexicon we have adopted here.

The argument we expect our critics to make in response to the assertion that the White House should have a more limited role in reviewing health and safety regulation is that, unlike the bureaucracy, the president is elected by the people. This type of accountability is and should be highly valued. We freely acknowledge that it is better to have elected officials making the big policy decisions involved in health and safety rulemaking, which is why we urge Congress to write more specific statutory mandates for the agencies. But centralized White House control does not mean that agencies deal with political appointees who have sufficiently high visibility that their decisions will become part of the record that the president runs on in the next election. Rather, in too many cases, the interference of relatively low-level staffers is not transparent to the public. Even when the official is high level (for example, Vice President Cheney) the implications of such interventions can remain hidden for years.

A fascinating empirical analysis performed by Professors Michael Vandenbergh and Lisa Bressman illustrates these points beautifully.[16] The analysis was based on a survey administered to a group of "presidential appointees"—meaning they were confirmed by the Senate—at the EPA during the Bush I (1989–93) and Clinton (1993–2001) administrations. Thirty-five individuals were identified and agreed to participate, fourteen from Bush I and twenty-one from Clinton. Professors Vandenbergh and Bressman administered a lengthy survey, by phone or in person, which was designed to characterize the appointees' experiences with presidential review. The survey focused on two aspects of the White House process: review by OMB's OIRA and review by other members of the White House staff. What is especially noteworthy about this survey is that because it involved the perceptions of political appointees and career civil servants, respondents were significantly more likely to be sympathetic to the president's efforts to control the bureaucracy.

The survey revealed that as many as nineteen White House offices were involved in reviewing EPA rules, with as many as 93 percent of the respondents explaining that they had become involved in debates with institutional entities other than the OMB. These other White House participants included the Vice President's Office, the Council on Environmental Quality, and a long list of other units within the domestic policy staff.[17] Some of these offices sought to represent the interests of other federal agencies in the disputes. So, for example, the Department of Defense typically opposes or seeks modification of rules that require the cleanup of toxic waste problems at military bases and might appeal to like-minded White House staffers for help in opposing an EPA rule in this area. One survey respondent said these battles got so "ugly" that the White House was compelled to mediate them. On other occasions, the intervention of other offices was provoked by EPA staff, who solicited their support in opposing changes demanded by OMB economists.

Bressman and Vandenbergh conclude that this ad hoc series of disputes could trump the more orderly and rational process followed by the agencies in adopting a rule, including meeting with relevant stakeholders, putting proposals out for public comment, analyzing the comments, and modifying the rules accordingly:

> It is not a sufficient response to say that the president gets involved in agency decision-making when he wants the public to understand that he is responsible for particular agency policies or rules. Even if such behavior promotes accountability on a limited basis, the concern is that it may not promote rationality in a systematic way, as a model of agency decision-making should.[18]

Two additional, related findings are noteworthy. First, 75 percent of survey respondents said that the OIRA's involvement in regulatory review made the outcome less protective of public health and the environment. They explained that OMB economists focused inordinately on regulatory costs as opposed to the benefits of a rule, such as improvements in public health, and on short-term costs benefits as opposed to long-term benefits. The short-term focus underestimates benefits like reduced cancer risks, which tend to be realized over the long run. Second, 97 percent of respondents said that White House intervention was not visible to the public or only somewhat visible to the public.

The utility of involving so many different White House offices and staff in internecine battles over a rule is highly questionable even from the perspective of maintaining presidential control over rulemaking. The most meaningful difference between the political appointees who serve at the five protector agencies and those who serve on the White House staff is that the agency group is far more likely to have actual expertise in the substantive issues under the agency's jurisdiction. The opacity of White House review frustrates democratic accountability, causes needless delays, and undermines the cabinet officials the president appoints to be responsible for policy making.


## Subverting Science

In theory at least, presidents find it more difficult to inject bad politics into agencies that require the evaluation of complex scientific and technological information. Sending technically unqualified but politically opportunistic appointees into such agencies provokes controversy. Conversely, if the appointees are qualified from a substantive perspective, they are likely to have appreciation for the civil service experts they supervise. These assumptions were turned on their head by the Bush II administration, which pursued an unprecedented and relentless campaign to subvert scientific and technical judgments throughout the government. Those efforts are the focus of a large body of critical scholarly and popular literature, to which we have contributed.[19] Critics make the case that the administration embraced bad politics over science in certain areas—for example, stem cell research and reproductive rights—and ignored science for bad political reasons in other areas—for example, climate change and the regulation of toxic substances such as mercury.

The implications of these efforts cannot be underestimated, especially from the perspective of sidelining the career civil service and elevating the preferences of political appointees. In 2008, the Union of Concerned Scientists (UCS), a nonprofit advocacy group, released the results of a survey it distributed to 5,500 career scientists who worked for the EPA.[20] The survey found that almost 60 percent of 1,600 survey respondents had experienced political interference in their work over the last five years. Forty-two percent said that commercial interests had inappropriately induced

reversal or withdrawal of scientific conclusions or decisions through political intervention. Twenty-two percent personally experienced selective
or incomplete use of scientific data to justify specific regulatory outcomes.
UCS sent a similar survey to 5,918 FDA scientists and achieved a 20 percent response rate.[21] Sixty percent of survey respondents knew of cases in
which commercial interests had inappropriately interfered with agency
decision making; 70 percent believed the FDA had insufficient resources
to achieve its mission of protecting public health; and 40 percent feared
retaliation if they expressed concerns about public health. Twenty percent
said they had been "asked explicitly by FDA decision makers to provide
incomplete, inaccurate, or misleading information to the public." In 2008,
UCS sponsored a petition signed by more than 15,000 scientists—including
fifty-two Nobel Prize laureates—asking Congress to codify "scientific
freedoms" for civil servants that included the "freedom to conduct their
work without political or private-sector interference" and to "communicate their findings to Congress, the public, and their scientific peers."[22]

Two case studies from the Bush II administration illustrate the pitfalls
of allowing bad politics to subvert health and safety policy making.

## Plan B

> I felt there was no role—not just for me but for the people who have expertise. I
> lose a lot of battles; normally you go to work to fight another day. But this time I just
> couldn't look in the mirror and live with myself. — Susan Wood[23]

In 2001, the last year for which statistics are available, 3.1 million pregnancies in the United States were unintended, with 44 percent resulting in
births, 42 percent ending in abortion, and 14 percent ending in miscarriage.
Obviously, despite a wide choice of before-the-fact birth control alternatives, unwanted pregnancies remain a significant social and public health
problem, for the mothers, for their children, and often for other children
and family members. In 1999, the FDA approved a medication known as
"Plan B" for sale by prescription only. The drug, which is administered in
two doses, must be taken as soon as possible—and no later than seventy-
two hours after unprotected sex—to have its intended effect.

In 2003, Barr Pharmaceuticals, the American manufacturer of the
drug, applied to have it converted to nonprescription status, as it is available in France, England, and more than thirty other countries. The FDA's

TABLE 6.1  **Plan B FDA Advisory Committee Votes**

| Question | Yes | No |
|---|---|---|
| 1. Does the actual use study (AUS) demonstrate that consumers used the product as recommended in the proposed labeling? | 27 | 1 |
| 2. Are the AUS data generalizable to the overall population of potential non-Rx users of Plan B? | 27 | 1 |
| 3. Based on the AUS and literature review, is there evidence that non-Rx availability of Plan B leads to substitution of emergency contraception for the regular use of other methods of contraception? | 0 | 28 |
| 4. Do the data demonstrate that Plan B is safe for use in the nonprescription setting? | 28 | 0 |
| 5. Are the plans for introduction of Plan B into the non-Rx setting adequate with respect to consumer access and safe use? | 22 | 5 |
| 6. Do you recommend Plan B be switched from Rx to non-Rx status? | 23 | 4 |

authorizing statute instructs it to allow prescription drugs to be dispensed over the counter if a prescription is "not necessary for the protection of the public health."[24] Following normal procedures, the FDA's career staff began to review the application. They also notified two standing panels of experts—one on reproductive health and the second on the efficacy and safety of over-the-counter drugs—that their assistance was needed in advising the FDA. Together, the panels fielded twenty-eight experts, mostly medical doctors.

The advisory panels had before them an Actual Use Study describing how patients typically used Plan B, along with reams of data summarizing all the scientific research relevant to these questions, including trials on pregnant women, health surveys done in countries where Plan B is readily available, and evidence about whether women who are not highly educated could understand the proposed package instructions for use of the product. The panels also heard several hours of presentations by FDA staff and experts representing the applicant, as well as testimony from the general public.

The questions that could be answered "yes" or "no" and the panelists' ultimate votes in response to them are presented in table 6.1.

The heart of the subsequent controversy over the FDA's refusal to approve Plan B for women under eighteen revolved around the minority views of the five panelists who answered "no" on question five and the four who responded "no" on question six. They said that very young girls (ages as low as nine or ten were mentioned) might not use the drug correctly or might overuse it, passing up more traditional birth control. They added that in the admittedly rare instances where a child that young was the victim of a rape or incest and sought to purchase Plan B, doctors should have the opportunity to counsel their patients, but over-the-counter access to Plan B would eliminate such visits. These concerns were articulated despite the panelists' unanimous agreement that Plan B was safe even if it was used incorrectly. Everyone agreed that the drug would not prevent pregnancy if taken too late but would not harm the patient's health in any way. The panelists also agreed unanimously that they did not have any data in front of them suggesting that over-the-counter access to Plan B caused less use of traditional birth control. Finally, these concerns conflicted with extensive evidence that access to a doctor is often limited, especially among lower income women, and that, as a practical matter, requiring a prescription would mean that the drug was inaccessible to many young women.

Four months after the advisory panels' lopsided vote in favor of approving the application, senior FDA political officials embraced the minority's views, announcing on May 7, 2004, that they wanted the manufacturer to do more studies on whether pregnant women under sixteen could understand the label without a doctor's assistance. The FDA had never before required research on the cognitive ability of young teenagers to understand other over-the-counter drug labels and had always allowed drug makers to extrapolate data on patient behavior from older to younger adolescents. James Trussell, a member of the reproductive health panel and the director of population research program at Princeton University, explained this history to a *New York Times* reporter, concluding, "The White House has now taken over the FDA."[25]

In August 24, 2006, the FDA approved the sale of Plan B without a prescription to women eighteen and older but required women seventeen and younger to have a prescription. Once again, this "dual status" approach was unprecedented. As Drs. Alastair Wood (a panel member who resigned in protest), Jeffrey Drazen, and Michael Green lamented in an editorial for the *New England Journal of Medicine* entitled "A Sad Day for Science at the FDA," acetaminophen is more dangerous than Plan B, causing "56,680 emergency-department visits, 26,256 hospitalizations, and 458 deaths" every year, with a "large number of these events affecting persons younger than 17 years of age":

> Studies presented to the advisory committee at its meeting about Plan B and additional studies published more recently demonstrate clearly that women given ready access to emergency contraception do not routinely use less effective regular contraception, do not engage more often in high-risk sexual behavior, do not become more promiscuous, and do not have increased rates of pregnancy or sexually transmitted diseases—all findings that contradict claims

made by those outside the FDA who oppose wider availability of emergency contraception.

Although the real reason behind the attempts to introduce an age restriction on Plan B are [sic] at best unclear, the effect would be to intimidate women of all ages. The only way to enforce such a restriction would be to insist that all those attempting to purchase emergency contraception provide proof of age — that they be "carded" . . . destroying any semblance of privacy.[26]

In a report on the decision-making process used to approve Plan B that was requested by nineteen senators and twenty-nine representatives, the GAO concluded that the FDA had approved all twenty-two previous switch applications filed between 1994 and 2004 when joint advisory committees had voted to recommend positive action.[27] In a further departure from normal procedure, the directors of the offices responsible for reviewing the application, both of whom were career civil servants, had refused to sign the action letter denying the Plan B application, and the letter was signed by higher level political appointees.

On March 23, 2009, federal district court judge Edward Korman upheld a challenge to the FDA's decision to not allow over-the-counter sales to women under eighteen, ruling that the action was arbitrary and capricious and "lacks all credibility."[28] Less than a month later, the FDA announced that it would not appeal the ruling and would initiate action to make Plan B available to all women.

An episode as egregious as Plan B is unlikely to be repeated in the Obama administration, at least with respect to an issue considered important by the religious right. But President Clinton engaged in similar, albeit less egregious and less publicized, behavior, refusing to follow the advice of Donna Shalala, his Secretary of the Department of Health and Human Services, to lift the ban on federal funding for needle exchange programs.[29] Clinton explained that he did not want to send the "wrong message" to children, acknowledging that he was overriding scientific research demonstrating the efficacy of such programs in curbing the spread of AIDS. The incident shows that presidents of all ideologies can succumb to the temptation to engage in social engineering.

## Mercury

The population at highest risk is the children of women who consumed large amounts of fish and seafood during pregnancy. The committee concludes that the risk to that population is likely to be sufficient to result in an increase in the number of children who have to struggle to keep up in school and who might require remedial classes or special education. — National Research Council[30]

The push to regulate mercury emissions from power plants is an attempt by extreme environmental groups to hinder economic growth and force jobs overseas. Recent science shows that fish consumption, the only major cause of mercury exposure is not harmful to Americans and should be an integral part of a healthy diet. . . . These anti-job, anti-growth extremists need to quit scaring the public with bogus information. — Bill Kovacs, U.S. Chamber of Commerce[31]

[The EPA's] explanation deploys the logic of the Queen of Hearts, substituting EPA's desires for the plain text [of the statute]. Thus, EPA can point to no persuasive evidence suggesting that [the statute's] plain text is ambiguous. — Judge Judith Rogers, D.C. Circuit Court of Appeals[32]

Considered in sequence, with a full understanding of the source of each quotation, these three statements should provide ample evidence that something was amiss in the EPA's decision making with respect to mercury emissions from coal-fired power plants. The authors of the first statement are scientists from a variety of disciplines who served on a panel convened by the National Research Council (NRC) to consider the EPA's reference dose on mercury. A reference dose is the level of mercury that can be ingested without causing adverse health effects. The NRC panel's conclusion was that the EPA's reference dose was valid. The NRC is a branch of the highly respected National Academies, self-described as "Advisers to the Nation on Science Engineering, and Medicine." Membership in the Academies is by invitation only and includes many of the most prominent scientists in the country. The Academies periodically convene panels of independent experts to advise government on difficult and controversial scientific issues. Their work is considered the gold standard for scientific peer review. Referral of major policy disputes to panels convened by the National Academies has become commonplace with respect to the most important work of all five protector agencies, especially the EPA.

The NRC report was issued in 2000. In 2003, as the second quote indicates, Bill Kovacs, lead lobbyist for the Chamber of Commerce, characterized the controversy as one between rational policy makers and radical environmentalists without mentioning the NRC report. Kovacs's position won the day at the EPA, where political appointees from a law firm that represented industry interests instructed career staff to stop working on a multiyear effort to regulate mercury in accordance with the detailed instructions of the Clean Air Act and instead to compile a significantly weaker rule that was favored by industry.

The third quotation is drawn from an opinion by a three-judge panel of the federal Court of Appeals for the District of Columbia. The panel included two Clinton appointees and a very conservative jurist named Janice Rogers Brown, whose appointment by George W. Bush had generated considerable controversy. They decided in 2008 that the EPA rule resulting from industry's intervention was illegal because it ignored the "plain language" of the statute. Barely able to contain their disdain for the agency's convoluted efforts to circumvent its highly specific statutory mandates, the panel analogizes EPA's decision to the "logic of the Queen of Hearts," the character in Lewis Carroll's *Alice in Wonderland*, who is as foul tempered as she is arbitrary and responds to frustration by shouting, "Off with their heads."

How did a single decision by the EPA trigger such disparate and intense reactions? We offer the basic facts of the episode as another example of politicizing decision making, rejecting expertise, and short-circuiting a statutory mandate, with the result—as in the Plan B case—that affirmative action is delayed indefinitely.

Congress first commanded the EPA to take specific action regarding mercury emissions in the 1990 Clean Air Act Amendments. The 1990 Amendments listed mercury among 188 substances labeled as "hazardous air pollutants," triggering a series of regulatory requirements for the industrial sources that emit this extraordinarily toxic heavy metal.[33] The 1990 Amendments afforded special treatment to coal-fired power plants, requiring the EPA to jump over a series of hurdles before deciding whether to regulate such emissions.

The first statutory mandate was the completion of a study analyzing the "hazards to public health reasonably anticipated to occur as a result of" power plant emissions of hazardous air pollutants; the report was due in November 1993 and completed in February 1998.[34] The second requirement was completion of a report regarding mercury emissions from power plants, municipal waste incinerators, and other sources; it was due in November 1994 and was completed in December 1997.[35] Finally, the EPA was instructed to consider whether regulation was "appropriate and necessary"; if it made an affirmative finding, it was to regulate "under this section."[36] The agency dawdled until December 20, 2000, shortly before President Clinton left office, and then issued a "regulatory finding" announcing that regulatory controls were in fact both appropriate and

necessary, thereby preparing the way for requiring the installation of pollution-control equipment to lower mercury emissions.[37]

For the next three years, EPA staff and a high-level working group of
outside advisors representing the states, environmental groups, and the
utility industry debated the details of how to choose and implement this
"technology-based" requirement. Everyone, including the industry representatives, assumed that issuance of such standards was a foregone
conclusion. But sometime in the spring of 2003, Jeffrey Holmstead, the
political appointee in charge of the EPA's air quality program, convened
a meeting of the career staff assigned to the mercury project and dropped
a bombshell. Forthwith, the EPA would no longer work on a technology
rule but would instead develop a cap-and-trade system strongly favored
by industry. This kind of system does not require each individual plant
to install pollution-control equipment but instead sets an overall cap on
total, nationwide, mercury emissions. The EPA allocates allowances to
individual plants based on their past emissions. Plants that clean up by
installing pollution-control equipment can sell allowances to plants that
do not. The total amount of allowances in the system is no larger than the
cap on emissions, thereby achieving the all-around reduction in emissions
sought. The use of cap-and-trade systems for highly toxic substances like
mercury is considered very controversial because the buying and selling
of allowances can cause emissions to pool around a given plant, creating a
hot spot that can jeopardize local populations.

Career employees were shocked by Holmstead's order and promptly
leaked the story to *Los Angeles Times* reporters Tom Hamburger and
Alan Miller.[38] They revealed that several paragraphs of the text of the
trading portion of the proposal were lifted verbatim from materials provided by industry sources, including Latham & Watkins, the law firm
where Holmstead practiced before he entered government service.

The EPA's final rule, issued in the spring of 2005, rescinded the 2000
finding that mercury was a hazardous air pollutant and embraced a trading
scheme that would not begin to operate until 2018, close to two decades
after Congress first instructed the agency to tackle the problem.[39] National
environmental groups and several Northeastern states promptly sued the
EPA in the federal Court of Appeals for the D.C. Circuit. As we explained
at the outset of this section, the three-judge panel upheld their petition
for review, ordering the EPA to go back to the drawing board and consider whether mercury emissions from coal-fired power plants still posed
a risk to public health, again as required by the statute. The utility industry

appealed the decision to the Supreme Court, which refused to review the D.C. Circuit's opinion. The Obama administration has announced that it will rewrite the rule in conformance with the court's ruling.

The scientific research developed since 1990 overwhelmingly supports Congress's original concerns. The primary pathway of human exposure to methylmercury, the most toxic form of the metal, is consumption of fish from water bodies contaminated by industrial sources. As the NRC concluded, prenatal exposure to methylmercury at very low doses causes neurological and other developmental damage, even if the mother herself does not appear to suffer any ill effects. The federal Centers for Disease Control (CDC) has assembled statistics showing that, as a result of this consumption, 7.8 percent of American women of childbearing age have levels of mercury in their bloodstreams that could harm their unborn children. On the basis of those statistics, the CDC estimates that as many as 300,000 babies are born each year with blood mercury levels above the NRC-approved standard.[40] Faculty members from the nation's leading medical schools say that even these disturbing statistics understate the problem because venous (from the vein) blood tests of pregnant mothers understate the levels of mercury in their babies' blood by 70 percent. Taking the higher concentrations of mercury in babies' blood into account, the scientists estimate that as many as 637,000 babies are born annually with blood mercury levels above the standard.[41]

## Ossification

As we explained in chapter 4, beginning with the Reagan administration, each president has issued executive orders requiring agencies to undertake analyses of the costs and benefits of proposed rules and submit them to the OMB for approval.[42] Congress has also imposed a menu of analytical duties. The Regulatory Flexibility Act mandates an assessment of proposed regulations on small businesses,[43] and the Unfunded Mandates Reform Act requires an assessment of proposed regulations on state, local, and tribal governments.[44] The Paperwork Reduction Act requires agencies to secure OMB's approval before they impose any requirement that creates a paperwork burden for a private sector entity, including the completion of questionnaires and the filing of reports.[45] These various analytical requirements are imposed in addition to the analyses already required by the agencies' authorizing statutes and the Administrative Procedure

Act (APA), which requires that agencies read, summarize, and respond to all significant comments that they receive from the public concerning rulemaking proposals.[46]

Law Professor Mark Seidenfeld has published a table showing that, depending on the content of a rule, agencies can be required to take as many as 111 different analytical steps before they can adopt a regulation.[47] His article came out in 2000 and does not take into account executive orders issued in the last several years, which would undoubtedly increase this daunting total. Because of these requirements, and the intrinsic complexity, major rules can take as long as five to seven and sometimes ten years to complete. These delays are often referred to by administrative law experts as "ossification."

Peter Barton Hurt, a former FDA general counsel now in private practice, has noted that the burden imposed on the agency is sufficiently overwhelming that the FDA tries to avoid rulemaking whenever possible:

> [I]n order to promulgate a regulation, the FDA must at a minimum include, in the preamble, not only full consideration of all substantive issues raised by the regulation itself, but also a cost-benefit and a cost-effectiveness analysis, an environmental impact discussion, a federalism evaluation, a small business impact statement, a determination whether there is an unfunded mandate impact on state or local governments, an analysis of paperwork obligations, and an assessment on the impact on family well-being. . . . However well-intentioned, these responsibilities place a major burden on the FDA and require that scientific resources be diverted from other areas in order to assure compliance. This has led the FDA to avoid rulemaking wherever possible and to substitute informal guidance, or to take no action whatsoever on important regulatory matters.[48]

At a 2005 conference at American University attended by the authors, Neil Eisner, an Associate General Counsel at the Department of Transportation who has advised the NHTSA for two decades, reported that the agency had hired a contractor to map out a flowchart of the rulemaking process. Eisner stepped into the aisle of the auditorium and rolled out a scroll over eighteen feet long as the audience dissolved into knowing laughter.

It is difficult to measure the costs of delay caused by ossification and impossible to prove that these costs are outweighed by improvements in the regulations that are adopted. We can say with some assurance, however, that even when Congress instructs the EPA to complete a regulation within a certain time frame, those deadlines are rarely met. For example, a 2005 GAO report on the EPA's struggle to implement the 1990 Clean Air Act Amendments found that the agency failed to complete 256 tasks (75 percent) on time, completing ninety-four actions (approximately 28 percent) more than two years after the statutory deadline.[49]

No doubt, shortfalls in funding are to blame for these delays and may have more to do with ossification than the long list of analytical requirements imposed by the White House and Congress. Yet we are deeply skeptical that the country can afford to retain the existing approach to regulatory impact analysis. No effort has ever been made to streamline the dozens of analytical steps that have been imposed on agencies.

## A Unitary Executive?

The administration of George W. Bush will be remembered for its unprecedented assertions of extensive executive power to curtail civil liberties, detain terrorism suspects, engage in preemptive war, and keep information about government operations secret. Bush's vision of executive branch prerogatives was so extensive that the White House was the overwhelmingly dominant force in government during his eight years in office. He did not originate the doctrine of the "unitary executive," as these assertions of broad authority to consolidate decision making are known in the legal lexicon, but he is likely to be judged as among the most determined practitioners of it in American history.

Supporters of the unitary executive doctrine range across the political spectrum, but only the most conservative commentators, many of whom were Bush II administration political appointees, defend these extreme interpretations of the Constitution.[50] Those defenses, which focus primarily on the extreme measures taken to fight the so-called war on terror, need not detain us here. Rather, we focus on more moderate interpretations of the doctrine advanced by scholars who support White House efforts to centralize control over domestic policy, a trend that we believe needs to be moderated.

Scholarship in the area ranges from the work of relatively conservative Professor Steven Calabresi, a cofounder and chairman of the board of the Federalist Society, to relatively liberal Professor Elena Kagan, the former dean of the Harvard Law School, who was appointed by President Obama to be the Solicitor General of the United States.[51] Coming at the question from opposite ends of the political spectrum, they argue that the president has the authority to resolve regulatory issues and that such centralized control by the White House leads to better policy making. Unlike Calabresi, Kagan does not justify her argument for strong White House influence over the implementation of statutory mandates on constitutional grounds, and she generally recommends a more accommodating White House regime than he would consider appropriate. For example, she argues that a president can do a great deal of good by elevating regulatory decisions to the White House, not because the agencies are untrustworthy, but because presidential attention enhances their importance and public prestige.

An opposing branch of scholarship, articulated well by professors Peter Strauss and Robert Percival, disputes the unitary executive doctrine, instead embracing what Percival has called the "not-so-unitary" executive theory of constitutional intent.[52] In this view, the president and his White House staff are "overseers" and not "deciders," possessing limited power to intervene in the interpretation and implementation of statutory instructions. Strauss and Percival argue that White House intervention typically results in significantly less sound public policy making.

Push comes to shove with respect to these opposing views when the White House decides that it wants to countermand a decision and the agency defends its position, albeit behind the scenes. Taking the unitary executive theory to its logical conclusion, the White House would be justified in insisting that the agency change its views, despite the fact that Congress delegated final decision-making authority to the agency, not the president. Opponents of the theory argue that the president's only recourse in this instance would be to fire the rebellious administrator, an action that could have unpleasant political ramifications. As a practical matter, few agency heads let matters get to this point, or, to be more precise, we rarely find out that they have taken such a stand. But the difference between one view of presidential prerogatives and the other is nevertheless very important.

At some point in every administration, the White House is going to demand a change that agency political appointees and career staff do not like. In these delicate negotiations, if the agency head sees herself as the person who is alone responsible for answering to Congress, the public, and her own staff for a decision, she will draw a line beyond which the agency is not willing to go. If, on the other hand, she sees the president and his White House staff as having the ultimate authority to make those determinations, compromise becomes far more acceptable.

Reporting by the *Washington Post* in a series on Vice President Cheney's influence on the operations of the federal government provided a rare glimpse behind the curtain that typically hides such machinations. As we explained earlier, one of its leading story lines involved Christine Todd Whitman, the former governor of New Jersey and President George W. Bush's first appointee to head the EPA. Whitman is a moderate Republican, and her appointment sent the signal that the president did not intend to repeat the disastrous mistakes made during Ronald Reagan's first term, when the appointment of conservatives James Watt as Secretary of the Department of the Interior and Ann Gorsuch Burford as the EPA administrator caused a firestorm of criticism. Initially, the Whitman appointment worked as the president intended. Environmentalists were mollified and Whitman was confirmed by the Senate with relative ease.

Despite this favorable public reception, Whitman soon discovered that she was overmatched by Vice President Cheney, the OMB, other members of the cabinet, and the White House staff, all of whom had considerably more restrictive and politicized views of how the EPA should exercise its authority. She ended up having little autonomy to make crucial decisions on climate change, power plant regulation, and other controversial issues, although she was expected to justify these decisions to the press and the public. Repeatedly reversed at the White House, Whitman resigned after two years on the job:

> "I just couldn't sign [a White House–written rule on power plant regulation]," she said. "The president has a right to have an administrator who could defend it, and I just couldn't."
>
> A federal appeals court has since found that the rule change violated the Clean Air Act. In their ruling, the judges said that the administration had redefined the law in a way that could be valid "only in a Humpty-Dumpty world."[53]

We will never know what would have happened to that rule had Whitman stood her ground, daring the president to fire her by refusing to lend her name to a policy she disdained.

## Conclusion

Four presidents have presided over American government in the past twenty-five years. Presidents Reagan and George W. Bush were exceptionally hostile to the missions of the five protector agencies; George H. W.

Bush was ambivalent; and President Clinton expressed support but never made health and safety regulation a priority. At times, Congress supported these presidential policies, and during other periods, it fought strenuously against them. Through all this political cycling, the five agencies continued on a slow downward trajectory. Budget problems explain much, but not all, of their susceptibility during this period. The other pieces of the puzzle include the centralization of White House authority, widespread disrespect for the civil service, manipulation of science, and the imposition of cost-benefit analysis. These problems reached their apex under the second President Bush but had been a long time in the making.

We do not know what to expect from our forty-fourth president. President Obama has announced that one of his top priorities will be combating climate change, and he has appointed people to head those efforts who are generally regarded as deeply committed to a strong, affirmative agenda on that issue. But he has also appointed economic advisers who are deeply skeptical that the cost of such strong action is affordable. One of those economic skeptics will head the OMB unit that has taken the lead in weakening affirmative regulatory proposals. Representatives of industries that oppose strong controls on climate change and other environmental issues are already predicting a contentious debate within the White House that will produce compromises they will find acceptable. Plans for the CPSC, FDA, NHTSA, and OSHA are unclear as this book goes to press.

## CHAPTER SEVEN

# The Judiciary

## Introduction

The only officials in American government appointed for lifetime terms are federal judges. Unless they are convicted by the Senate of gross malfeasance in office—an extraordinarily rare occurrence historically—they serve until they resign voluntarily or die in office. What strange vision persuaded the Framers of the Constitution to create this privileged kingdom when they had just emerged from a devastating revolutionary war to overthrow a foreign monarch? The most obvious answer is that the federal judiciary was intended to be the last bulwark against corrupt elected officials and the "violence of faction" so feared by James Madison.[1]

The Constitution reposes in federal judicial hands the ultimate authority to keep the other two branches of government within their legal boundaries, in relation to each other and, as important, in relation to individual citizens. The Framers reasoned that in light of their lifetime tenure, federal judges should be beholden to no one, thereby bringing otherwise unattainable wisdom and objectivity to their work. The trade-off is the creation of a slow-moving, entrenched elite that, at its worst, could prove impervious to the changing circumstances of the nation. Once these invulnerable wise men made a decision (women and people of color came late to these appointments), the nation lived with it for a very long time. As just one glaring example, the Supreme Court's decision to uphold segregation in *Plessy v. Ferguson*[2] at the turn of the century took fifty-eight years to overturn in *Brown v. Board of Education*.[3]

While the power of the judiciary is extensive, it is not unlimited. Courts serve as decision makers of last resort. Because the vast majority of cases settle before judges are asked to render an opinion, the courts serve as a safety valve far more often than they determine the outcome of the parties' disputes. Judges cannot identify issues that they find interesting and bring them into the judicial system. Rather, they preside over "cases and controversies" brought to them by private and public sector parties. They do not have the freedom to study a problem from scratch at their own initiative. Rather, they must take the facts pretty much as the parties to the lawsuit present them. Litigation is expensive and can only be pursued by parties with access to substantial resources, further narrowing the scope of judicial decision making. And parties may not run to court every time they are angry. Instead, they must demonstrate that they have standing to bring the case before the courts.

These threshold rules mean that, in order to be adjudicated, a dispute must have matured to the point that the parties will suffer concrete injury if the matter is left unresolved. That injury need not be financial. Interference with a right to speak freely or practice one's religion confers access to the courts. And the major federal environmental laws allow citizens to enforce their provisions, assuming the status of "private attorneys general." So, for example, if I am an avid paddler on a river anywhere in America, I can bring a lawsuit challenging the EPA's failure to fulfill a nondiscretionary duty to control pollution from factories along its banks that threaten water quality.[4]

Although the legal community expends tremendous energy criticizing the courts, few have seriously suggested abandoning the lifetime tenure of federal judges. A cynic might suggest that the judges do a good enough job of bobbing and weaving that they have convinced every power constituency in the country—from Fortune 100 companies to national civil rights organizations—that they have some hope of winning their cases some day. An optimist might acknowledge that the federal judiciary is not a perfect system but ask the Churchillian question, Compared to what?

We agree with both assessments. However, we have some advice for federal judges regarding their consideration of the health, safety, and environmental issues problems that are the focus of this book. We believe that judges have overreached in this arena, moving beyond resolving disputes into the dangerous territory of superimposing their own relatively uninformed interpretations of statutes crafted by Congress. Recently developed empirical evidence further demonstrates that federal judges increasingly make decisions in environmental cases on partisan grounds, with Republican appointees proving far more likely than their Democratic counterparts to block the access of nonindustry parties to the courts. Republicans are also more likely than Democrats to endorse less protective agency decisions and to overturn more protective decisions.

As readers have no doubt gathered by now, we are troubled by these outcomes. But even if judicial trends had headed in the opposite direction, with liberal judges egging agencies on, we would object to the means used to get to that end. Biased federal judicial activism introduces destructive instability into the system because it focuses agencies on satisfying courts that are erratic. Instead, agencies should devote their time and attention to interpreting their statutory mandates, under consistent and balanced oversight by Congress, presidential appointees, and senior civil servants.

This chapter opens with an explanation of cases involving the OSHA's attempts to regulate toxic chemical exposures in the workplace because they are good illustrations of the harm caused by unwarranted judicial interference. Next, we explain the evidence demonstrating judicial bias. We examine the incentives that motivate judges in order to discover why such bias arises. We discuss how ideological judging creates regulatory dysfunction. The chapter concludes with a series of recommendations for arresting these trends by defining the appropriate role of judges as last-resort or "border patrol" overseers.

## Toxics in the Workplace

Congress authorized OSHA to protect workers from dangerous chemicals in two stages. To start, it instructed the agency to adopt safety and health standards within two years of the Occupational Safety and Health Act's passage in 1971. As part of this effort, OSHA promulgated "permissible exposure limits" (PELs) for over four hundred substances that are emitted into workplace air. Each PEL limits worker exposure to levels that are acceptable from a health perspective. All but a handful were borrowed straight from consensus standards, such as those issued by the American Council of Governmental Industrial Hygienists (ACGIH). Second, Congress expected OSHA to update and supplement these PELs and address new threats to workers through rulemaking. When adopting a health regulation, OSHA has the authority not only to establish an exposure limitation but also to adopt additional protections for workers, such as a requirement of medical monitoring or the use of safety equipment.

The agency has largely failed in this second phase. Many of the four hundred original PELs are dangerously out of date because they were promulgated in 1971 and no longer reflect the latest scientific evidence about the risks to workers. OSHA has promulgated comprehensive workplace regulations for only two chemicals in the last ten years. Taking both the PELs and comprehensive regulations into account, the agency has legally enforceable exposure limitations for fewer than two hundred of the approximately 3,000 chemicals that the EPA characterizes as "high production volume" chemicals because more than a million pounds of each substance are circulated in commerce annually.

Although we would be the first to admit that resource shortfalls are a major cause of OSHA's overall problems, in this area we believe that even a fully funded agency would have suffered a paralyzing failure of will because of the merciless thrashing administered by the courts early in its tenure. A landmark Supreme Court decision in *Industrial Union Department v. American Petroleum Institute* concluded that OSHA had to prove that benzene—or any other toxic chemical—poses a significant risk before it can order employers to reduce workers' exposure.[5] The Occupational Safety and Health Act has no language referring to an obligation to prove significant risk. Justice Stevens, who wrote the plurality opinion, invented this language out of whole cloth. Compounding this constraint, the opinion required OSHA to present quantified evidence of significant risk, also reading words into the statute that are not there. Justice Marshall, who authored a dissenting opinion joined by Justices Brennan, White, and Blackmun, correctly predicted that the opinion would stymie OSHA's capacity to protect workers:

> The critical problem in cases like the ones at bar is scientific uncertainty. While science has determined that exposure to benzene . . . creates a definite risk of health impairment, the magnitude of the risk cannot be quantified at the present time. The risk at issue has hardly been shown to be insignificant, indeed, future research may reveal that the risk is in fact considerable. But the existing evidence may frequently be inadequate to enable the Secretary to make the threshold finding of "significance" that the Court requires today. If so, the consequence of the plurality's approach would be to subject American workers to a continuing risk of cancer and other fatal diseases, and to render the Federal Government powerless to take protective action on their behalf. Such an approach would place the burden of medical uncertainty squarely on the shoulders of the American worker, the intended beneficiary of the Occupational Safety and Health Act.[6]

Benzene causes a range of chronic effects including cancer. Ten years after the decision was issued, OSHA promulgated a PEL setting the exact same level for benzene exposures in the workplace that the Supreme Court majority had rejected. By that time, scientific research indicated that thousands of workers were subjected to levels in excess of the standard, at grave risk to their health. As is consistently true in such cases, the delay caused disease and death among the people who should have been protected, rather than resulting in research exonerating the chemical, the possibility that apparently troubled the plurality who signed the Stevens opinion.

OSHA was devastated by this opinion and has never recovered. But just in case it forgot this harsh judicial guidance, the Eleventh Circuit Court of Appeals administered a reminder a dozen years later. That episode began with the Reagan administration's appointment of John Pendergrass, an industrial hygienist who had formerly worked for the 3M Corporation, as OSHA administrator in 1985. Pendergrass immediately expressed his interest in updating the PELs that OSHA had adopted in 1971. He argued that many of OSHA's legally mandated PELs were less protective of workers than new and updated voluntary exposure limitations of the ACGIH, the professional association that was the source of most of the original PELs. He asked OSHA staff to update the original PELs based on ACGIH standards, as well recommendations from the National Institute of Occupational Safety and Health (NIOSH), a government-sponsored agency dedicated to scientific research. In a single rulemaking, the agency promulgated a final regulation that reduced PELs for 212 substances and set new PELs for 164 substances that were not previously regulated.

This innovative effort ran aground when the Eleventh Circuit Court of Appeals held that the OSHA omnibus regulation was illegal under the agency's statutory mandate, as interpreted in the benzene case.[7] The problem with OSHA's effort, according to the court, was that the agency failed to demonstrate that each chemical exposed workers to a significant risk. OSHA had cited scientific evidence that the chemicals were harmful to workers, and it noted that the ACGIH and the NIOSH had recommended similar protections. But it did not assume what would have been the staggering burden of quantifying the precise, numerical risk posed by each one of these many hazards.

In his dissenting opinion in the OSHA benzene case, Justice Marshall wrote,

> In cases of statutory construction, this Court's authority is limited. If the statutory language and legislative intent are plain, the judicial inquiry is at an end. Under our jurisprudence, it is presumed that ill-considered or unwise legislation will be corrected through the democratic process, a court is not permitted

to distort a statute's meaning in order to make it conform with the Justices' own views of sound social policy.[8]

We would take this wise observation one step further. Not only should the courts defer to Congress, they should also give great weight to an agency's interpretation of its authorizing statutes. As we explain shortly, the Supreme Court eventually embraced this view, although it and the lower courts often evade its impact by analyzing cases in a different fashion. In any event, the combined pressure of the two decisions paralyzed OSHA's toxic chemicals program and also influenced other agencies to self-impose unduly high burdens of proof. The decisions were not preordained by the records before the courts; other judges could have produced results supportive of worker protection and many lives could have been saved.

## Judges as Overseers

Judges are latecomers to an administrative process that can take years and sometimes a decade or more. The first step in the process is development of a rule by agency scientists, engineers, economists, lawyers, and other professionals, as we described in chapter 4. If the rule will impose costs of more than $100 million or is otherwise significant for policy reasons, it must undergo review by the OMB's OIRA. The Administrative Procedure Act (APA) then requires the agency to issue a notice of proposed rulemaking, which is published in the *Federal Register*, the compendium of federal government actions that is published daily on-line and in hard copy.[9] The rulemaking notice includes the text of the proposed rule and a preamble, a detailed explanation of why the agency is proposing the rule. The APA also requires an agency to invite public comments on its proposals. Controversial regulations can generate hundreds, sometimes thousands, of comments.

The agency's rulemaking team then begins the development of the final version. Before, during, and after the comment period, the agency will meet with or receive telephone calls, letters, or electronic mail from trade associations and business groups, individual companies subject to the regulation, public interest groups, members of Congress, and various offices in the White House, including the OIRA. Once the agency has a draft of the final rule, it must return to the OIRA for a second review. The agency then issues a final regulation, which is again published in the *Federal*

*Register.* This version includes another preamble, justifying the rule in light of the comments and evidence submitted to the agency. For complicated and controversial regulations, it is not unusual for final preambles to cover dozens, and even hundreds, of pages.

Agencies are routinely sued after a rule is promulgated by regulated industries, one or more public interest groups, and, on occasion, the states. Congress has authorized the federal courts of appeals, also known as circuit courts, to hear these cases. (The country is divided into twelve circuits, each covering several states.) Many health and safety statutes require that "petitions for review" be filed in the District of Columbia Court of Appeals, also known as the D.C. Circuit, because Congress wanted one circuit court to develop expertise in hearing such disputes. All cases before the circuit courts are heard by a three-judge panel; the judges are chosen by lottery to prevent parties from manipulating the outcome of their cases by shopping for sympathetic judges. An appeal normally takes two to three years to be resolved. Approximately 250 circuit court judges sit on cases across the country, including ninety-six on senior status, which allows them to take a reduced caseload. The D.C. Circuit includes thirteen judges, with four of those on senior status.

Appellate cases based on the APA and other health and safety statutes revolve around three distinct types of problems. The first is whether the plaintiff is eligible to sue the agency. The Constitution imposes the limitation that plaintiffs must have cases and controversies to get before the court, a requirement also known as standing to sue.[10] As we will discuss, conservative judges have interpreted this vague requirement to prevent environmental and consumer groups from suing to challenge agency regulations.

A second set of problems is whether the agency has statutory authority to support the rule that it adopted. This issue usually arises because the plaintiff argues that the agency did not read the statute correctly. Courts engage in statutory interpretation to determine the validity of the agency's position. In the case involving the OSHA benzene PEL, the Supreme Court engaged in an aggressive form of statutory interpretation. As that case illustrates, a court's decision to limit an agency's statutory authority can cripple entire regulatory programs for years afterward.

Third, the courts are often asked to review the rationality of an agency's decision to issue a specific rule. Congress has instructed the courts to ensure that rules are not "arbitrary [or] capricious," a scope of review intended to require the courts to defer to an agency's fact-finding and policy decisions unless the agency seems to have acted in an irrational or erratic way.[11] This requirement serves the important function of ensuring

that a regulation has the potential to serve the purposes that Congress intended, but, as we will demonstrate, it has also been used to make it more
difficult for agencies to regulate.

When judges resolve issues of standing, statutory interpretation, and
rationality, they are functioning in a principal-agent relationship. As overseers of the regulatory process, along with members of Congress and the
president, the courts also serve as agents of the public. The goal of the
principal (the public) is to ensure that regulatory agencies carry out their
statutory missions effectively. But, as in other principal-agent contexts,
without sufficient constraints, the agent may pursue its self-interest rather
than the principal's goal. Because federal judges have lifetime appointments, the public has even less control over how well judges perform their
role as overseers than it does over the president or Congress, who periodically stand for reelection. This limited accountability suggests that courts
should confine their oversight to clear departures from the public interest,
as opposed to crossing an admittedly blurry line and undertaking review
that substitutes judicial opinions on policy questions for the agency's conclusions. To the great detriment of health and safety agencies, judges have
routinely crossed that line, especially in the last two decades, and in the
process they have become a major factor in the agency dysfunction we
chronicle throughout this book.

## Biased Judicial Review

Ideally, judges should rule on issues of standing, statutory interpretation,
and regulatory rationality in a neutral and unbiased manner, taking each
case as they find it and applying the precedents established by earlier
cases to ensure the long-term stability of the law. This neutrality, after
all, was the primary justification for giving them lifetime appointments,
to insulate them from short-term political pressure. But recent empirical evidence suggests that judicial neutrality has eroded in the arena of
health and safety regulation. The evidence shows that judges appointed
by Republican presidents are significantly more likely to decide regulatory review cases in favor of regulated industries than judges appointed
by Democratic presidents.

Table 7.1 summarizes recent empirical studies addressing judicial review
of regulatory agencies. The studies correlate the outcome of a case with
whether a judge was appointed by a Republican or Democratic president,
which is used as a proxy for ideology. It is worth noting that Republicans

TABLE 7.1 **Judicial Voting Patterns in Agency Review Cases**

| Subject | Scope | Probability That Republican/Democrat Voted to | Republican Results, % | Democrat Results, % |
|---|---|---|---|---|
| Industry procedural challenge against EPA[1] | D.C. Circuit (1987–93) | Uphold industry challenge | 54–89 | 2–13 |
| | | Percentage of Cases in Which Judges Voted to | | |
| Deny standing to environmental plaintiff[2] | D.C. Circuit (1992–98); all courts (1992–98) | Deny standing Same | 79.2 43.5 | 18.2 11.1 |
| Industry challenge to EPA regulation[3] | D.C. Circuit (1970–2002) | Deny industry challenge | 46 | 64 |
| Statutory interpretation by EPA and NLRB[4] | All circuits (1989–2005) | Validate liberal interpretation | 60 | 74 |
| | | Validate conservative interpretation | 70 | 51 |
| Arbitrariness review of EPA and NLRB[5] | All circuits (1989–2005) | Validate reasoning in liberal decision | 58 | 72 |
| | | Validate reasoning in conservative decision | 72 | 55 |
| | | Percentage of Cases in Which Panels with Two Republicans/Democrats Voted to: | | |
| Challenge to stringency of EPA regulation[6] | D.C. Circuit (1991–95) | Affirm challenge | 27.8 | 50.3 |

*Note*: The National Labor Relations Board (NLRB) covers issues outside the scope of this book except to the extent that judicial opinions regarding its work may reflect an antilabor bias.

[1] Richard L. Revesz, "Environmental Regulation, Ideology, and the D.C. Circuit," *Virginia Law Review* 83 (1997): 1717, 1763.

[2] Richard J. Pierce, Jr., "Is Standing Law or Politics?" *North Carolina Law Review* 77 (1999): 1741, 1759–60.

[3] Cass R. Sunstein, David Schkade, and Lisa Michelle Ellman, "Ideological Voting on Federal Courts of Appeals: A Preliminary Investigation," *Virginia Law Review* 90 (2004): 301, 318, 322–23.

[4] Thomas J. Miles and Cass R. Sunstein, "Do Judges Make Regulatory Policy? An Empirical Investigation of *Chevron*," *University of Chicago Law Review* 73 (2006): 823.

[5] Thomas J. Miles and Cass R. Sunstein, "The Real World of Arbitrariness Review," *University of Chicago Law Review* 75 (2008): 761.

[6] Richard L. Revesz, "Congressional Influence on Judicial Behavior? An Empirical Examination of Challenges to Agency Action in the D.C. Circuit," *New York University Law Review* 76 (2001): 1100, 1104.

outnumber Democrats 162 to 91 among all judges. Because four of the six measurements summarized in the table involve the D.C. Circuit Court of Appeals, it is conceivable that they are not representative of the judiciary as a whole. However, in the health and safety arena, polarity on the D.C. Circuit is a significant problem because so many cases go to that court.

Ideological and partisan voting patterns are expected in Congress. But to see judges tilt for or against business in such a pronounced way is disquieting. The legal profession as a whole has always understood that judging involves some discretion and that judges, consciously or unconsciously, use this discretion to further their views of what makes for a good society. Yet the polarization suggested by these results indicates that ideological behavior may be a larger influence than originally thought; indeed, it may be among the most important factors determining the outcome of regulatory review cases.

## Judicial Incentives

What incentives lead judges to interject their own ideology into decision making, and are there incentives that cut against this behavior? The legal literature suggests judges generally respond to three incentives: (1) respect—from fellow judges, practicing lawyers, and academics; (2) ideological utility—or the temptation to interject their own views of the world in determining the outcome, as opposed to legal precedent or the specific circumstances presented by the case at bar; and (3) leisure—or the sheer amount of effort they devote to their jobs that lack a traditional supervisory structure.[12] Obviously, if judges choose to do less work than more, they are less likely to be effective overseers, but the first two incentives are the most important for our purposes.

Judges value the prestige associated with being on the bench and try to maintain and enhance their reputation with lawyers and other judges. A good reputation is also valuable to judges because it enhances their ability to influence other judges. Judicial reputations are forged by crafting well-reasoned applications of legal rules to the circumstances of a particular case, described many years ago by Karl Llewellyn as the judicial "craft."[13] Craft behavior enhances a judge's reputation because it demonstrates competence in performing legal analysis and decision making. This behavior also generates legal decisions that are consistent and predictable, two results the legal profession values highly. A "pure" craft orientation is outcome-neutral in the sense that the judge does not consider the implications of a given result for society in general.

A judge will also value influencing public events according to his or her worldview, which is the "ideological utility" factor in this construction of judicial incentives, otherwise known as an "outcome orientation." Judges achieve ideological goals from outcome behavior, which focuses on the implications of the result in a case for society as a whole. Their satisfaction derives from the exercise of substantial judicial power and from achieving a result that corresponds to the judge's overall sense of social justice and welfare. This motive is other-regarding in the sense that it does not depend on an enhancement of the judge's own self-interest, although judges may gain considerable respect from the perception by others that they are part of a movement to restore or enhance the judiciary's impact on society. Judges have the freedom to engage in such other-regarding behavior because they are not burdened by the necessity of being reelected.

Craft and outcome behavior can conflict or they can coincide. If the two behaviors are not clearly in conflict, the judge may choose either approach depending on the relative satisfaction gained from each choice. The judge does not have to sacrifice the respect that comes from following a craft-oriented approach in order to obtain ideological utility. If the two behaviors lead to clearly conflicting results in a case, we would expect the judge to engage in craft behavior. In theory, the judge should default to craft behavior because this approach is the expected norm in the legal and judicial professions, taught to law students as the only appropriate behavior for a judge and reinforced continuously in the official rhetoric of the profession.

Determining whether a judge has followed these craft norms in a given case depends on the clarity of the legal rules or precedents that guide him or her. When the legal rules are indeterminate, vague, and ambiguous, judges have more freedom to be outcome oriented. If judges choose outcomes that are consistent with an ideological preference, they are more likely to avoid detection and unlikely to lose respect for a failure to engage in craft behavior. Opinions that depart from those precedents expose judges to intensified scrutiny and the accusation that an ideological—or outcome—motivation has determined the result. Conversely, when a legal doctrine is more specific and clear, outcome behavior is easier to detect and judges find it more difficult to engage in such behavior without suffering a loss of respect.

The legal doctrines used in judicial review of administrative decisions—for example, whether an agency interpreted its authorizing statute correctly or whether it was arbitrary or capricious—tend to be less, rather than more, determinative for several reasons. First and most important, unlike disputes over contracts (agreements to undertake transactions) or torts (efforts to recover damages from people or companies alleged to have negligently caused injury), which have a long recorded history going back hundreds of years, this area of the law is relatively new. Administrative agency activities did not become sufficiently robust to provoke lawsuits until the mid-1970s. The large variety of relatively youthful health and safety statutes also means that cases present issues of "first impression"—that is, the courts have not yet addressed the issues and judges are free to write on a clean slate (sometimes called a tabula rasa). The technical complexity of the cases can make outside scrutiny and the discovery of ideological bias quite challenging. The research we cited demonstrating the partisan polarization on the D.C. Circuit Court of Appeals, for example, undoubtedly was time-consuming and difficult to perform.

The indeterminate nature of administrative law opens the door for judges to engage in outcome behavior that reflects their ideological preferences. In addition, judges have a stronger motivation to pursue an outcome orientation in regulatory cases because, unlike most private litigation, regulatory cases are more likely to involve important issues of public policy. Judges harboring ideological motivations are therefore more likely to obtain greater utility from deciding a case in a manner that favors their worldviews.

## Craft or Ideology?

The opportunities provided by administrative law for judges to respond to ideological incentives and depart from craft-oriented norms are painfully evident in the context of health and safety cases involving the three categories of problems we mentioned earlier: standing, statutory interpretation, and regulatory rationality.

### Standing

As we explained earlier, Article III of the Constitution empowers the judiciary to hear cases and controversies, and people who present such matters are said to have standing to sue. Large membership organizations, such as the Consumer Federation of America or the Sierra Club, were formed in part to bring lawsuits on behalf of their members, but they must show that one or more members have standing. No one can sue the federal government without its permission, but Congress has generally authorized those persons who are the beneficiaries of regulations to sue an agency if they are "aggrieved" by its actions, as, for example, when the agency fails to regulate as stringently as Congress intended.[14]

The Supreme Court's decision in *Lujan v. Defenders of Wildlife* illustrates how outcome behavior is assisted by the use of indeterminate legal terms.[15] The 1992 decision held for the first time that even if Congress authorizes a plaintiff to sue, the person must still meet the additional standing requirements devised by the Court, including an "injury in fact," that is, "concrete and particularized" and "actual or imminent" rather than "conjectural or hypothetical." The injury must be "fairly . . . trace[able] to the challenged action" of the agency being sued. It also must be "likely," rather than "speculative," that the injury will be "redressed by a favorable decision." Prior to *Lujan*, the Court generally deferred to congressional intent to allow a case to proceed.

Legal scholars have vigorously criticized the Supreme Court for overinterpreting the Constitution's vague language to require such strenuous requirements for standing, finding no indication that the Framers intended Article III to impose an injury-in-fact requirement. The authors of a prominent administrative law textbook observe,

> It is impossible to read the complicated and conflicting opinions issued in the Court's over one hundred cases resolving standing disputes without drawing the inference that the Justices are greatly influenced by their personal political and ideological values and beliefs. The concepts of injury-in-fact, causality, and redressability are extraordinarily malleable. The Justices can, and do, manipulate these concepts to obtain results they prefer on political and ideological grounds. Some Justices are sympathetic to environmental plaintiffs, while others are not.[16]

Compounding the problems caused by *Lujan*, the lower federal courts have enthusiastically expanded the reach of constrictive standing rules. Readers will recall the empirical study that found Republicans on the D.C. Circuit voted to deny standing to environmental plaintiffs in 79 percent of the cases in which the issue arose, while Democrats voted against standing in only 18 percent of the cases. A similar pattern was found in all of the circuit courts.

The Supreme Court's current standing doctrine creates a gap in judicial enforcement. When judges kick consumer or environmental plaintiffs out of court, there is no judicial review of the merits of the plaintiff's claims. The lack of judicial review contributes to agency dysfunction when the agency makes a decision that a court would have appropriately reversed or remanded. Assume, for example, that EPA interprets its statutory mandate in a way that is obviously illegal. If this interpretation favors the corporations it is regulating, they are unlikely to sue to contest it. If no environmental plaintiff has standing to challenge the interpretation, it is unlikely that it will be challenged at all, paving the way for the agency to succeed in its misreading of the statute.

*Public Citizen, Inc. v. National Highway Traffic Safety Administration (NHTSA)*, a 2008 decision by the D.C. Circuit, illustrates this gap in accountability.[17] Public Citizen, a consumer interest group, sought to challenge a regulation requiring new vehicles to have a warning system indicating to drivers when a tire was significantly underinflated. Congress had passed legislation requiring NHTSA to promulgate such a regulation in the wake of the tire failures involving Ford SUVs and Firestone tires. Public Citizen claimed NHTSA had adopted a weaker regulation than Congress permitted under the legislation. The court denied Public Citizen's standing. According to the court, Public Citizen could not prove that one of its members might be injured as a result of the agency's failure to adopt a more stringent regulation. Public Citizen had argued that one of its thousands of members was at substantial risk of having automobile accident involving a tire failure and therefore would suffer injury because the NHTSA rule was too weak to prevent such incidents. The court ruled the injury alleged by these consumers was neither actual nor imminent, but it permitted Public Citizen to file additional evidence from a statistician about the likelihood of such an injury. The court then rejected the statistical evidence as speculative.

This result is not without its irony. Congress passes legislation to protect consumers from tire blowouts, but the Court concludes, in effect, that no consumers have standing to argue that NHTSA failed to implement Congress's mandate because they have not been injured yet. In this instance, the D.C. Circuit was clearly refusing to defer to Congress's judgment that persons benefiting from regulation should be able to sue to protect their interests when an agency adopts weaker regulations than may be required.

The Supreme Court has not justified its strict approach to standing except on the basis that the Constitution restricts courts to hearing cases and controversies. The architect of this momentous shift in doctrine, Justice Scalia, has explained in his extrajudicial writings that the Constitution delegates to the president exclusive power to ensure the proper execution of the laws.[18] Therefore, the courts should defer to presidential determinations of whether agencies have adopted strict enough regulations. The judges in *Public Citizen* echoed this concern. They noted that allowing the members of Public Citizen to have standing "would expand the proper—and properly limited—constitutional role of the Judicial Branch beyond deciding actual cases or controversies; and would entail the Judiciary exercising some part of the Executive's responsibility to take care that the law be faithfully executed."[19]

This justification for standing reflects the unitary executive theory that we discussed in chapter 6. The theory is that the president has broad discretion to interpret the law consistent with his own policy preferences. As Justice Scalia interprets this theory, the courts must be careful not to intrude on executive power. But the results of such decisions can enable the misuse of executive power. When an agency has made an illegal decision that benefits regulated entities and disadvantages the beneficiaries of regulatory action, only that latter group has an incentive to challenge the agency's action. If they are disabled from doing so, the rule of law cannot be upheld. This failure is an issue for the courts to resolve, not merely a political matter, as Justice Scalia would prefer to characterize it. The benefits from ensuring the rule of law simply outweigh an intrusion on executive power when the executive branch has engaged in illegal action.

We hope that the addition of more moderate appointments to the Supreme Court will result in a return to a pre-*Lujan* approach to standing that broadly defines injury in fact and defers to congressional intent that the potential beneficiaries of regulation should be able to sue to hold agencies accountable for a failure to regulate or regulate sufficiently. Some evidence suggests that several justices are already rethinking this restrictive approach to standing. While the Court continues to follow the *Lujan* tests, it sometimes applies them in a manner that increases, rather than decreases, the possibility of a court reaching the merits of a plaintiff's claim.[20]

### Statutory Interpretation

Although the clear trend in Congress is to write increasingly detailed statutory mandates in order to ensure that agencies do what Congress wants and to forestall wasteful lawsuits over congressional intent, the health and safety laws vary quite a bit in specificity, leaving agencies considerable interpretive discretion. To some extent, this result is both inevitable and commendable. Expecting Congress to resolve every technical issue likely to come up in a rulemaking is unreasonable, would be wasteful and duplicative, and could bring already slow lawmaking to a standstill. On the other hand, as our description of the Supreme Court's decision to overturn the OSHA benzene standard earlier in this chapter indicates, enthusiastic second-guessing by the courts can also cause enormous difficulties for agencies.

In 1984, seven years after the benzene decision, the Supreme Court decided to establish a clear standard of review for such cases. *Chevron U.S.A. Inc. v. Natural Resources Defense Council, Inc.* sets up a two-step test for determining the validity of an agency rule.[21] In the first step, a court asks whether Congress has "directly spoken to the precise question at issue," and, if so, a court "must give effect to the unambiguously expressed intent of Congress." If the statute does not have a plain meaning, "the court does not simply impose its own construction on the statute, as would be necessary in the absence of an administrative interpretation. Rather, if the statute is silent or ambiguous with respect to the specific issue, the question for the court is whether the agency's answer is based on a permissible construction of the statute." *Chevron* was a landmark case because it removed the primary authority to conduct statutory interpretation from judges to the agencies. By turning this relationship on its head and instructing courts to defer to an agency interpretation, the decision had tremendous potential to tilt the balance of power over rulemaking in an agency direction.

The rationale underlying *Chevron* is that agencies are in a better position to resolve the meaning of ambiguous statutory language than the courts because these determinations involve policy issues about which agencies have considerably more scientific and technical expertise than generalist judges. Agencies further understand the full scope of the problems that they must surmount when implementing complex programs and can therefore read a statute holistically, as Congress intended when it drafted such integrated regulatory blueprints. *Chevron* was further motivated by the Supreme Court's determination to make it more difficult for courts to engage in outcome-oriented, or ideological, behavior. Because judges have lifetime appointments, their ideological influence can extend well beyond electoral changes that put people who have different beliefs in the White House and Congress. If judges defer to an agency's construction unless Congress has unambiguously expressed its intent, the theory went, they will have considerably less opportunity to define statutory terms in a way that serves an outmoded ideological preference. Unfortunately, the courts did not depart quietly from the field of battle.

The empirical research reflected in Table 7.1 suggests that *Chevron* is honored in the breach. Republican appointees were 19 percentage points more likely to validate an interpretation by the National Labor Relations Board (NLRB) and the EPA that had a conservative impact than Democratic appointees. Conversely, Democrats were 14 percentage points more likely to vote for a construction that had a liberal impact than Republicans.

One reason that *Chevron* may not be working as intended is because a majority of the justices on the Supreme Court have decided to take periodic detours around the decision. Empirical research conducted by professors Thomas Miles and Cass Sunstein looked at validation rates among Supreme Court justices in cases involving statutory interpretation.[22] The study found

1. The most conservative justices (Rehnquist, Scalia, and Thomas) are 30 percentage points more likely to vote to validate conservative agency interpretations than to validate liberal interpretations;
2. The liberal justices (Stevens, Breyer, and Ginsburg) are 27 percentage points more likely to vote to validate liberal agency interpretations than to validate conservative interpretations;
3. The most conservative justices had a validation rate that was 19 percentage points lower when reviewing interpretations made by agencies in the Clinton administration as compared with voting to validate agency interpretations during the two Bush administrations; and
4. By comparison, validation rates of more moderate or swing justices (Kennedy, Souter, and O'Connor) were less consistently correlated with the ideological content of the agency decision.

The authors of the study conclude, "If judicial decisions under the *Chevron* framework are assessed in crudely political terms, the voting patterns of Supreme Court justices fit with the conventional groupings of the justices along political lines—a clear signal that the *Chevron* framework is not having the disciplining effect that it is supposed to have."

While ideological behavior is observable in the Supreme Court's application of *Chevron* to subsequent cases and we consider these outcomes unfortunate, we strongly support decisions in which judges have reversed agencies that violate a clear statutory command. A good example is *Natural Resources Defense Council v. EPA*.[23] The Natural Resources Defense

Council, a national environmental group, challenged a rule promulgated under the Clean Air Act (CAA) that regulated emissions of formalde-hyde, a chemical used by plywood manufacturers that is a known human carcinogen (cancer-causing agent). The CAA requires industries to reduce emissions of hazardous air pollutants to levels that could be achieved by the maximum achievable control technology, but the statute also permits the EPA to exempt entire categories of pollution sources from stringent regulation if the probability that a pollutant causes cancer is less than a one case per one million people (a relatively low level of disease).[24] The EPA sought to circumvent this limitation because it wanted to give a regu-latory break to eight plywood plants that had emissions projected to cause adverse health effects above the 1/1,000,000 threshold. So the EPA cre-ated a new category of low-risk plants that was never authorized in the statute, announcing that it would oversee such facilities on an individual basis to make sure they did not endanger the public.

*Los Angeles Times* reporter Tom Hamburger and Alan Miller reported that the EPA's novel legal theory was developed by Jeffrey Holmstead, the political appointee who headed the agency's air pollution programs and was formerly a lawyer at Latham and Watkins, a prominent Washington, D.C., law firm, where he represented timber interests.[25] (For a similar *Los Angeles Times* story concerning the EPA's decision to drastically weaken regulation of mercury emitted by coal-fired power plants, see chapter 6.) The theory received the enthusiastic endorsement of John Graham, then head of OIRA, but was strongly opposed by the EPA's career lawyers, who warned that the legal theory "results in a regulatory approach equiva-lent to the one Congress specifically rejected in 1990. . . ." As it turned out, the D.C. Circuit Court of Appeals agreed with the career lawyers' advice, reversing the EPA decision because it "is contrary to the plain language of the statute [and therefore] fails at *Chevron* step one."[26] The panel consisted of Judge Judith Rogers (a Clinton appointee), who wrote the opinion, and judges Douglas Ginsburg (a Reagan appointee) and Thomas Griffith (a George W. Bush appointee).

The formaldehyde case is not an anomaly. Although dominated by con-servative judges, the D.C. Circuit Court of Appeals has upheld a series of challenges to EPA CAA regulations issued during the Bush II adminis-tration. A 2008 investigation by the House Committee on Oversight and Government Reform revealed that the EPA lost all or part of two-thirds of the CAA cases decided by that court, and, in a majority of those chal-lenges, the court concluded that the agency had misinterpreted the plain language of the law.[27] These outcomes indicate the importance of very specific statutory provisions to the courts' efforts to supervise agencies; the CAA is the most detailed health and safety statute now on the books. They also demonstrate the extreme efforts of the Bush II administration to produce industry-friendly results, leading us to suspect that senior political appointees wanted to delay regulation, as opposed to promulgating rules that they honestly thought would survive judicial scrutiny.

*Regulatory Rationality*

Much of an agency's time and effort is spent identifying and characterizing a problem and then determining the best remedial approach for solving it. Congress clearly intends for an agency to take the lead in this effort, but it also expects the courts to review the substance of the rule to ensure that it is supported by the administrative record the agency developed during the rulemaking and is not arbitrary and capricious.[28] Administrative records include every recorded piece of information and policy advice that the agency received regarding the rule since its inception, as well as all the information that the agency itself generated and intended to rely on when it promulgated the rule. This type of review is supposed to be deferential, but not so deferential that agencies are free to adopt regulations that are unsupported by the record and entirely fail to meet Congress's expectations about protecting the public.

In a 1971 case, *Citizens to Preserve Overton Park, Inc. v. Volpe*, one of the most important decisions in administrative law, the Supreme Court instructed judges to determine whether agency decisions were "based on a consideration of the relevant factors and whether there has been a clear error of judgment."[29] Under this approach, judges first ask whether an agency has considered factors other than those Congress indicated were to be used to decide on the substance of a rule. They then ask whether, in light of the evidence available to it and the purpose of the agency's mandate, the regulation is clearly unreasonable. In a subsequent and equally important case, *Motor Vehicle Manufacturers Ass'n v. State Farm Mutual Automobile Insurance Co.*, the Supreme Court expanded on these duties, creating an expectation that to survive judicial review, agencies must articulate "a satisfactory explanation for its action including a 'rational connection between the facts found and the choice made.' "[30] We wholeheartedly agree that such basic requirements keep agencies honest, forestalling any nascent tendency to fudge or obscure the reasons why they decided to adopt a major rule.

But some courts have overreacted to these requirements, using them as an excuse to engage in excessively critical review of the agency's rationale for its regulation. Known as "hard look review," judges defend this scrutiny as necessary to their fulfillment of the obligation to determine whether an agency has rigorously analyzed the evidence and arguments presented by persons filing comments. The origins of hard look review date back to the 1970s when liberal judges sought to ensure that regulatory agencies had not ignored the evidence and arguments presented by consumer and environmental advocates.[31] These concerns should sound familiar. In essence, they are the judiciary's version of preventing agency capture by second-guessing their decisions on a very detailed level. Yet such scrutiny can cut both ways. Like their more liberal predecessors, today's more conservative judges consider, often in excessively painstaking detail, an agency's factual predicate, its analytical methodology, and its chain of reasoning. Their intent is to see whether the agency ignored evidence offered by regulated industries that less stringent regulation is appropriate.

As the consequences of judicial review for OSHA indicate, outcome-oriented and hard look review is a tremendous problem for health and safety agencies, contributing greatly to agency dysfunction. The harshness of such review, whether originating from the left or from the right, saps agency confidence, diminishes predictability, and encourages agencies to overcompensate in anticipation of what courts may eventually say. The courts' unreasonable demand for satisfactory reasons increases the potential that any mistake in analysis, no matter how minor, may cause a court to overturn a rule. Agencies overcompensate to avoid judicial reversals, with results that severely undermine their effectiveness.

Perhaps the most debilitating example of overcompensating is the construction of excessively lengthy administrative records that attempt to demonstrate an agency's scrupulous examination of all the information and opinion that outside public commenters have presented. Douglas Costle, a former EPA administrator, provides a discouraging example of this damaging, pervasive problem.[32] For one rulemaking during his tenure, the EPA received 192 comments that produced four hundred separate issues. The agency's effort to respond to all of these issues filled up 1,600 pages in the *Federal Register*. The chilling effects of hard look review not only slow down the progress of individual regulations, they constrain an agency's overall capacity to issue rules, thereby reducing the scope of federal regulation.

We recognize that some progressive scholars support hard look review as a necessary check on capture.[33] We are sympathetic to the concern of these scholars that captured agencies will give short shrift to proregulatory arguments. Nevertheless, on balance, hard look review is more likely to be a cause of agency dysfunction than a solution for it. This approach gives judges a false impression about how precise agency decision making can be, which invites judges to hold agencies up to a standard of perfection impossible to meet in the real world. When agencies fail to offer more perfect justifications for rules, the reason is far more likely to be that they face very difficult policy choices than that they have negligently disregarded evidence or arguments. Under hard look review, the pursuit of the perfect becomes the enemy of the good.

Hard look review creates the significant potential for outcome-oriented behavior. What is a "satisfactory explanation" is in the eye of the beholder. Administrative records typically contain thousands—even tens of thousands—of pages and include multiple, highly technical positions on conflicting scientific evidence. A skeptical judge can easily find flaws in the way that the agency responds to this morass of information, even though the individual analytical or evidentiary errors are relatively unimportant. The research on appellate review summarized in Table 7.1 supports this conclusion. The authors of the study concluded,

> Our findings offer a clear prediction for the future: when a judiciary consisting mostly of Democratic appointees confronts a conservative executive branch, the rate of invalidations will be unusually high, and so too when a judiciary consisting mostly of Republican appointees confronts a liberal executive branch. The conflict between a Democratic administration and a Republican-dominated judicial branch should be expected to produce a large number of invalidations in the most important domains of regulatory policy.[34]

## A Border Patrol Judiciary

Federal appellate courts are ill suited to the task of preventing capture because they lack the resources and the expertise to review administrative records in any great detail. Of course, they can make exceptions in specific cases, deciding to mount an extraordinary effort because they dislike the agency or are otherwise interested in the issue. The problem with this approach is that each time it happens, it reignites the hope of hard look review among parties who can afford expensive appellate litigation—generally, regulated industries that already have a substantial stake in delay.

For this and other reasons, the judiciary is not the right institution to fine-tune health and safety regulatory policy. Its review comes late in the development of a rule. Judges lack relevant technical and scientific expertise. And they have demonstrated a disturbing propensity to abandon professional craft-oriented norms in favor of ideological outcomes in this arena. Because they enjoy lifetime appointments, their ideological views are often out of sync with electoral preferences. For example, we cannot predict with any certainty when conservative Republican judges will cease to dominate the federal bench, and the country has already headed in a significantly different direction as a result of the 2008 national election. Swings in judicial ideology deprive health and safety agencies of the predictability they should have under an increasingly detailed set of statutory mandates. Well before the 2008 election, congressional lawmaking in all the areas we have discussed—from environmental protection to food, drug, and consumer product safety to occupational health—has trended toward more stringent requirements even as Republican judges have done their best to push policy in the opposite direction.

With the election of Barack Obama, health and safety advocates may well decide to bide their time and wait for progressive appointments to replace conservative judges. Gradually, the direction of outcome-oriented, ideologically based judging should swing in the direction favoring safety and health regulatory agencies. Assuming that agencies in the Obama administration will issue more protective regulations than they did during the Bush II administration, a reconfigured federal bench should favor stronger regulatory protections.

We fear that this strategy is expedient but unwise, especially from the perspective of building long-lasting and stable reform of the regulatory system. Judges across the spectrum should shun outcome-oriented judging and return to a craft-oriented approach. The profound changes promised by *Chevron* should come to pass, even if they mean that agencies under Republican presidents receive deference for regulations that are less vigorous than we might prefer.

Instead of tolerating ideological judging when one's own side has hope of dominating the judiciary, we urge the adoption of what we call a "border patrol" role for the federal judiciary. This approach is entirely consistent with the *Chevron* doctrine as written, if not as applied. Border patrol judges would scrutinize agency decisions primarily to determine whether they are consistent with the nonambiguous meaning of the statute. They would not reverse those determinations unless an agency failed to articulate a reasonable justification for how it resolved an ambiguity in its mandate or made a decision clearly contradicted by the administrative record the agency compiled. Judicial review would become far more predictable: agencies would win unless they strayed far beyond reasonable interpretations of their mandates or were too incompetent to marshal the evidence for what they wanted to do.

We see two avenues for accomplishing this redefinition of the judiciary's role. The first would require an epiphany among a majority of Supreme Court justices, who would choose the right opportunity to write a "Chevron II" opinion, reiterating its intention that the lower courts defer to agency interpretations of ambiguous language and promising to do so themselves. (Unlike the other federal courts, the Supreme Court chooses the cases it is willing to consider. Federal court of appeals cases stand as precedent unless the Supreme Court chooses to reconsider them.) We recognize that, given its existing workload, the Supreme Court may be reluctant to take the second step that would be necessary to accomplish this change: policing the appellate courts to ensure that they follow these dictates, but we think the project would in fact be a worthwhile use of the Court's resources given the grim status of the agencies today.

Another avenue would require extensive congressional action. By taking the time and attention it needs to write better reasoned, more detailed statutes, Congress could curtail the judiciary's penchant for reinterpreting its intent. We recognize that Congress labors under constraints that would make it difficult to achieve this kind of lawmaking. As we noted in chapter 2, Congress chooses vague and ambiguous language because it recognizes that health and safety regulation requires a level of scientific and technical expertise that it cannot always muster. As important, the most talented legislators know that a certain degree of ambiguity is essential to grease the skids for a controversial bill politically because vague language allows warring stakeholders to read legislation in their own favor. Congress should also monitor judicial decisions and intervene when courts misinterpret an agency's authority. For example, we can think of no justification for Congress's failure to rescue OSHA from the implications of the *Industrial Union Department* decision.

## Conclusion

As overseers, the federal judiciary has its good and bad points. Judges remain a reliable check of agency excess, especially where statutory mandates are clear and specific. In those cases, the judge risks a significant loss of reputation if he or she looks the other way. The record in other cases is more mixed. Judicial review doctrines are ambiguous and access restrictive, inviting judges to pursue an outcome orientation instead of a more neutral approach. When these results occur, the courts can become a source of agency dysfunction rather than a solution.

What we know about judicial incentives suggests that the most promising remedy for judicial overreaching is to make the law more determinate. The Supreme Court should formulate a clear test for standing that defers to congressional judgments. Congress should avoid vague and ambiguous statutory mandates whenever possible, and it should overrule judicial decisions that take advantage of ambiguity to impose restrictions on an agency's mandate that makes it more difficult for the agency to regulate. The Supreme Court should make it clearer to the lower federal courts that *Chevron* was intended to increase judicial deference to agency statutory interpretation of vague and ambiguous statutory terms, and the Court should itself respect this intention. The Court should also make it clear to the lower federal courts that it does not sanction hard look review.

Should they occur, these steps will not make the courts into exemplary agents of the people. Judges will continue to engage in outcome behavior because of the strong pull of ideology in regulatory cases involving important issues of public policy and because judicial discretion is an unavoidable part of judging. A reduction in outcome-oriented behavior, however, would be an improvement and should reduce agency dysfunction that arises from biased judicial review.

PART III
# Solutions

## CHAPTER EIGHT

# Positive Metrics

## Introduction

A s this volume draws to a close, we turn our attention to a pervasive question that is the quid pro quo for every recommendation we have made: how will the urgent need to revitalize the CPSC, EPA, FDA, NHTSA, and OSHA inch its way to the top of the national agenda, receiving the time, attention, political capital, and money that these issues so badly need? Or, to put the problem in institutional terms: will Congress, President Obama, the courts, and the next two or three presidents be able to overcome the momentum of neglect and ride to the rescue, revitalizing these agencies as they near forty?

We understand that revitalization cannot simply turn the clock back to an earlier era. Without new approaches, such efforts are bound to falter. The central problem is the failure to hold agencies accountable for accomplishing their statutory missions and to provide them with what they need to turn the corner: additional resources, statutory authority, and less interference from the White House and the courts. Instead, political leaders blame the agencies for what goes wrong until the next time something goes wrong, when leaders blame them again. To help break these destructive cycles, this chapter proposes to harness the power of the World Wide Web with a new version of an old idea: the independent development of rigorous and concise "positive metrics" that should alert us when health and safety agencies have run into trouble.

Others have traveled this road before us. Some federal and regional agencies have experimented with "indicator" reports, which are generally focused on ambient conditions, or pollution levels, in various environmental media (air, water, or soil).[1] These efforts have attracted enough attention that conservative groups have followed suit with their own reports designed to show that conditions are not nearly as grim as the government and environmentalists claim.[2] But the most aggressive effort to exact accountability is the Government Performance and Results Act of 1993 (GPRA), passed with bipartisan support and embraced by then newly elected President Bill Clinton in 1993.[3] The statute requires agencies to compile "strategic plans" that establish goals for evaluating their performance. Agencies devote thousands of hours to complying with the statute annually, but these efforts have a surreal quality, typically failing to acknowledge the impediments that produce regulatory failure.

The GPRA has failed to promote effective regulatory government because it has two fundamental flaws. First, as interpreted by conservatives in Congress, its major goal is to ferret out waste, fraud, and abuse in government performance. Predictably, agencies try to defend themselves by creating euphemistic performance goals in order to ensure that they can "pass" their own evaluation criteria. The upshot is a sunny set of invented statistics designed to reassure their overseers that they are doing fine, ending any possibility that the real causes of regulatory failure are discovered, much less addressed. Second, and related, the GPRA is so nonspecific in its effort to be one size fits all for the entire government that the products it generates have devolved into a meaningless overlay on the actual daily management of agencies. GPRA does not so much guide agency priorities and management as mirror those efforts from a level of 8,000 feet.

The concept underlying the GPRA—holding agencies accountable by scrutinizing their actual performance—is unassailable. But, we would argue, performance must be measured on the basis of positive metrics that invite a diagnosis of the impediments that prevent agencies from achieving their statutory missions. The regulatory metrics that we propose are designed to attract public attention to agency successes and shortcomings, producing early warning signs that will motivate a search for potential solutions.

Our proposal differs from previous reporting requirements in another fundamental way. While the elaborate paperwork that these programs have generated is easy to recover from the World Wide Web, one has to be a knowledgeable stakeholder to get any satisfaction out of reading these arcane narratives. These documents represent the essence of "inside baseball," making them unintelligible to congressional staff and reporters, much less the general public. In contrast, we intend positive metrics to be sufficiently concise and accessible that they could interest and inform regulatory outsiders.

We do not underestimate the challenge of boiling down the existing morass of data about agency performance, and we recognize the crucial distinction between identifying regulatory gaps and actually addressing the causes of these problems. It will take a sea change in attitudes toward government for the spirit and not just the letter of positive metrics to work as they should. Nevertheless, this chapter explains why positive metrics have a realistic chance of jump-starting a political dynamic that would root out the causes of regulatory failure and spur action to correct those deficiencies.

We begin with an examination of how national policy agendas get set. We analyze why the GPRA and other similar efforts have failed. We then explain the key attributes of positive metrics.

## Agenda Setting

### Policy Windows

Common wisdom has it that major health and safety legislation requires a precipitating crisis—or series of crises—to get passed. In this context, "crisis" is defined as something really big—a tragedy of major proportions that repeatedly makes front-page news. In 1937, for example, 107 people (including many children) died after ingesting a patent medicine known as elixir of sulfanilamide, which was used to treat streptococcal infections and was converted to liquid form by dissolving its basic ingredients in the poisonous solvent diethylene glycol. The incident led to the 1938 passage of the Federal Food, Drug, and Cosmetic Act.[4] Liquid wastes seeping into basements near Love Canal prompted passage of the Comprehensive Environmental Response, Compensation, and Liability Act in 1980.[5] And a chemical explosion at a Union Carbide pesticide plant in Bhopal, India, killed 3,000 people, prompting passage of the Emergency Planning and Community Right-to-Know Act of 1986.[6]

The converse of this rule of thumb—that in the absence of a crisis, nothing happens, no matter how much an agency degenerates over time or how much convincing evidence shows that changes are necessary—is often overlooked by proponents of the common wisdom. Nor do they seem to consider the possibility that even very significant crises sometimes are not enough to spur legislative action.

So, for example, the attacks of September 11, 2001, seemed to present a golden opportunity to strengthen the security at chemical plants containing large quantities of acutely toxic chemicals. Despite television exposés showing unaccompanied reporters wandering around factory grounds, numerous editorials, and a series of reports pinpointing vulnerabilities, the chemical industry prevailed in its argument that it can take care of any problems through voluntary self-regulation.[7] Similarly, the 2008 amendments to the Consumer Product Safety Act were ostensibly targeted at tightening up controls on imports, but the CPSC was not given anywhere near enough money to construct an effective inspection program at the nation's borders. Instead, Congress instructed the agency to write a report on the subject and submit it to Congress for future consideration.[8] If recent history is any guide, reforming the five agencies could take many decades, and the upshot could well be that they remain hobbled by short-term fixes and impulsive mandates, becoming even less effective than they are now.

Dissatisfied with these prospects, we reexamined the common wisdom, with the assistance of political scientist John W. Kingdon, whose well-known book, *Agendas, Alternatives, and Public Policies*, offers a more nuanced and complex picture of how public policy gets changed.[9] Although we think that Professor Kingdon's theories accurately portray the past, and could be applied retrospectively to all the legislation that we have written about here, we value them even more as a framework for testing whether our positive metrics have the capacity to, in Kingdon's terminology, "open the policy window" and provoke constructive change. His most crucial insight is that while catastrophic events can serve as catalysts for change, they only work when effective solutions are available and when the national political atmosphere is receptive to those changes. Positive metrics, then, must prompt inquiry into the causes of regulatory failure and a search for regulatory solutions, in addition to alerting policy makers that something is gravely wrong.

At outset of his analysis, Kingdon distinguishes between the policy "agenda"—meaning which issues get focused attention from decision makers—and policy "alternatives"—meaning the solutions they select to deal with the agenda item so elevated. Both factors are essential. It does no good to elevate an issue to the top of the agenda if acceptable solutions are not at hand. At the same time, the availability of those solutions is rarely enough, on its own, to elevate an issue.

A variety of "players," as Kingdon refers to them, or "stakeholders," as they are labeled in the current lexicon, have influence on agendas and alternatives, but those with the most power are the most adept at big picture agenda setting, while less visible participants provide the details of feasible alternatives. A president and his cabinet or a particularly effective member of Congress has the capacity to identify the four or five issues that will dominate the domestic agenda. But these leaders also need menus of cost-effective, practical, and politically saleable programs for implementing those broad goals. Kingdon emphasizes that nongovernmental players, including reporters, public interest groups, academics, and campaign managers, play a role both in assisting high-visibility players to affect agenda selection and in developing alternatives.

Kingdon identifies "three major process streams" in the federal government that affect agenda setting, development of alternatives, and policy change: "(1) problem recognition, (2) the formation and refining of policy proposals, and (3) politics."[10] He suggests that unless and until these three streams converge, significant reform cannot occur and that their convergence is dependent on the full tableau of players carrying out their disparate roles fully. Our "positive metrics" fall squarely within the first stream. As Kingdon explains:

> Fairly often, problems come to the attention of governmental decision makers not through some sort of political pressure or perceptual slight [sic] of hand but because some more or less systematic indicator simply shows that there is a problem out there. Such indicators abound in the political world because both governmental and nongovernmental agencies routinely monitor various activities and events.
>
> . . .
>
> Another type of information that indicates a problem is a failure to meet stated goals. If the administrators of a program have themselves set targets that they then do not meet, various overseers wonder if there is a problem to which they should devote some attention.[11]

As for the two other process streams, Kingdon describes the formation of policy proposals in a conventional way to include debates prompted by problem identification that occur within agencies and among agency personnel and outside stakeholders. His explanation of the political process is more innovative and worth quoting. It includes "swings of national mood, vagaries of public opinion, election results, changes of administration, shifts in partisan or ideological distributions in Congress, and interest group pressure campaigns."[12]

But perhaps Kingdon's most significant insights are that real change occurs incrementally, as many categories and levels of players work on a problem, and that, as the national mood shifts, problems are yanked out of the back of the queue and pushed into a place much closer to the policy window. Kingdon acknowledges the importance of "focusing events"

like the crises that feature so prominently in the common wisdom we explained earlier.[13] But he dismisses their staying power, arguing that they
can bring problems to the fore but that real change will only occur if those
problems were already undergoing sufficient discussion that policy alternatives are near at hand.

This model suggests that the nation is poised for big changes after the
pent-up, slow-moving domestic policy making that occurred in the aftermath of September 11, 2001, when the nation was preoccupied with two
seemingly unwinnable wars. Eight years of conservative neglect of government's affirmative mission, the anxiety of a deep, worldwide economic
recession, and President Obama's large margin in the popular vote also
suggest opportunities for profound changes in government. The question
is not whether change will occur, but rather how many issues can fit on the
agenda. The answer to that question depends in turn on whether players at
all levels are prepared to identify problems and develop solutions so that
they are ready to enter the policy window when it opens even a crack.

For two decades, participants in the health and safety debate, especially
public interest advocates, have operated on the assumption that the common wisdom is right and have done everything they could to exploit the
crises that erratically came their way. Unfortunately, this entirely understandable effort to "rip progress from today's headlines" has often failed.
In Kingdon's terms, this concentration on focusing events has occurred at
the expense of work in the first and middle streams: identifying problems
in government performance and developing policy alternatives to resolve
the problems so identified.

The positive metrics we envision would jump-start the discussion of an
agency's most important problems, both within the agency and between
the agency and its overseers. These discussions should propel experts to
develop alternatives with the expectation that the policy window will open
and permit their adoption. But to accomplish these results, designers of
positive metrics must avoid the problems that plagued previous efforts.


## Performance and Results?

*Indicators as Practiced*

In a 2004 report evaluating the "hundreds of environmental indicator sets"
developed throughout the country, the GAO offered the following working definition of this concept:

Environmental indicators track changes to the quality and condition of the air, water, land, and ecosystems on various geographic scales, and related human health and economic conditions. Whereas definitions of "environmental indicator" vary, most of them emphasize that an environmental indicator is a selected quantifiable variable that describes, analyzes, and presents scientific information and its significance.[14]

The GAO criticizes indicators as they are practiced for four reasons. First, negotiations to develop a single set of indicators are heavily politicized because the sponsors of the effort must contend with the anxieties of participants that the information will make them look bad. Second, available environmental data exhibit large and significant gaps between what is monitored and what should be monitored, making it difficult to collect a meaningful set of statistics regarding actual conditions. Third, federal efforts to coordinate data gathering and analysis among other governments and the private sector are weak. Finally, and most important for our purposes, indicators often do not reflect the connection between regulatory activities and actual results. Without measuring that cause and effect, indicators fail as a vehicle for inspiring government accountability.

Among the best examples of the gap—a cynic might even say yawning chasm—between indicators and the government activities designed to address environmental problems is the Chesapeake Bay Program (CBP), which has come under fire from the GAO and its congressional overseers for consistently failing to improve environmental conditions in the nation's largest estuary. The Chesapeake Bay watershed covers 64,000 square miles, measuring two hundred miles in length and thirty-five miles at its widest point. The watershed is one of the most beautiful and economically productive in the world. Tourism, which depends to a large extent on the preservation of pristine environmental conditions, contributes billions of dollars to the economies of the states nearby, especially Maryland, Delaware, and Virginia. Unfortunately, the bay is plagued by so-called nutrient loading, a condition in which a river or stream is choked with organic matter discharged from sewage treatment plants and manufacturing facilities or washed into the water by rainwater runoff from agricultural lands and urban centers. Nutrient loading kills fish and other aquatic life, accelerates the growth of algal blooms, and, at its worst, results in "dead zones" where such natural resources cannot survive.

Between 1995 and 2004, the federal government provided $3.7 billion dollars in direct spending for bay restoration, and an additional $1.9 billion was spent on programs that have an indirect effect on improving the bay's conditions. Although these amounts sound like a great deal of money, most experts agree that significantly more funding will be necessary to complete the job. But the restoration effort is in crisis at the moment because environmental conditions have not improved significantly over the last decade.

Founded in 1983, the CBP combines representatives from the EPA and its state regulatory counterparts in Delaware, Pennsylvania, Maryland, Virginia, West Virginia, and the District of Columbia. The CBP is a voluntary endeavor that has no independent regulatory authority. Instead, it depends on dozens of committees, working groups, and task forces to jawbone, shame, and cajole the partners to redouble their pollution-control efforts. The CBP has established a series of goals for reducing nutrient loading. It has failed to meet any of them by large margins. In recent years, critics have ridiculed it for producing a large array of beautifully illustrated reports that put the most favorable gloss on environmental conditions in the bay and the CBP partners' activities.

A slew of reasons explains these misfires.[15] Large population increases in the bay watershed have increased pollution, and technology to prevent nutrient loading has lagged behind. Some states benefit significantly more than others from tourism, and the partners are competitive with each other economically, producing distrust and even outright animosity on occasion. Local politicians jockey for credit and flee from criticism. The EPA, the only partner with the legal clout to make everyone toe the line, has consistently ducked any leadership role. And the law that determines the scope and content of such efforts—the Clean Water Act—is woefully outdated and inadequate.[16] In a pointedly negative 2005 report, the GAO estimated that the CBP had established 101 "measures" that track environmental conditions in the bay watershed:

> Mirroring the shortcomings in the program's measures, the Bay Program's primary mechanism for reporting on the health status of the bay—the *State of the Chesapeake Bay Report*—does not provide an effective or credible assessment on the bay's current health status. This is because these reports (1) focus on individual species and pollutants instead of providing an overall assessment of the bay's health, (2) commingle data on the bay's health attributes with program actions, and (3) lack an independent review process.
>
> . . .
>
>     We believe that the combined impact of these deficiencies has already resulted in a situation in which the Bay Program cannot effectively present a clear

and credible picture of what the restoration effort has achieved, what strategies will best further *Chesapeake 2000's* restoration goals, and how limited resources should be channeled to develop and implement the most effective strategies.[17]

Our assessment is even grimmer. The CBP's 2007 document, entitled *A Report to the Citizens of the Bay Region, Chesapeake Bay Health & Restoration Assessment*, contains close to forty pages of lavish graphics, photographs, and text explaining all the man-made threats that impair the watershed. None explain which institutions are responsible for addressing specific problems. Instead, on page six, the authors include the following throwaway line: "Program scientists project that little more than half of the pollution reduction efforts needed to achieve the nutrient goals have been undertaken since 1985."[18] This remarkable statement suggests that the reason the bay's conditions continue to worsen is that the CBP partners have not gone nearly far enough in developing and implementing concrete regulatory programs that would prevent discharges of nutrients into the already polluted water. Or, in other words, not only does the report recite worsening environmental conditions in the bay without tying these conditions to the regulatory efforts designed to improve them, the report ignores—and CBP partners have overlooked—a series of unnamed regulatory approaches that are necessary to restore the bay to a healthy condition.

If we were members of Congress, we would write and request that the program scientists send us the full list of "pollution reduction efforts" they have in mind and take matters from there.

*GPRA's Edicts*

The federal GPRA was inspired by analogous reforms at the state and local level. According to its mission statement,

> [W]aste and inefficiency in Federal programs undermine the confidence of the American people in the Government and reduces [*sic*] the Federal Government's ability to address adequately vital public needs. . . . [The purpose of this Act is to] improve [that] confidence . . . by systematically holding Federal agencies accountable for achieving program results.[19]

The statute asks agencies to indicate the constraints under which they operate and how these constraints may affect their performance, but agencies compelled to function in an antiregulatory, even hostile, political atmosphere are predictably reluctant to speak truth to power. Instead, their goal has become convincing congressional and White House overseers that they are performing well, despite budgets that are extraordinarily inadequate for effective implementation of their missions.

The GPRA orders all agencies to submit strategic plans covering a period of not less than five years to Congress and the director of the OMB.[20] Those plans must contain a "comprehensive mission statement," as well as general "goals and objectives." Agencies must explain how they intend to achieve their goals and then describe the "human, capital, information, and other resources" they will need to do so. They must identify the "key factors external to the agency and beyond its control" that could affect the achievement of their general goals and objectives. The agencies are instructed to consult with Congress and also to "solicit and consider" the views of all entities that are "potentially affected by or interested in" their plans.

Strategic plans, apparently intended to be visionary and "big picture," must be supplemented by "performance plans," covering each "program activity" set forth in the agency's budget.[21] Performance plans must establish goals, expressing them in "objective, quantifiable, and measurable form." They must identify the indicators that agencies will use to assess "outputs, service levels, and outcomes" and the "means" they use to "verify and validate measured values." The GPRA further requires the agencies to prepare annual "program performance reports" that compare their goals and indicators with their "actual program performance." If they fail to achieve success, they must explain why, what they intend to do about it, and whether the goals or indicators themselves are the problem and must be changed. This last requirement is rarely followed.

As we mentioned at the outset, the GPRA has generated volumes of positive sounding numbers, cheerful narrative, and assurances that all is well at whichever regulatory agency is justifying its performance. Probe beneath the numbers, however, and these assurances lose their credibility. To illustrate these deficiencies, we circle back on two prominent examples of regulatory failure explained in previous chapters, neither of which were mentioned in the agencies' GPRA reports.

*Strategic Planning in Practice*

The first example involves Vioxx, which was released in 1999 as a prescription painkiller for use in the treatment of arthritis. Merck, the manufacturer of Vioxx, voluntarily withdrew the drug in 2004 because studies indicated it significantly increased the risk of heart attacks. Although the FDA was actively engaged in trying to persuade Merck to feature more prominent warnings on Vioxx packaging in the months preceding the voluntary recall, it was not sufficiently forceful in these negotiations, either because it feared it was not ready to go to court to force action or because it was under pressure from top-level political appointees. Dr. David Graham, an associate director in the FDA's Office of Drug Safety, estimated that between 88,000 and 139,000 Americans suffered a heart attack or stroke as the result of taking Vioxx and that as many as 30–40 percent of these patients died as a result.

The Vioxx crisis was the most visible symptom of serious problems that began a decade earlier, when the FDA began to rely on pharmaceutical industry fees generated by the Prescription Drug User Fee Act of 1992[22] (PDUFA) to fund its work on new and existing drugs. The money came with conditions attached. First, the law said that fees could only be used to support the FDA's review of applications to market new prescription drugs. Second, it required the FDA to devote at least as much money to new drug reviews as it spent in 1992 (later changed to 1997), adjusted for inflation. These provisions forced the FDA to reallocate money from other areas of its drug safety and efficacy programs—in particular, the monitoring of existing drugs for long-term safety problems—in order to continue the generation of fees. A 2002 GAO report found that the FDA's efforts to rob Peter to pay Paul allocated about 1,000 more full-time equivalents (FTEs) to drug and biologic review activities and 1,000 fewer FTEs to other FDA programs regarding food safety and medical devices (for example, heart valves and pacemakers).[23] Funding was further distorted within the FDA's Center for Drug Evaluation and Research, with 74 percent of its resources in 2002 spent on reviewing new drug applications and just 6 percent on the safety and efficacy of existing drugs.

Not only did the FDA's GPRA paperwork fail to acknowledge these funding disparities, it obscured the brewing Vioxx scandal by emphasizing inappropriate priorities far removed from the FDA's core mission. The thirty-two-page 2003 *FDA Strategic Action Plan* was preoccupied with what the agency could do to promote pharmacological and food technology developments.[24] The document worried aloud about the decreasing number of new drug applications received by the FDA, speculating without much justification that the agency's approval process might chill innovation, posing a competitive disadvantage for pharmaceutical companies locked in races with foreign competitors to develop the next blockbuster drug. This concern even extended onto the factory floor, with the FDA pledging to update its "Current Good Manufacturing Practices" in order to "encourage" what it believed could be "large savings in production costs."[25] The FDA never explained why American companies' profitability should be a top priority for the only regulatory agency charged with policing the safety and efficacy of new and existing drugs in a period of budget shortfalls.

The second example involves the Superfund toxic waste cleanup program and the unfortunate facts that the corporate tax authority intended by Congress to fund the bulk of the program expired in 1995 and that Congress has never revisited the issue. Cleanups at priority sites have slowed to a crawl, and the program is now dependent on a trickle of general taxpayer revenue to support these efforts.

The EPA is one of the more ambitious agencies when it comes to compiling GPRA reports. The *2006–2011 EPA Strategic Plan*[26] is a beautifully illustrated, 180-page publication; the 667-page *2007 EPA Performance Plan*[27] is less polished in presentation but considerably more detailed. Yet neither of these reports mentions the expiration of Superfund's taxing authority, nor do they have anything to say about the funding challenges facing the program. In fact, both reports omit the number of sites on which the construction of remedies (for example, caps to prevent infiltration of rainwater or slurry walls to block seepage of waste) was completed.

Instead, both reports contain statistics that are puzzling at best and misleading at worst because they suggest the agency is making progress when it is not. For example, the *2006–2011 EPA Strategic Plan* promises that by 2011, the agency will "achieve and maintain at least 95 percent of the maximum score on readiness evaluation criteria in each region."[28] The statement refers to the EPA's ability to respond to emergencies involving hazardous substances. The 95 percent figure is clear enough, but the report makes no effort to explain what each region's "readiness criteria" entail. In another section, the EPA promises to "complete an additional 975 Superfund-lead hazardous substance removal actions," noting that "[i]n FY 2005, 175 of these actions were completed."[29] Not only does this promise lack any objective context (how many removals are needed?) or historical context (how many were done in years when funding was at full strength?), but it also lacks ambition: simple math shows that the EPA expects to do 162 removal actions in each of the six fiscal years between now and 2011, a 7 percent drop from the 175 done in fiscal year 2005.

## A Plan for Positive Metrics

### Working Definition

*Webster's Dictionary* defines "metric" as "a standard of measurement."[30] "Standard" means "something established by authority, custom, or general consent as a model or example."[31] We embrace these broad definitions, which have the advantage of including measurements of the status quo, measurements of current and future activities and their expected results, and measurements of normative goals within the ambit of an agency's statutory mission.

Positive metrics would focus on agencies' core statutory mission or missions, explaining what the agency is trying to accomplish, who is responsible for achieving those results, and when they will complete those activities. Because positive metrics would be concise and would be made available on the World Wide Web, they should have the potential to generate publicity and oversight concerning why agencies have experienced regulatory failure, fulfilling the problem identification phase of Professor Kingdon's agenda setting. In isolation, positive metrics would not indicate why an agency has failed. Instead, they would alert the agency's senior leadership, as well as its oversight committees in Congress, White House staff, advocacy groups, the media, and the public, that those causes of regulatory failure must be found. To make the best use of positive metrics, a system of routine oversight focused specifically on improvements in the metrics should be created.

### Metric Characteristics

STATUTORY MISSION.    Positive metrics should be based, first and foremost, on an agency's statutory missions and, if available, more detailed statutory mandates to take specific actions. For the FDA, the authority to approve new drugs and monitor the safety and efficacy of drugs already on the market are two distinct statutory functions.[32] Each needs its own metric. As another example, the Clean Air Act (CAA) requires the EPA to identify "criteria air pollutants," set standards for each such pollutant (limits on their concentrations in ambient air), and oversee the development of "state implementation plans" that will bring air quality into compliance with these standards—accomplishing each task under strict deadlines.[33] Geographic areas that do not meet the standards are called "non-attainment areas." The CAA mandates suggest metrics that disclose the levels of criteria pollutants in the ambient air across the country and explain how long it will take the agency to catch up on its work.

SHORT AND CONCISE.    If metrics are to have any hope of serving as a catalyst for supportive oversight, they cannot devolve into what Senator David Pryor (D-AR) characterized as "routine reports written by contractors using largely boilerplate language."[34] The excessive detail and mind-numbing length of GPRA reports has proven self-defeating from an oversight perspective. Positive metrics should therefore number no more than a few dozen for each agency and should be based on quantitative data or measurements that need empirical data to be complete.

INDEPENDENT ADVICE.    Permanent committees of independent experts familiar with each of the five agencies' work should advise agencies on the selection of positive metrics, but the agencies themselves should have the final say over which are chosen. The independent entity assigned the task of compiling an initial list of positive metrics could be established within existing institutions that have expertise in an agency's mission. The National Academy of Sciences, Institute of Medicine (for the FDA), or preexisting agency science advisory boards are all possibilities. Alternatively, Congress and the president could establish new advisory groups.

The best historical examples of what we have in mind are two reports issued in 1987 by the EPA in an effort to reexamine national environmental priorities. The first was an analysis by career staff of the environmental problems that should be on the EPA regulatory agenda, which was entitled *Unfinished Business: A Comparative Assessment of Environmental Problems*.[35] Three years later, the EPA asked its Science Advisory Board to review this document and prepare its own recommendations for the agency's future direction. *Reducing Risk: Setting Priorities and Strategies for Environmental Protection* was issued in 1990:

> For the past 20 years, EPA has been basically a "reactive" agency. As environmental problems were identified, the public conveyed its concern to Congress, and Congress passed laws to try to solve the problems within some, often well-defined, timeframe. EPA then implemented the laws using the resources—budget and staff—allocated by Congress.
>
> . . .
>
> This reactive mode, although understandable when seen in its historical context, has limited the efficiency and effectiveness of EPA's environmental

protection efforts. Because of EPA's tendency to react to environmental problems defined in specific environmental laws, the Agency has made little effort to compare the relative seriousness of different problems. Moreover, the Agency has made very little effort to anticipate environmental problems or to take preemptive actions that reduce the likelihood of an environmental problem occurring.[36]

In addition to helping agencies select metrics, independent advisors should routinely review and suggest revisions as information emerges and progress is made.

We emphasize the importance of engaging objective, independent help in order to avoid the elaborate logrolling that would undermine this effort if each portion of the agency assembled its outside constituencies to lobby for metrics that would make that unit look good. For example, the FDA staff responsible for reviewing new drugs would assemble pharmaceutical companies to ensure that fast disposition of such applications remains a top priority, while staff responsible for reviewing the safety and efficacy of existing drugs would press for metrics highlighting the need for additional funding of those efforts. Such negotiations are likely to produce an overly lengthy and complicated list because agencies would compromise by accepting everyone's proposals.

EVOLUTION OVER TIME.    Wherever possible, metrics should be based on information that is already available rather than waiting to perfect such data. However, if an especially probative piece of information is missing, the metric should call for its development over time. For example, the EPA's 2002 *Water Quality Inventory* of "impaired" waters—those polluted to the point at which they are unfit for a "designated use" such as drinking, swimming, or recreational boating—indicates substantial regulatory failure.[37] The agency estimates that 45 percent of assessed river and stream miles and 47 percent of assessed lake acres were not clean enough to support uses such as fishing and swimming. An assessed water body is one that has been monitored by a state.

Unfortunately, these numbers are at best rough guesses for two reasons. First, according to the EPA, the states have assessed only 19 percent of the nation's total river and stream miles and 37 percent of its lake, pond, and reservoir acres. Second, the statistics reported by the states are too unreliable to create a national picture of regulatory success or failure. According to a 2002 report by the GAO, the EPA's database of impaired waters is of "questionable reliability" because states categorize and sample water quality inconsistently.[38] No one would argue that monitoring must occur every few feet along the banks or in the middle of the nation's great lakes, rivers, and streams. But measuring the water quality of a river segment that runs through agricultural lands and using those figures to characterize problems along a ten-mile segment that runs through a major urban area does not establish the baseline needed to craft effective controls.

To tackle this problem, a positive metric on impaired waters could adopt a phased approach. In its first year, the EPA and its state partners would estimate how much it would cost and how long it would take to synchronize federal and state data and expand monitoring to a statistically valid sample of surface waters. In its second year, the program would require an explanation of progress made on that work, hopefully prompting greater investment if those efforts were lagging. These reports would continue until a valid set of statistics was assembled, reflecting water quality in real time and allowing the work of evaluating restoration activities to begin.

OUTCOMES VERSUS OUTPUTS.    The GPRA's inventors had one overriding claim to make about why their solution would succeed when so many other efforts had failed: the statute would compel civil servants to stop "counting beans" and stand accountable for results.[39] This distinction is described in the political science literature as the difference between procedural accomplishments (rules written, permits issued, enforcement actions taken) and outcomes (pollution reduced, accidents avoided, dangerous drugs kept off the market). As James Q. Wilson explained in his classic book, *Bureaucracy*,

> First, identify a course of action . . call it the treatment. A "treatment" can be a police tactic, a school curriculum, or a welfare program. Second, decide what impact the treatment is intended to have; call this the outcome. The outcome can be a crime rate, an achievement score, a work effort, a housing condition, or an income level.[40]

Or, as President Clinton explained in his GPRA signing statement,

> It may seem amazing to say, but like many big organizations, [our government] is primarily dominated by considerations of input, how much money do you spend on a program, how many people do you have on the staff, what kind of regulations and rules are going to govern it, and much less by output, does this

work, is it changing people's lives for the better, can we say after we take money and put it into a certain endeavor that it was worth actually having it away from the taxpayers, into this endeavor, and their lives are better?[41]

Since the GPRA was enacted, the GAO has repeatedly acknowledged the difficulties agencies face in making the transition from listing treatments or inputs to quantifying outcomes or results.[42] Not only must they struggle with the deeply embedded habit of counting what they do, as opposed to what they cause to happen, health and safety agencies often lack the resources they need to monitor environmental quality. When records are readily available, the problem boils down to making the effort to compile it. However, when the data do not exist it is often expensive to set up a system to generate the information, and the data may not be obtainable in some cases.

While we recognize the importance of driving agencies to develop outcome information, in many circumstances, input information may be a perfectly reasonable substitute. For example, in a perfect world, OSHA's performance should be evaluated on the basis of trends in workplace fatalities, injuries, and illnesses. But the task of gathering these data is much easier said than done. The Bureau of Labor Statistics (BLS), a division of the Department of Labor, publishes such statistics, but the data are extraordinarily incomplete and inaccurate for two reasons. First, the system relies on employers to report fatalities, injuries, and illnesses, and second, occupational diseases often do not appear until after years of exposure to toxic chemicals, long after a worker has left the employment where the exposure occurred.

It is unclear what kinds of resources and time OSHA or the BLS would need to develop more reliable methods of tracking an occupational illness. In the meantime, positive metrics should focus on OSHA's regulatory input. OSHA has established permissible exposure limits (PELs) for only five hundred chemicals, a small fraction of the thousands of substances present in the American workplace. It has established exposure limitations for fewer than two hundred of the approximately 3,000 chemicals characterized by the EPA as "high production volume" chemicals (meaning more than a million pounds of the substance is produced or imported each year). Many of OSHA's existing emissions limitations, which were adopted at the time that the agency was founded, are out of date, and OSHA has promulgated new occupational disease regulations for only about thirty substances since it was founded.

Output information is also necessary in the assessment of agency enforcement activities. Deterrence-based enforcement depends on high-profile prosecutions of entities in all segments of an industrial sector. Focusing on only one outcome—for example, the prosecution of a large emitter to reduce its excess pollution—would create a twisted incentive for an agency to ignore routine violations committed by smaller emitters, undermining the deterrence of the system.

EVOLVING METRICS.    Metrics that remain static would come close to being worse than no metrics at all because they would rapidly degenerate into a rote effort that would not push agencies to improve their performance. As our Clean Water Act example illustrates, initial metrics would ask agencies to take stock of the problem, admitting when they do not have the information necessary to fully characterize the milestones they must reach to achieve a statutory mission. Over time, as that information is developed, metrics should shift to an evaluation of the progress agencies are actually making in achieving these milestones. Or, in other words, initial metrics would be replaced by more demanding metrics that gradually ratchet up expectations for the agency's performance.

DIAGNOSTIC METRICS.    Metrics should have the potential to help diagnose the causes of regulatory failure—including funding gaps, technical complexity, lack of political will, inadequate statutory design, and agency capture. Once these shortfalls are made obvious, it would be up to Congress and the president to decide whether to remedy them. Public interest advocates would have the information they need to advocate for those results.

READY AVAILABILITY.    Agencies should feature positive metrics on their Internet sites and avoid what appears to be a powerful motivation to bury information about poor performance behind a wall of non-obvious links requiring multiple clicks to reach the desired data, thereby rendering Internet sites accessible only to the very patient or to the already well-informed.

FUNDING FOR OTHER GOVERNMENTS AND INSTITUTIONS.    Inevitably, the five protector agencies will be dependent on sister governments and other institutions for assistance in gathering information for positive metrics. Perhaps the clearest example is the EPA, which delegates much of the work of implementing major environmental laws to its state counterparts.

Without financial assistance from the federal government to cover the extra costs of assembling the data, state governments are likely to resist such reporting, which many will view as extraneous to what they are required to do.

## Conclusion

The five protector agencies share a paradoxical problem. They are not accountable to their true principals—the American people—in any real sense of the word. But they are accountable—overly accountable—to other agents for the wrong things. Over the past decade, and in some instances longer than that, all five agencies have been examined, excoriated, reviewed, and punished for overperforming, or overregulating, and for underperforming, or committing regulatory underkill.[43] The vast majority of this faultfinding was not done to engage in a constructive dialogue about solving the root of the problem. If much of it had been focused in an affirmative way, many of the crippling conditions we have described, from funding shortfalls to centralized decision making to intrusive judicial review, would have come to light. Instead, these abortive efforts to impose accountability were launched primarily to exonerate the overseer from responsibility in whatever health and safety fiasco had come to light.

For all of these reasons, we propose positive metrics with full awareness that the approach will have huge obstacles to overcome, the most important of which will originate from within the civil service. Convinced that they are already audited to the point that they cannot get their jobs done, understandably cynical officials could view our proposal as one more set of meaningless reporting requirements that will be used, if at all, to make them look bad. All we can say at this point is that this outcome is the last result we intend. Rather, we are looking for a way to communicate what the agencies do—and are unable to do—to people who will be distressed enough by that result to ask the crucial follow-up questions: what does the agency need to accomplish this crucial mission? Why has it failed? How can other agents of the people, whether in Congress or the White House, help it to surmount obstacles and succeed?

## CHAPTER NINE

# Renewing the Civil Service

> The fact that government agencies are having trouble doing their work has never been of serious concern in American democracy. After all, constitutional arrangements in the United States were not designed to smooth the way for the exercise of power by the instrumentalities of the state. No amount of antibureaucratic rhetoric, however, can obscure the fact that effective national policymaking in the United States, as in other democracies, requires that the elected officials responsible for making policy decisions receive as much help as possible from the permanent organizations of government. — Francis E. Rourke, Professor, Johns Hopkins University[1]

## Introduction

According to the Office of Personnel Management, the typical federal civilian employee is 46.9 years old and has been in her job for 16.3 years, earning averages of $66,371 worldwide and $86,444 in the Washington, D.C., metropolitan area. Supervisors and managers constitute 11.4 percent of the total. About 43 percent of the workforce has a bachelor's degree or higher. Some 56 percent are male, and 44 percent are female. Minority workers represent 32 percent, African Americans 17.2 percent, Hispanics 7.4 percent, and Asians 5 percent of the workforce. Veterans make up 22.3 percent of the total.

The five protector agencies employ approximately 30,000 people—a little over 1 percent of the total federal workforce. But the EPA alone has 17,000 employees. The remaining 13,000 people are responsible for keeping nine million workplaces safe, ensuring the purity of 80 percent of the food supply, spotting defects in billions of consumer products, and preventing traffic accidents. Even if the protector agencies had sufficient staffing, they face another daunting prospect: 76 percent of Senior Executive Service (SES) employees are eligible to retire in 2012; 36 percent are expected to exercise the option.

Civil servants, or, to use the more pejorative term, bureaucrats, have experienced three decades of antipathy from national political leaders. Democrats Jimmy Carter and Bill Clinton bought into this trend, although they used disdain for the civil service more as a defense against the charge that they were free-spending Democrats than a battle cry. Republican George H.W. Bush was moderate on the issue. But presidents Ronald Reagan and George W. Bush staked their legacies on bringing bureaucrats to heel. As just one vivid example of the distrust of the civil service common during this period, consider the "jigsaw puzzle management" theory developed by Michael Sanera and published as part of the Heritage Foundation's 1984 handbook *Mandate for Leadership II*:

> Career staff will supply information, but they should never become involved in the formulation of agenda-related policy objectives. . . . [O]nce controversial policy goals are formulated, they should not be released in total to the career staff. Thus, the political executive and his political staff become "jigsaw puzzle" managers. Other staff see and work on the individual pieces, but never have enough of the pieces to be able to learn the entire picture.[2]

During the same period, the government as a whole went through a series of broad-based reforms that further shook up the workforce without addressing its most intractable problems. These time-consuming campaigns ranged from President Reagan's effort through the Grace Commission to apply corporate management methods that would weed out "waste, fraud, and abuse" to Vice President Gore's reinvention initiative, which centered on the edict that agencies must become "customer oriented." This second notion was especially inappropriate and corrosive as applied to the five protector agencies because they are expected to police—not assist—the harmful activities of businesses large and small.

The second President Bush did not launch a comparable reinvention initiative. But his determined efforts to maintain control over agency decision making were extensive in their breadth and depth and largely effective. The most persistent charge leveled against these efforts was that the administration systematically ignored scientific evidence of risks to the safety and health of Americans. Yet the Bush II era cannot be dismissed as an outlier that is irrelevant to future administrations. These episodes are simply examples of the White House succumbing to the inevitable temptation to control regulatory decisions. This trend toward centralization has increased in intensity for several decades. Further, the administration had enough time to establish powerful institutions and processes that perpetuate centralization, most notably the OMB, leaving a legacy that will require significant effort to reverse.

This chapter considers the paradox of these attacks and the dilemmas they create for presidents. American government cannot possibly be strong, effective, and efficient—not least in the arena of health and safety policy—without the renewal of its battered civil service. But powerful cultural and political trends pull the weight of history against such reforms. The civil service is beleaguered by excessive layers of review, constant second-guessing, scant public recognition, insufficient resources, and growing disparity between public and private sector pay scales. Presidents of both parties seem irretrievably committed to the centralization of decision making. But this preoccupation has been taken to the point that it demoralizes the career civil service, slows policy making to a crawl, and introduces inappropriate political considerations into decisions intended to be based on scientific and policy criteria.

We argue here that political leaders, especially the president and senior members of Congress, must distinguish between "macropolicy" decisions best made by elected officials and "micropolicy" decisions that should be left to the professional civil service in consultation with the political appointees who lead the five agencies. The authorizing statutes of all five agencies delegate regulatory decisions directly to those leaders, specifying the criteria for carrying out their missions. Officials at the FDA are instructed to determine whether individual drugs are safe and effective and categories of food meet scientifically based standards of purity. Officials at the EPA are instructed to determine what kind of pollution-control equipment should be required for manufacturing plants. In contrast, decisions about our national position on the import of drugs manufactured abroad or whether we should curb the proliferation of coal-fired power plants should be left to the president and the Congress.

In drawing these distinctions, we do not pretend that the dividing lines are blatantly obvious. Science blends into policy and policy blends into politics. In the late nineteenth century, the Progressive movement argued that the civil service should be composed of the best and brightest "scientists" who would drain politics out of decisions to the point that only one right answer would miraculously emerge. This approach was discredited over time. But in rejecting the feasibility of a perfect objectivity in government, while at the same time allowing the career civil service to degenerate in composition, morale, and power, we have arguably pushed our expectations for government too far in the opposite direction.

In urging that we give the career civil service a central role in defining the public interest and implementing the programs that will achieve it, we understand that we are swimming upstream, against political currents and a spate of recent scholarship that overwhelmingly favors the locus of ultimate authority in the White House. Commentators from both the liberal and conservative ends of the political spectrum emphasize presidential prerogatives. We do not doubt the president's ability to send his White House staff to the bridge and shout out orders to the crews laboring below. We argue, however, that if the goal is to promote sound policy making within reasonable periods of time, centralization and top-down control are unlikely to accomplish that result over the long run. The fulcrum of power must shift from the White House back to the agencies.

We begin with a brief history of the civil service, explaining the model of neutral competence that a century of arduous change was designed to produce. We explain the distinctions we would draw between the exercise of neutral competence and decisions more appropriately centralized in the White House, using examples from the recent history of the CPSC, OSHA, and the EPA. We consider the most significant problems confronting efforts to revive the career civil service, including the "brain drain" that will deplete its crucial midlevel management, the disparities in pay that propel the best employees out the door, the "thickening" of supervision that depletes initiative and accountability, and the poor image of government that confounds recruitment of qualified replacements. All of these problems were analyzed by the 2003 National Commission on the Public Service, which assembled the best political scientists and public management experts in the country to sound the alarm about civil service dysfunction.[3] It developed several recommendations that we enthusiastically support, as we explain in the conclusion.


## The Civil Service and the Republic

Several prominent political scientists have attributed the civil service's most severe problems to the Constitution's omission of any clear role for a professional workforce, and it is certainly true that the Framers of the Constitution ignored the issue. The Constitution says simply that the president has the power to appoint "Officers" of the United States with the approval of two-thirds of the Senate and that Congress can vest the appointment of "inferior" officers in the president, heads of departments, or courts of law.[4] The Framers may well have ignored the need for a large civil service because they were committed in principle to a small national presence regarding domestic governance. As many observers beginning with Alexis de Tocqueville have noted, Americans' deep-seated, love-hate relationship with government is determined in large part by the country's historical legacy of resisting distant control by monarchical entities. Nevertheless, a behemoth federal government is clearly here to stay. Correcting the most negative elements of common attitudes toward the bureaucracy will require a national leader with the patience to explain why government is necessary to help and protect people when they cannot help and protect themselves.

With these debates swirling in the background, the civil service has expanded steadily as the country has grown, going through growth spurts during the Civil War, western expansion, the First World War, the New Deal, the Second World War, and the Great Society. For the first half century of the country's existence, the bureaucracy was made up of upper-class white men, with fathers handing their positions down to their sons. In 1829, Andrew Jackson converted this system of inherited power to a system of patronage, in the process doing his best to democratize the civil service from a class perspective. The operating assumption at the time was that the jobs were sufficiently fungible and easily performed that no particular preparation or expertise was required. Recipients of patronage paid party dues as high as 6 percent of their salaries, and the vast majority of jobs were located outside of Washington, D.C. The spoils system had its minor exceptions, protecting from electoral turnover certain jobs for auditors, comptrollers, clerks, and scientific personnel.

Pressure to change the patronage system grew steadily through the Civil War, as the nation grew in size and a broad coalition of urban merchants, bankers, lawyers, journalists, and clergy coalesced to support broad-based reform. The Progressive movement advocated a professionalized civil service bureaucracy in the 1880s; one of its first successes was to engage "sanitarians" (today's industrial hygienists) in the design of sewage systems for America's developing urban centers, eliminating widespread bouts of infectious disease and setting the stage for modern health and safety programs. In 1883, Congress passed the Pendleton Act, creating for the first time a merit-based civil service; a law granting formal job tenure and protection from partisan dismissal followed in 1890.[5] And in 1939, Congress passed the Hatch Act, closing the last opening for patronage by prohibiting political activity by civil servants.[6] Of course, political appointees remained at the top rungs of the management pyramid and served at the pleasure of the president.

In 1953, urged on by stalwart Republicans who were determined to make the most of their return to the White House, President Dwight Eisenhower pulled these trends a short distance in the opposite direction, creating the Schedule C system for lower level political appointments. He was determined to rein in the sprawling New Deal bureaucracy established by Democratic presidents Franklin Roosevelt and Harry Truman over two decades, and this effort had significant effect. Subsequent presidents have followed his lead, using Schedule C appointments to assert control over allegedly unfriendly civil servants. In 1978, Congress established the SES, a category of employees operating at the edge of the merit-based and political appointments system. Career SES personnel cannot be fired with a new administration, but they can be summarily transferred, assuring the president and his appointees the flexibility to appoint their preferred representatives and hound those they dislike from office.

Political scientist Francis Rourke, quoted at the outset of this chapter, characterizes the history of the civil service as an effort to work toward a goal of "neutral competence"—civil servants are the technocrats who maintain a strong grounding in the objective technical and scientific information that undergirds an agency's missions and are also the guardians of the agency's institutional memories. This image does not sit well with presidents who view themselves as "agents of change," as Ronald Reagan, Bill Clinton, and George W. Bush certainly did:

> Thus, presidents who regard themselves as trail-blazing innovators (and no self-respecting White House is likely to see itself in any other way today) may look upon neutral competence as having about it an aura of passivity, whereas the hallmark of an administration with path-breaking policy goals is activism. Even a bureaucracy with genuine neutral competence as its outstanding characteristic may thus have little attraction for a White House committed to making dramatic breakthroughs in policy.[7]

The problem with this response is that presidents do not enter the field of health and safety regulation with blank slates upon which they may write freely. Instead, each agency has elaborate mandates, generally developed by Congress in two phases—an authorization in the early 1970s and, especially in the environmental arena, a subsequent reauthorization that toughened and expanded the law. These statutory mandates place a premium on highly demanding technical and scientific judgments and continuity of policy making.

While civil service laws broke the back of patronage and the spoils system, relapses have occurred, sometimes to the great disadvantage of the public. One glaring example was the appointment of Michael Brown, the former head of a trade association representing breeders of Arabian horses, to run the Federal Emergency Management Administration. His and his agency's grotesque incompetence during Hurricane Katrina is among the most prominent examples of catastrophic failure of government in the nation's history. When the reversion to patronage is this stark, it is easy to combat, although the people who paid the price for this inexplicably stupid mistake were far removed from the core of government. For the most part, however, the professional credentials of the 3,000 political appointees deployed to the front lines of agencies have steadily improved as a twenty-four-hour news cycle gives presidents a vested interest in the competence of agencies in both crises and routine operations.

Ensuring that political appointees have the right substantive credentials is a crucial first step, but presidents must expect much more if they want effective leadership from what political scientist High Heclo has dubbed the "in-and-outers":

> In contrast to the results produced by a patronage operation, the in-and-outers are a technocratic group called upon to fill jobs that are far from routine. They are asked to play challenging roles as policy managers and administrative leaders. Their previous involvement in policy matters is often substantial, but their attachments to government or politics as organizational enterprises are always transient.[8]

Heclo further notes that the periodic entry of senior-level outsiders can bring fresh ideas, political accountability, and a healthy, skeptical perspective to the bureaucracy, preventing it from becoming entrenched. On the other hand, appointees who have little experience in management and scant respect for the civil service can demean and ignore their professional advice advice, repeating historical mistakes and making serious errors in judgment in both framing and choosing policy options. In the end, Heclo concludes, and we agree, that a balanced and respectful relationship between appointees and civil servants within an agency, which is given substantial deference by the White House staff, is the best chance of stabilizing and improving government.

One solution is to appoint from within, promoting senior career staff to serve as high-ranking political appointees. Presidents are historically reluctant to make this choice, even at agencies like the five we profile here, where professional credentials and substantive background are indispensable. They have been more willing to recruit from the ranks of both elected and appointed state and local officials, a viable alternative that can provide candidates with both technical and managerial expertise.

## A Day in the Life

How can we distinguish between macro regulatory decisions most appropriately made by politicians and their high-level appointees, with technical advice from careerists, and micro decisions that should—and arguably must—be left to the civil service, under the general guidance of in-house political appointees? Once again, as we have done throughout this book, we return to practical examples that illustrate what we mean more effectively than theoretical statements.

### CPSC

NEUTRAL COMPETENCE AND DANGEROUS TOYS.    The Consumer Product Safety Act instructs the CPSC to determine the risk of injury that could be caused by a consumer product, considering the results of research, development, testing, and investigation conducted by the manufacturer and the CPSC's professional staff. Before issuing a rule, the staff must state the number and types of consumer products it would cover, consider how the CPSC might reduce adverse effects on competition in writing the rule, describe the potential costs and benefits of the rule, and explain what alternatives to the final rule were considered by the agency.[9] Beginning in 1973, the CPSC has developed through numerous rulemakings a section of the *Code of Federal Regulations* entitled "Banned Toys and Other Banned Articles Intended for Use by Children."[10] Here are selected excerpts:

> (a) . . . [T]he Commission has determined that the following types of toys or other articles intended for use by children present a mechanical hazard . . . because in normal use, or when subjected to reasonably foreseeable damage

or abuse, the design or manufacture presents an unreasonable risk of personal injury or illness.

. . .

(5) Caps (paper or plastic) intended for use with toy guns and toy guns not intended for use with caps if such caps when so used or such toy guns produce impulse-type sound at a peak pressure level at or above 138 decibels, referred to 0.0002 dyne per square centimeter, when measured in an anechoic chamber at a distance of 25 centimeters (or the distance at which the sound source ordinarily would be from the ear of the child using it if such distance is less than 25 centimeters) in any direction from the source of the sound.

(6) Any article known as a "baby-bouncer," "walker-jumper," or "baby-walker" and any other similar article. . . . [T]he design features of such articles which classify the articles as banned hazardous substances are:

(i) The areas about the point on each side of the article where the frame components are joined together to form an "X" shape capable of producing a scissoring, shearing, or pinching effect.

. . .

(iii) Exposed coil springs which may expand sufficiently to allow an infant's finger, toe, or any other part of the anatomy to be inserted, in whole or in part, and injured by being caught between the coils of the spring or between the spring and another part of the article.[11]

To develop these standards, CPSC experts conducted a survey of children's products available throughout the country, tested them to discover defects, developed technical specifications like those quote above, proposed the language of a ban, put that language out for public comment through publication in the *Federal Register*, reviewed all the comments they received including lengthy technical analysis from the products' manufacturers, wrote a rulemaking notice summarizing and responding to those views, and issued the technical rule in final form. We have little doubt that if they were given a choice, the American people would prefer for career specialists to write such rules, as opposed to Congress or the White House staff.

POLITICAL INTERVENTION AND DANGEROUS TOYS.    Without radical changes in policies and funding, imported consumer goods and food present insurmountable challenges to the CPSC and the FDA. The value of Chinese imports in the United States marketplace is estimated to be approximately $246 billion, about 40 percent of the value of total products that the nation imports and about 20 percent of consumer products sold in the country.

Over the last decade, these imports quadrupled, from $62 to $246 billion annually. In 2007, dubbed the "year of the recall" by consumer groups, millions of toys made in China were pulled off shelves because they were coated with lead paint or designed in an unsafe manner. At the time, the CPSC had fifteen inspectors nationwide to police these and billions of dollars' worth of other products, although President Obama has proposed a $7 million increase in its $100 million budget for 2010.

Despite this increase, Congress must give the CPSC significantly expanded resources if it expects the agency to inspect its way out of this growing threat, requiring the addition of hundreds—maybe thousands—of inspectors to the agency's ranks and costing hundreds of millions of dollars. Diplomacy is also unlikely to bear fruit any time soon. Chinese manufacturing operates in a close to lawless environment.[12] Even if the Chinese central government wanted to implement a comprehensive regulatory system, it would take several years to get one up and running, especially given the global economic downturn, the decentralization of Chinese manufacturing, and the likely resistance of local and regional governments in that vast country.

One option that deserves full consideration by the president and Congress is to exert pressure on American companies that import consumer goods to use their considerable economic leverage to compel foreign suppliers to address these problems at the point of origin. Investigative reporting provides some pressure. Faster and more effective reform could be accomplished by enactment of a comprehensive law imposing stringent legal liability on high-ranking corporate officers if companies do not establish their own routine inspection programs on the floors of all their suppliers' factories.[13] The CPSC does not have the legal authority to make such a major policy decision and would appropriately need the full support of the president and majorities in Congress.

NEUTRAL COMPETENCE AND WORKPLACE TOXICS.    Beryllium is a highly toxic metal, lighter than aluminum but stronger than steel.[14] It is used in weapons production and for a variety of other purposes, including the manufacture of alloys used to fill cavities in teeth. At some point in every production process using beryllium, including dentistry, the metal is ground into fine particles, which workers can then inhale. The metal is so poisonous that within days, workers exposed to extremely small amounts of such particles develop a form of chemical pneumonitis, with symptoms including labored breathing, coughing, and chest pains. When beryllium was used in the early 1940s to produce fluorescent lamps, 30 percent of workers contracting this illness died. In the half century since, ample medical evidence documents these hazards and shows that beryllium also causes cancer at even lower doses.

The OSHA standard for beryllium was set in 1949 at two micrograms per cubic meter of air. A microgram is 1/100,000 of a gram, one of the smallest units of weight/mass commonly used. Despite what seems to be an unimaginably low level, this standard has been battered into disrepute by subsequent science and is now widely viewed as inadequate to protect public health. In 1999, the Department of Energy (DOE) lowered this standard to 0.2 micrograms per cubic meter of air, a tenfold reduction from the OSHA standard. But because of expensive and highly effective lobbying by beryllium's leading manufacturer, Brush Wellman, the OSHA standard was never changed. This intolerable result—protecting one set of workers subject to DOE regulation to such a significantly greater extent than workers subject to OSHA regulation—remains a glaring embarrassment for the government.

To make the determination that the standard should be lowered, DOE experts examined animal studies that experimented with the results of various levels of beryllium exposure, epidemiological studies on human populations, medical observations from doctors who had treated afflicted workers, and reports on the industrial practices used to process the metal. They also considered a barrage of conflicting evidence provided by manufacturers and users of the metal, including the Department of Defense and its contractors. All of this information was developed over a half century of study, conducted in response to the first manifestations of beryllium poisoning.

In 2001, thirty-year OSHA veteran epidemiologist Peter Infante wrote a special bulletin warning dental technicians that they could be exposed to beryllium when grinding fillings.[15] Political appointees at the agency immediately turned his draft over to a public relations firm hired by Brush Wellman. The company's scientists marked up the draft, and Infante incorporated what he considered to be reasonable changes. The revised version was returned to the company for another review, and it continued to raise objections. Infante refused to make further changes but was overruled by OSHA's political leadership; the bulletin was eventually issued with a footnote challenging a recommendation that the firm opposed:

> A single report to the literature by Brush Wellman, Inc. researchers . . . concludes that the [Beryllium Lymphocyte Proliferation Test] BeLPT does not

meet the criteria for a screening test, but is useful for a disease surveillance tool. In this report, 46% surveillance-identified workers with sensitization had [chronic beryllium disease] CBD at initial clinical assessment. In other studies, 49–100% of surveillance-identified sensitized workers had CBD at initial clinical assessment for the disease.[16]

For readers puzzled by the significance of this dense prose, allow us to translate. Brush Wellman wants to note for the record that if dental health workers are afraid that they have been exposed to beryllium and want to determine whether they are at risk for adverse health effects, their doctors should not use the blood test recommended by the OSHA staff. Or, perhaps more accurately, if doctors use this test in accordance with the OSHA recommendation, and workers subsequently try to sue the company for damages, Brush Wellman will object to the test's validity.

We have little doubt that if the American people were given a choice, they would rather have Peter Infante write the bulletin without interference from the company that makes the metal. And once again, as tempting as it is to chalk this episode up to the proindustry bias of the Bush II administration, remember that in 1999, when the DOE lowered its standard and OSHA refused to follow suit, President Clinton was in office.

POLITICAL INTERVENTION AND WORKPLACE TOXICS.   The penalties available under the Occupational Safety and Health Act against companies who violate the law with impunity are so low that they do not provide any deterrent to corner cutting that saves compliance costs but injures workers, especially because amounts employees can recover for such injuries are sharply curtailed by the workers' compensation system. The penalty for a "serious" violation—defined as circumstances in which there is a "*substantial probability*" that death or serious physical harm could result" is $7,000 per incident.[17] Penalties for willful violations, involving situations in which an employer evinces plain indifference to the law, are capped at $70,000 per incident, even when a worker dies.[18] Compounding the gross inadequacy of these provisions, the statute does not give OSHA any authority to recoup the profits earned as a result of the lawlessness—the avoided costs of forcing workers to operate without safety equipment, for example.

Adding insult to injury, OSHA is notorious for an unbroken history of permissive enforcement.[19] The average penalty for enforcement cases involving fatalities in FY 2007 averaged just $10,133 for federal and state plans combined. Between 1982 and 2002, OSHA investigated 1,242 cases in which it concluded that worker deaths were caused by willful safety violations, but it declined to seek prosecution in 93 percent of those cases. In addition to a lack of political will, these failures are caused by acute shortfalls in funding for enforcement. Together, OSHA and its state partners rarely field more than 2,000 inspectors. The agency generally averages about 40,000 inspections annually, employing a variety of tactics to pick the worst industries, worst workplaces, and emerging hazards. At that rate, it would take 212 years for OSHA inspectors to visit all the workplaces that were under its jurisdiction in 2006. President Obama asked Congress for FY 2010 funding to support an additional 160 inspectors, an important step in the right direction but not yet enough to make the agency's enforcement program credible. Real reform will require more extensive action by Congress.

NEUTRAL COMPETENCE AND COMMON AIR POLLUTANTS.   The heart of the Clean Air Act is a provision requiring the EPA to set national ambient air quality standards (NAAQS) for seven "criteria pollutants," one of which is ground-level ozone, commonly referred to as smog.[20] Criteria pollutants are the most plentiful, ubiquitous, and harmful air pollutants in the country. In addition to ozone, they include particulate matter, carbon monoxide, sulfur oxides, nitrogen oxides, and lead. Ozone is formed when nitrogen oxides combine with volatile organic compounds in the presence of sunlight. Excessive amounts of ozone are quite harmful to people and animals, exacerbating respiratory diseases like asthma. Ozone pollution is also harmful to crops, forests, and other vegetation, which can die or have their growth severely stunted. Consequently, the act instructs the agency to set a "primary" standard to protect people and a "secondary" standard to protect natural resources.[21] The statute requires that limits be set without regard to cost, at whatever level is sufficient to protect health and the environment with an "ample" margin of safety.[22] The Supreme Court has interpreted this language to mean that the EPA can only consider adverse effects and not the costs of reducing ozone, an outcome fiercely opposed by industry groups.[23]

The act requires that the agency review the standards every five years, revising them downward if scientific evidence indicates they are not sufficiently protective. The EPA set the first standards for ozone in 1971. It has revised the primary and secondary ozone NAAQS several times over the last four decades but has often been late with these reviews. Before the episode at the center of our story,[24] the EPA had last revised the ozone standards in 1997. In 2003, the American Lung Association sued the EPA over the delay, and the agency agreed to a court order stipulating that it would promulgate revised standards no later than March 12, 2008. In the intervening decade (1997–2007), 1,700 additional scientific studies of ozone and its effects on public health had become available.

The agency's revisions were based on an elaborate process that took several years and involved the preparation by staff scientists of lengthy documents that assessed and summarized the state of the relevant research. Those documents were then reviewed by the Clean Air Science Advisory Committee (CASAC), a panel of outside scientists established by the Clean Air Act.[25] The CASAC met with EPA staff seven times in extended public sessions to discuss the science and in the end recommended unanimously, in itself an unusual outcome, that the EPA revise both the primary and the secondary standards to even lower levels than those selected by Stephen Johnson, the EPA administrator. The proposed new standards were published for comments, the EPA staff reviewed all the comments, and a final notice was prepared. Johnson sent it over to the White House, expecting it to be approved in time for a press conference he had scheduled for March 12, 2008.

On March 6, 2008, Susan Dudley, the director of the OMB's OIRA, wrote Johnson a memorandum explaining that she disagreed with the secondary NAAQS issued by the EPA and planned to appeal the issue to the president. The secondary standard was set on the basis of what cumulative ozone levels would be during the growing season for crops, a new approach ratified by the EPA's science advisors, to replace the old standard, which measured ozone over an eight-hour period. Dudley argued that the EPA should have considered economic values in setting the standard. Johnson's deputy administrator, Marcus Peacock, responded on behalf of the agency that cost was not a legally permissible criterion under the act. President Bush ultimately sided with Dudley, and the secondary standard was revised to be the same as the primary standard. Administrator Johnson announced the decision, defending it as a loyal soldier representing his president. But Dr. Rogene Henderson, chair of the CASAC and a leading national expert on air pollution, subsequently told Congress that as a result of the OMB's interference, "Willful ignorance triumphed over sound science."[26]

POLITICAL INTERVENTION AND COMMON AIR POLLUTANTS. The day that he announced the new ozone standards, which included the revisions demanded by the White House, Administrator Johnson also called upon Congress to amend the Clean Air Act to allow, among other things, the consideration of costs in setting NAAQS.[27] Declaring that the act "is not a relic to be displayed in the Smithsonian," Johnson announced four principles to guide Congress, including changes that "should allow decision-makers to consider benefits, *costs*, risk tradeoffs, and feasibility in making decisions about how to clean the air."[28] Although we believe that Johnson should have resigned in response to the OMB's extralegal interference, he was clearly fulfilling his responsibilities as EPA's top political appointee when he explained how he thought the law should be changed. This approach is exactly what we mean by macro regulatory decision making that falls within the realm of Congress, the president, and senior political appointees. Making a decision to issue the cost-based standard that OMB economists had demanded as if the law had already been changed, however, is an example of undermining the neutral competence that the public has a right to expect from the bureaucracy.

## The National Commission on the Public Service Report

The 2003 National Commission on the Public Service was convened by the Brookings Institute, funded by private foundations, housed at the National Academy of Public Administration, and led by former Federal Reserve Board chairman Paul A. Volcker. Members included former Comptroller General Charles Bowsher; former Senator Bill Bradley (D-NJ); former Secretary of Defense Frank Carlucci; former Reagan administration Chief of Staff Kenneth Duberstein; former Director of Presidential Personnel Constance Horner; former OMB Director Franklin Raines; Co-Chair of the Millennial Housing Commission Richard Ravitch; former Secretary of the Treasury Robert Rubin; former Secretary of Health and Human Services Donna Shalala; and former Representative Vin Weber (R-MN). The report is notable for its strong tone of alarm and foreboding:

> Trust in government—strong after World War II, with the United States assuming international leadership and meeting domestic challenges—has eroded. Government's responsiveness, its efficiency, and too often its honesty are broadly challenged as we enter a new century. The bonds between our citizens and our public servants, essential to democratic government, are frayed even as the responsibilities of government at home and abroad have increased. Gov-

ernment work ought to be a respected source of pride. All too frequently it is not.[29]

The notion of public service, once a noble calling proudly pursued by the most talented Americans of every generation, draws an indifferent response from today's young people and repels many of the country's leading private citizens. Those with policy responsibility find their decisionmaking frustrated by overlapping jurisdictions, competing special interests, and sluggish administrative response. Those who enter the civil service often find themselves trapped in a maze of rules and regulations that thwart their personal development and stifle their creativity. The best are underpaid; the worst, overpaid. Too many of the most talented leave the public service too early; too many of the least talented stay too long.

. . .

There are too many decisionmakers, too much central clearance, too many bases to touch, and too many overseers with conflicting agendas. Leadership responsibilities often fall into the awkward gap between inexperienced political appointees and unsupported career managers. Accountability is hard to discern and harder still to enforce. Policy change has become so difficult that federal employees themselves often come to share the cynicism about government that afflicts many of our citizens.[30]

The commission recommended "radical change" in the form of a massive reorganization of the entire government.[31] Its members were experienced enough to acknowledge that reorganization would require such difficult political negotiations and so much disruption of crucial, ongoing work that it might take a national emergency to bring it about. They undoubtedly had on their minds the creation of the Department of Homeland Security the previous year, in response to the terrorist attacks on September 11, 2001. They could not have known how profoundly the new department would fail its first test when Hurricane Katrina hit the Louisiana and Mississippi coasts.

A primary reason for the commission's emphasis on reorganization was its concern about duplicative and overlapping federal programs, laid out in painstaking detail in its report. We acknowledge this problem and have respect for these concerns, although we are puzzled by the methodology used to quantify duplication. One chart entitled "Shared Federal Responsibility for Environmental Protection," for example, decries the overlapping efforts of the Tennessee Valley Authority and the National Academy of Sciences without acknowledging that the first entity generates pollution and so needs programs to ensure its compliance with federal environmental laws, while the second entity fields high-level scientific panels to evaluate the pollution-control challenges confronted by the public and private sectors.

We find it difficult to imagine that any president in the foreseeable future would feel that he or she had the breathing space to reorganize the entire government. Admittedly, we write these words during the worst economic recession since the Great Depression and when the country is engaged in two wars. Things could, and hopefully will, get better. We also acknowledge that we are not public management experts and may not have a full appreciation for how much duplication damages the government. On the other hand, we are certain that of all the problems experienced by our five protector agencies, overlapping jurisdiction is not among the most prominent or the most acute. For all these reasons, we will not pursue these recommendations here. Instead, we focus on the Commission's recommendations regarding morale, pay, and turnover because these issues are central to the chronic failures of our five agencies and represent a compelling agenda for the immediate future.

*Brain Drain*

According to the nonprofit Partnership for Public Service and several news accounts, by 2012, the federal government will lose nearly 530,000 employees, largely because it has a workforce aging far faster than that of the private sector—58 percent of federal workers are over 45, compared with 41 percent in the private sector.[32] The implications of this "brain drain" are compounded by the fact that downsizing throughout the 1990s reduced the size of the federal workforce by 400,000 jobs, leaving many crucial positions unfilled. The attrition will cripple the government at the highest levels—the partnership projects that 36 percent of SES employees will retire by 2012 but that because 76 percent will be eligible to retire, the vacancy rate could be significantly higher. Similarly, 27 percent of supervisors who direct daily work throughout the government are expected to retire by 2012. While most of these retirements are motivated by length of service, morale problems are also acute:

> Far too many talented public servants are abandoning the middle levels of government, and too many of the best recruits are rethinking their commitment, either because they are fed up with the constraints of outmoded personnel sys-

tems and unmet expectations for advancement or simply lured away by the substantial difference between public and private sector salaries in many areas. Some employees leave federal service because they can no longer tolerate the dismal facilities and working conditions in many agencies.[33]

One likely result of this brain drain will be dramatic increases in contracts to private companies that do work that an underfunded government cannot accomplish. The partnership notes that by some estimates, as many as seven million people work for private contractors doing government work, or close to four times the size of the federal civilian workforce. Enlarging privatization will drastically increase the expense of getting the job done from the taxpayer's perspective, both because competent federal contract officials who monitor private sector performance and billing will be in short supply and because, in their absence, contractor costs are likely to escalate. A private sector employee who lacks a long-term stake in how a policy plays out for an agency is likely to make expedient decisions that reflect immediate pressures from lobbyists representing narrow interests in the debate. To our regret, the implications of privatization are beyond the scope of this volume, although the subject is vital and we hope to return to it soon.

As disruptive as this mass exodus from government is likely to prove, the difficulties that government will experience in recruiting whatever replacements are needed after private contractors push their way into the fray has the potential to prolong the civil service's recovery for many years. The commission observed, "The entry-level situation is equally dismaying. Rarely in recent history has there been a time when public service was so far from the minds of America's young people."[34] In our experience, a fundamental change in attitudes toward government must occur before these trends can be arrested.

In the 1970s, an entire generation of baby boomer lawyers, scientists, and newly minted political science and public management graduates, including the two of us, migrated to Washington, D.C., to become part of an idealistic revival of public service not seen since the New Deal. We knew, of course, that the battle for the future of government was by no means resolved—Reagan's election on a platform based on bureaucracy bashing made that dilemma painfully apparent. But we sincerely believed that we had a better chance to accomplish great things on behalf of the public interest inside the government than out. Based on our cumulative experience teaching young people about government, we see little sign that

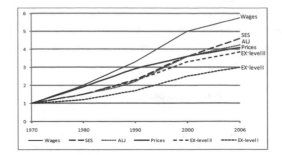

FIGURE 9.1. Trends in executive and judicial pay. *Source*: U.S. GAO.

these attitudes exist among today's college and professional school graduates. Recruitment and retention are systematically undermined by three
related problems: (1) disparities in pay, especially for professionals trained
in highly desirable categories such as pharmacology, toxicology, law, and
engineering; (2) the agencies' poor image in news accounts, exacerbated
over the last eight years by the frequent controversies we have described
throughout this volume; and (3) the perception that decision making has
become sufficiently politicized that the agencies' inspiring missions are
secondary to those considerations.

*Pay Disparities*

Gross disparities between private sector and public sector pay at the highest levels of management are illustrated in figure 9.1 from a 2006 GAO
report entitled *Human Capital: Trends in Executive and Judicial Pay Suggest a Reexamination of the Total Compensation Package*:[35]

The GAO report urged Congress to consider the total compensation
offered to employees, including basic pay, locality pay (jobs in certain
metropolitan areas pay more to account for higher costs of living), cash
awards and bonuses, and noncash benefits such as annual and sick leave,
health insurance, and life insurance.

In a comparable vein, a 2008 report from the Partnership for Public
Service urged the next president to make the restoration of the federal
workforce's prestige the centerpiece of his administration's reform efforts.
The partnership noted that the country's compensation system is nearly
sixty years old and is "inflexible, antiquated and lacks market sensitivity."[36]
The system is "widely criticized for providing too little latitude to recruit
top talent and reward exceptional workers, while also making it difficult
to discipline poor performers. Longevity is the primary determinant of

worker's pay increases, denying federal managers a potentially valuable tool for attracting new workers and motivating existing ones."[37]

The partnership said that the outmoded system for recruitment is incapable of correcting the public's vague understanding of federal job opportunities and has not effectively combated the negative impressions that are the heritage of a steady drumbeat of criticism of the bureaucracy by politicians over four decades. To replace the retiring baby boomer generation, the partnership recommended that the government appeal to midlevel and middle-aged managers from the private sector.

## Thickening

"Thickening" has become a term of art in the public management literature and refers to the multiple layers of review interposed between frontline civil servants and the people who ultimately are charged with making a final decision. Coined by prominent political scientist Paul Light, the term is defined as adding more layers of management and expanding the number of people within each layer. In a 1995 book, *Thickening Government, Federal Hierarchy and the Diffusion of Accountability*, Light traces the historical development of thickening and explains why it is stifling the effectiveness—and not just the efficiency—of government.[38] The primary impetus for the addition of so many management layers are presidential efforts to control the bureaucracy, both through centralization of decision making in the White House and through the deployment of political appointees deep into the ranks of the agencies. Another source of thickening is the instincts of the civil service itself, which has organized its own structures for supervision.

Light notes that thickening is expensive. Under an estimate developed during the National Performance Review conducted under the leadership of then Vice President Al Gore, as much as $35 billion annually could be saved by reducing the ranks of the 700,000 federal employees whose job it is to manage, control, or audit others.[39] But Light emphasizes other effects of excessive management, including and especially the diffusion of responsibility. Because line employees have little confidence that their proposals will survive scrutiny, they are less committed to getting it right the first time.

With decisions that involve enormously complex analyses of ambiguous scientific and technical information, the prospect that years of work will be derailed by unanticipated problems with the White House is profoundly discouraging. Consider, for example, the experience of career EPA staff who worked on the ozone NAAQS matter we described earlier. Staff had worked for a decade to prepare this final rule, had the unanimous support of the agency's statutorily mandated panel of science advisers, and expected little trouble when they forwarded their final decision to the White House. In a rare glimpse behind the opacity that typically shrouds such decisions, Representative Henry Waxman (D-CA), chair of the House of Representatives Oversight and Government Reform Committee, obtained a series of e-mails that EPA staff exchanged among themselves on March 11 and 12, 2008, as the OMB elevated the dispute.[40]

> From John Vandenberg to Linda Tuxen: EPA was moving to have a new form of the secondary standard (SUM06, an important change); OMB last Friday said "no." I hear final decision came down last night seeing the wisdom of OMB on this point, so secondary standard will be equal to the primary. To hell with the trees . . .
>
> From Jenny Noonan to Jeffrey Clark: Bad day for EPA. Primary has held but we lost the 2ndary.
>
> From Karen Martin to Susan Stone: we talked about how we could restructure the secondary standard section of the preamble—I'm going to do some cutting and pasting from the proposal to create a new version tonight—John's going to go through the RTC to see what we can keep, what needs to be dropped, and what can survive with minor edits. I talked with Vicki—she'll follow up on changes to the RTC in the morning. So, try to relax tonight—I know how incredibly frustrated and disgusted we all are at the moment. Times like this, I really, really appreciate what a wonderful group of people you are to work with. See you in the morning.
>
> From Erika Sasser to Sara Terry: Hi—[the draft powerpoint] looks good, just a few suggested changes, on slide 11 (in blue)—especially I don't think that we need to repeat all this . . . um . . . stuff. . . . about "parks and forests" when we're not doing anything to protect them. Just say that we're tightening the secondary, but keeping same form, and this will have the effect of providing some additional protection to sensitive vegetation, and leave it at that. No need to distinguish which types of vegetation are in need of additional protection, since we're not really protecting any of them properly!
>
> From Lewis Weinstock to Dave McKee: Thanks. My sympathies to all and you in particular for all the work that went down the drain.
>
> From Chris Trent to Dave McKee: My favorite excerpt from the AP article I saw on Yahoo: The science boards had told the agency that limits of 60 to 70 parts per billion are needed to protect the nation's most vulnerable citizens, especially children, the elderly and people suffering from asthma and other re-

spiratory illnesses. Johnson said he took those recommendations into account, but disagreed with the scientists. "In the end it is a judgment. I followed my obligation. I followed the law. I adhered to the science," said Johnson in a conference call with reporters.

From Dave McKee to Chris Trent: I guess that means that he doesn't have to pay attention to the scientists, who were overly worried about vulnerable citizens.

From Lea Anderson to MaryAnn Poirier: One additional thought did occur to me today in discussing with my client what we would do if we were to change the rule at this late date to set a secondary standard equal to the primary. In short, we would have a hard time doing anything other than putting out an obviously legally deficient notice given the time frames. You may have already thought of this, but it occurred to me that we could be in the position of having to fend off contempt proceedings for that sort of action. The obligation to promulgate a rule arguably means to promulgate one that is nominally defensible, i.e., that meaningfully responds to at least most significant comments and has a clear explanation of the basis for the decision.

To translate the last entry for readers who may not be familiar with legal jargon: the author of the e-mail is in the EPA General Counsel's Office and serves as the agency's in-house counsel for this particular rulemaking. Obviously shaken by the last-minute reversal, which required EPA staff to hurriedly revise thick documents that they needed to issue the next day to meet a court-ordered deadline, she shares her concern that in the event of a court challenge to the decision, the documents will look sufficiently arbitrary and half-baked that the agency will risk a contempt finding by the court—a harsh form of censure reserved for the worst cases of inappropriate conduct.

## Revival

### Obama's Mission

We do not underestimate the Obama administration's potential to bring change in the way that government service is perceived among young people. For the first time, the presidency will be occupied by a post–baby boomer, African American who won his office by making extensive use of the latest technology and turning out a record number of first-time voters. If Obama avoids the pitfalls of bureaucracy bashing, and he has given little sign of falling prey to that occupational hazard, we can hope that his relative youth, energy, broad definition of government's mission, and determination to be a president who pivots the fortunes of the country will combine to change the atmosphere and therefore the appeal of government employment.

His early effort to explain the role of government as doing "that which we cannot do for ourselves—protect us from harm; provide a decent education for all children—invest in new roads and new bridges, in new science and technology"[41] is a very good sign, as are his declarations that "we don't need bigger government or smaller government, we need smarter government, we need better government, we need more competent government. We need more honest government, a government that fights for you and that fights for the values we hold in common as Americans."[42] To have a lasting impact, however, the Obama administration's commitment to change must have concrete expression in the areas of diminishing centralization, reversing trends toward the distortion and suppression of scientific research, and shrinking the gap between private and public sector pay.

### Diminishing Centralization

The Commission on Public Service urged Congress and the president to "work together to significantly reduce the number of executive branch political positions."[43] Not only does the multiplication thicken government, but the culture has increasingly become one of sending watchers to watch appointees who are supposed to watch careerists:

> Political appointees may enter their jobs with too little trust in the competence and loyalty of career executives. Newly selected department and agency heads are often unable to keep control their own subordinate appointments due to pressure from the White House, special interest groups, or determined members of Congress. Thus these department and agency heads are forced to lead disparate teams of strangers, some of whom owe little loyalty to the senior leadership. Talented and experienced senior career managers find themselves forced further and further away from the centers of decisionmaking, even as they create new management layers to compensate for pay freezes and the lack of opportunity for advancement created by an aging workforce.[44]

We strongly endorse these recommendations and would offer two additional reforms that could make a world of difference in preventing unwarranted politicization at the five protector agencies. We hope that despite his extensive reliance on former officials from the Clinton administration to organize his transition and make up his highest level appointments, President Obama will reconsider the Clinton legacy of expanding the White House staff and giving so many "councils" within the White House wide-ranging portfolios to interject themselves in the business of the five protector agencies. One indispensable place to start would be to terminate the practice of giving the OMB the opportunity to review individual rules. Instead, its role should be to communicate broad policies, especially those having to do with regulatory impact analysis, to agencies and departments throughout the government.

We expect regulated industries and their allies in the White House to protest this approach, arguing that the White House cannot afford to lose control over regulatory decisions that could cost a weakened economy a fortune. We understand this concern, and we do not expect the importuning of White House officials over specific rules to cease miraculously once the OMB is read out of those appeals officially. What we hope to accomplish by this admittedly sharp departure from past practice is for presidents to learn to rely—and for agency heads to internalize the responsibilities implied by that reliance—on the experienced professionals they have deployed to the front lines of the agencies for the final advice they receive on the merits of a rule, rather than anonymous, lower ranked, and professionally limited economists at the OMB.

Another important reform is to overturn the existing practice of keeping agency recommendations secret until they have undergone White House review. All of the EPA staff electronic messages we quoted earlier were printed on paper bearing the legend "Internal Deliberative Document of the U.S. Environmental Protection Agency, Disclosure Authorized Only to Congress for Oversight Purposes." The EPA turned some of the documents over to the Congress; the White House refused to release the rest, asserting executive privilege.[45]

The Freedom of Information Act (FOIA) exempts from disclosure "inter-agency memorandums . . . which would not be available by law to a party other than an agency in litigation with the agency. . . ."[46] The legislative history of the statute makes it clear that the exemption was intended to incorporate the government's privilege to resist "discovery" when it is involved in litigation with private parties.[47] (Discovery means requests that opposing counsel turn over documents that shed light on the merits of litigation.) The Supreme Court has held that this privilege includes "executive privilege" material, or predecisional documents.[48] The reason for the privilege is to protect open and frank advice and recommendations from government employees to their superiors. Under the FOIA exemption, scientific advice and reports from agency staff to agency officials are generally not available to the public because they fall within the ambit of predecisional documents.[49]

Allowing agency staff to freely exchange ideas in writing during the formulation of a rule has important advantages, and we do not seek to disrupt this process. However, we urge the Obama administration and Congress to consider one important exception to the presumption that predecisional documents can be kept secret by either agency staff or the White House. This exception would be triggered by a scientific recommendation that marks a clear watershed in the deliberative process. So, for example, existing law already requires that the staff memorandum submitted to the CASAC for review, and the CASAC's response to those documents, be disclosed on the World Wide Web. This practice is appropriate given the high profile of such consultations. It should be extended to all decisions involving a specific piece of scientific advice exchanged intra- or interagency. Disclosure should deter the most blatant examples of mischaracterizing science-based policy recommendations for bad political reasons.

## Pay Scales and Management Structures

The Commission on Public Service was preoccupied with salary disparities at the highest levels of government, noting that cabinet secretary salaries declined 44 percent in constant dollars between 1969 and 2001. It also noted that "recent research suggests that pay disparities at the middle and lower levels of the federal workforce may be less significant than previously believed" but does not identify which studies it consulted.[50] Finally, it acknowledged that the "relevant markets" for comparison of federal and private sector pay are not profitable corporations but rather the "independent sector," which it defined as "universities, think tanks, and nonprofits. . . ."[51] The commission recommended with customary urgency that these pay disparities at the highest level of government be addressed, suggesting that the government allow each agency to develop its own system for personnel management and compensation, within broad guidelines that would establish a "broad-band system" for compensation "under which the 15 pay grades and salary ranges would be consolidated into six to eight broad bands with relatively wide salary ranges" within each.[52]

We agree with the commission's sense of urgency on these issues, although we disagree with its apparent view that salaries at the top levels of the civil service are the primary ones deserving attention. In the context of the five protector agencies, the markets for comparison are all the companies that have business with them: drug companies seeking new drug approvals or negotiating new warning labels on existing drugs to take into account emerging research on adverse health effects; toxicologists who understand how to write—and dispute—chemical profiles that determine how stringently a product or waste will be regulated; or experts in fuel efficiency standards who can advise companies how to meet their fleet-wide averages under the rules they helped write while in the government. Viewed from that perspective and based on anecdotal observation, we are confident that midlevel government pay lags far behind what the best and the brightest can earn if they step through the revolving door into the private sector.

The management flexibility recommended by the commission is equally, if not more, important. Each of the five agencies is unique in comparison with the largest portions of the bureaucracy that administer either benefits or tax collection programs. The Commission on Public Service recommendations for the reorganization of the civil service urge that government be divided into six or seven large departments grouped by mission. We could envision all five agencies being reassigned in this way, removed from their "mother" departments—OSHA from the Department of Labor, NHTSA from the Department of Transportation, and the FDA from the Department of Health and Human Services—and recombined into a single health and safety department. Even without such drastic changes, however, we think the five have enough in common to justify allowing them to develop their own specially designed personnel system.

In addition to pay disparities, we recommend that such reforms consider the wisdom of a final commission recommendation: the division of the SES into "an Executive Management Corps" and a "Professional and Technical Corps":

> Unfortunately, the Senior Executive Service (SES), created in 1978, has never developed into the hoped-for corps of experienced managers that would move across agencies, deploying their skills and bringing the benefit of their experience to a broad array of management venues. Because the SES is the main route for senior employee advancement, many members of the SES are not managers at all but scientists, other professionals, and technical specialists. Few SES managers have ever worked, or applied to work, outside of the agency in which they

are currently employed. The original design also included a rewards and incentive system where compensation for senior managers would be closely tied to performance. Those who performed at the highest levels would get bonuses and merit awards equal to a substantial portion of their annual pay. But Congress has often failed to appropriate the funds necessary to fuel that reward system. . . . Although there are six levels on their pay scale, 70 percent of all SES members now earn the same compensation. So much for performance incentives. We believe that dividing the Senior Executive Service into a corps of professional and technical specialists and another of highly talented executives and managers can address these problems.[53]

In our experience, the funneling of superior expert and exemplary management employees through the same system for promotions and pay raises causes substantial confusion and does not adequately reward either group's expertise. The need for senior scientists who are seasoned enough to lead complex regulatory deliberations and senior managers who can inspire line employees to enforce the law effectively is acute enough that making such individuals compete against each other for a small number of ostensibly fungible executive positions makes little sense.

## Conclusion

No challenge is more important at this juncture in the nation's history than redefining our shared understanding of the federal government's affirmative role and responsibilities so that people can be clearer about government's failures and its success. The 2008 election definitively rejected the reactionary argument that has done so much damage to health and safety protections over the past two decades: namely, that government needs to get out of the way of free market capitalism in order to allow an incoming tide of prosperity to lift people up. Instead, the election gave the new president a mandate for restoring government as the arbiter, moderator, and regulator of the ways in which industrialization can impinge on the public good.

Some might argue that the election was nothing less—and certainly nothing more—than a reaction to a bad economy. As soon as the downturn is finished, "small" government will get back to its modest business as usual. Only time will tell which interpretation is correct. As we explained at the outset, however, our purpose is to chart a new path for government,

assuming the nation's political leaders have the determination to implement and enforce the powerful statutory mandates that have never been
repealed.

Disparagement of the civil service's competence and integrity has not
led Congress to exert self-control with respect to the tasks assigned to the
five agencies, not has this rhetoric translated into the elimination of regulatory regimes. No single set of reforms is more important to that outcome
than reviving the morale, strength, and youth of the professional civil service. Without its help, the people's interests, as expressed in elections large
and small, cannot be satisfied.

## CHAPTER TEN

# The Road Forward

## Introduction

The completion of this book during the summer of 2009 occurred at the end of a very damaging decade for the protection of health, safety, and the environment, in the midst of an unprecedented and so far unrelenting global recession, and following six months of President Barack Obama's first term. We are more hopeful about the fate of the five protector agencies than we were when we began the book, even though we are better informed about the granular details of the challenges they face. But we would be jumping to unsupported conclusions if we were to predict their resurrection with any certainty. This closing chapter distills our most important arguments and solutions.

When Congress created four of the five agencies (the CPSC, EPA, NHTSA, and OSHA) and strengthened the authority of the fifth (the FDA) in the 1960s and 1970s, the nation was embroiled in social and political upheaval that transformed the legislative landscape. The public was receptive to a momentous expansion of government. Its elected representatives in Congress—the primary "people's agents" of our title—responded with a series of interventions more ambitious than any since the Great Depression and the New Deal.

The major reason for optimism about the future of the five agencies is the resonance that we discern in the nation's current affairs with this history. The majority of the people, as exemplified by the campaign themes and promises of the president elected in 2008, believe that the government's approach to business and the regulation of the economy must change profoundly. Because a majority of Americans are angry at what they perceive to be the rapaciousness of private sector financial institutions and anxious about what the future holds, the door appears open to profound changes in the way government is configured and operates. A strong majority of the public rejects the proposition, promoted during the Reagan and Bush administrations, that government should play a secondary role, standing on the sidelines and deferring to free enterprise.

As we have mentioned several times in this volume, President Obama appears intent on mustering this backlash in public opinion and using it to achieve a series of sweeping reforms. He has embraced the common wisdom—first attributed to President John Kennedy—that a crisis breeds political opportunity. We like the way he has framed government's role—to help people in circumstances where they cannot help themselves—and we believe that he is sincere in his commitment to harness economic upheaval in the service of compelling hard choices that will improve the quality of life enjoyed by the poor and the middle class.

Yet President Obama has already made some mistakes along the way that could undermine his ability to achieve change. By centralizing control over regulatory policy in the White House through the appointment of "czars" for energy, environment, regulatory affairs, and health policy, he has undercut the power and effectiveness of the experts he has appointed to lead departments and agencies, potentially congealing policy making and further demoralizing the career civil service. The president has promised to advocate legislative and administrative changes to reduce greenhouse gases but has pushed health care reform to the front of the queue of his legislative priorities, slowing and potentially dooming the progress of climate change bills in Congress. The Obama administration clearly understands the gravity of the threat posed by the nation's severely weakened system for ensuring food safety but has given no indication that it comprehends the urgency of reforming other regulatory regimes, from workplace safety and health to protecting the public from dangerous products imported from countries like China, where health and safety regulation simply does not exist.

These misguided managerial arrangements and substantive blind spots are not fatal to a comprehensive reform effort in and of themselves. But they have negative ripple effects. Running domestic policy from the White House causes delay and wastes considerable resources at a time when the five agencies have neither to spare. Environmental programs in desperate need of new authority and new money—exposure of children to toxic air pollutants and pesticides, for example, or hobbled efforts to deal with runoff from agricultural lands into rivers, lakes, and streams—are stalled behind climate changes. If that big initiative reaches gridlock, the other issues could languish for years. And we literally have no time to waste in taking action on import safety, a severe problem that imposes many hidden costs. These drags on the momentum for change will inevitably combine with factors beyond the president's control, including a fragile economy, a strident opposition reluctant to reach compromise on any issue, and the deep-seated institutional problems of the other branches of government. Together, these potent challenges could thwart real reform over the long run.

In the past, efforts to address the dysfunction of the protector agencies were sideswiped by the argument that the country cannot afford more stringent regulation. This argument proceeds from two extraordinarily persistent myths: health and safety agencies impose unreasonable regulatory costs on American industry, and, at a time of large government deficits, we cannot afford the money it would take to make the protector agencies more effective. The threshold premise of cost-benefit analysis— that people should only get the protection that economists think they are willing to buy—is one major cause of this false paradox. The apparently precise measurements of regulatory benefits are based on outdated and deeply flawed wage premium studies from the 1970s that do not accurately measure either how people perceive safety and health risks or what amounts of money people would spend to avoid them. As damaging, the typical cost-benefit study ignores benefits that cannot be easily converted into monetary amounts, even though these benefits are undoubtedly real and significant—consider, for example, the damage to irreplaceable natural resources that will confront our children. Nevertheless, enthusiastic practitioners of this troubled methodology have succeeded in convincing each new president that agencies should spend millions of dollars and considerable time and energy attempting to measure the costs and benefits of proposed regulations before they are allowed to promulgate important new controls.[1]

The second plank in the argument that we cannot afford more protection is persistent confusion about how much this aspect of government actually costs. Far too many people are confused about the difference between the inflated estimates of the compliance costs businesses must pay to reduce hazards and the money we actually spend on the five agencies. The second number—approximately $10.3 billion, or 0.29 percent of the $3.5 trillion budget Congress approved on April 2, 2009, and 0.89 percent of the $1.2 trillion deficit projected for FY 2010—is truly small by any measure.

Despite our anxiety about President Obama's prospects for reaching the problems we address here before he runs out of political capital and momentum, we are hopeful that their visibility is increasing and that Americans will maintain their expectations that protecting people and the environment is the right job for government. The question then becomes whether the institutional reforms we advocate will lead to the improvements we seek.

The remainder of this chapter reviews those reforms, considers the potential of changes within the bureaucracy to steer policy making in the right direction, and concludes with a few suggestions on how we can determine that change has happened.

## Institutional Changes

### The First Branch

The public has gradually absorbed the unmistakable and accurate impression that warring factions devoted to partisan bickering have produced gridlock in Congress. Even though such polarization is motivated by deep fault lines among Americans in different regions of the country, which suggests that individual members of Congress are only acting as they think they must to achieve reelection, a reservoir of hostility to the legislative branch is established and growing. At some point, this hostility could become more important than individual electoral interests, forcing a critical mass of members to support the institutional reforms that would break gridlock and get Congress back to the business of forging workable compromises on a large backlog of legislative priorities, including amendments to health and safety statutes last updated more than two decades ago.

The most important legislative reforms Congress could take to get its houses back in order are the institution of a longer work week, the restoration of concerted oversight, a return to the "regular order" of considering legislation at the committee level and on the floor, strengthened capacity to tackle ethical problems, and diminished exploitation of parliamentary maneuvers such as closed rules that prohibit floor amendments in the House and secret holds and threatened filibusters in the Senate. As important to the revival of health, safety, and environmental protection is the construction of procedures for compelling consultation between the authorizing committees that establish regulatory programs and the appropriations committees that decide how many resources the agencies will receive to implement them. The disconnect between these two crucial functions, especially when authorizing committees neglect their oversight and reauthorization responsibilities, is a major reason for the dysfunction that plagues the five protector agencies. To the maximum extent practicable, Congress should craft specific agency mandates with clear deadlines for agency action and make sure that the resources it provides to fulfill these prescriptive requirements are adequate to accomplish them.

Congressional resumption of lawmaking and oversight would restore its constitutional position as coequal with the presidency, especially with respect to domestic policy. The prevailing imbalance is bad for the country in ways that are obscured by seemingly more dangerous foreign policy threats and the expansion of presidential power to fill the vacuum left by congressional paralysis.

## A Managerial Presidency

We would have difficulty overstating the profound differences between the administrations of George W. Bush and Barack Obama, which overshadow the nevertheless significant differences between how George H.W. Bush and Bill Clinton ran the government. Yet history is likely to view these modern presidencies as unified by a strong trend toward the accretion of power within the executive branch in relationship to Congress and, to a lesser extent, the courts. That development is arguably the most important trend in American government in half a century. When we suggest that the president should revert to a managerial role with respect to the health and safety agencies, we are advocating reforms that conflict with these powerful developments, running the risk of appearing naïve or ignorant.

We do not shoulder the burden of swimming upstream lightly. It would be far easier to accept the presidency as the domineering branch it has become, especially because we generally favor the positions of the current occupant of the White House. After many years of watching the relentless deterioration of the five agencies' capacity, however, we are convinced that accepting presidential assertions of discretion to reshape the law are unlikely to serve the public interest well no matter who is in the White House.

The government has increased in size and complexity to the point that no president, however well intentioned, can micromanage its far-flung operations. Presidents who are fundamentally hostile to government may think they can afford to ignore the implications of congressional neglect, while presidents with ambitious and progressive agendas for what government should accomplish need far more active engagement and support from the legislature. Asserting White House control by constraining agency and department heads from active involvement with their authorizing and appropriations committees cripples executive branch efforts to chart new directions.

Regardless of the ideological motivations, the centralization of decision making in the White House has exacerbated the effects of a demoralized and aging government workforce that is having great difficulty replenishing itself. Only by allowing the five protector agencies to stabilize themselves and achieve more control over their daily work can the president preside over functioning and effective institutions once again.

## Judges and the Borders of the Law

The federal courts are responsible for ensuring that the five agencies neither invade constitutional rights nor stray beyond their statutory boundaries. Because federal judges are granted lifelong terms, either party's control of the presidency creates a long tail of influence that can take decades to shift. In the 1970s and early 1980s, relatively liberal judges established the precedent of intrusive review, goading agencies into action. From an ideological perspective, this approach backfired as more conservative appointees took over, and the second-guessing remained intrusive but shifted in the opposite political direction. For some agencies—most notably OSHA—a handful of critical opinions saddled the agency with unrealistic evidentiary obligations, slowing affirmative rulemaking to a crawl.

Even for agencies that managed to keep marching despite such harsh reversals, empirical research indicates that Republican judges are significantly more likely to decide cases in a manner that is hostile to regulation than Democratic appointees, who tend to vote the other way. We recommend a concerted effort to reverse these trends, a change that probably can only be accomplished by development of a consensus that ideological splits have gotten out of hand in the lower courts, diminishing the reputation of the judiciary as a whole for objectivity in the review of rulemaking. We urge the courts to retreat to a position of affirming agency decisions unless an agency has overstepped its statutory mandate by a large margin or has taken action with plainly insufficient evidence to support it, regardless of whether the agency has made a decision favoring or disfavoring strong regulation. Removing the courts from the thick of the fray over what regulatory policies are preferable will also have ripple effects in a positive direction, making the agencies less timid, more nimble, and quicker to both issue and revise rules.

## Reform of the Bureaucracy

*Opening the Policy Window*

Congress has a long road to travel toward true institutional reform, and the development of a mechanism for jump-starting its interest in reviving the five protector agencies was among our top priorities in writing this book. We propose the development of positive metrics that would replace the discredited system of glossy reports produced under the Government Performance and Results Act of 1993.[2] These metrics would focus agencies on their core statutory missions by explaining what the agency is trying to accomplish, who is responsible for meeting those milestones, and when the agency will complete those activities. Because positive metrics would be concise (no more than a dozen or two for each major area of regulatory activity—for example, water quality or existing drug safety and efficacy) and would be available on the World Wide Web, they have the potential to generate publicity and oversight regarding the reasons why an agency has experienced regulatory failure.

Our ambitions for metrics stop short of the expectation that an individual measure would disclose the causes behind the failure. We might discover, for example, that a large percentage of follow-up studies promised by drug manufacturers regarding medicines already on the market had never been completed, at least so far as the FDA knew. This disconcerting fact could indicate that the drug makers had simply ignored this commitment, or it could suggest that the studies were taking longer to complete than anticipated. Or it could mean that the study sponsors were delaying submission of the results because they were not positive. Rather than appearing as an isolated story on page A14 of the *New York Times* once every few years, however, these delays would be reported to Congress and featured on the FDA's Web site on a yearly basis until steps were taken to investigate, identify solutions, and correct the problem.

*Performance-Based Budgeting*

Among the most disturbing manifestations of the hostility to regulation that dominated three of the last four administrations is the notion that agencies failing to demonstrate the effectiveness of their own programs should have their budgets cut, regardless of the importance of the program to the public. In fact, we have not discovered any prominent examples of instances in which such counterintuitive penalties were actually meted out. But the threat that they would be has been enough to transform reports filed under the Government Performance and Results Act into self-serving narratives that omit or obscure the reasons why agencies are having difficulty fulfilling their statutory missions.

To remedy this self-defeating state of affairs, we have urged the executive branch—specifically, the OMB—to use its routine analysis of the effectiveness of agency programs as an opportunity to require agencies to compose "true-up budgets." The methodology OMB uses to assess agency effectiveness is the Performance Assessment Rating Tool (PART), a vehicle that is already the target of Obama administration reform efforts. True-up budgets should contain good faith, amply substantiated analyses of the resources an agency would need to fulfill its statutory mandates, broken down by mandate.

We harbor no illusions that true-up budgets will produce needed increases in agency resources immediately. Congress is innately suspicious of claims that agencies need more money, and the president may choose to emphasize other priorities in the integrated budget he sends annually to Capitol Hill. But the exercise of comparing existing resources to the resources that would be needed to mount an effective enforcement program and produce timely updates of rules should prove eye-opening to all of an agency's constituencies, including the regulated industries that are as frustrated as public interest groups by chronic delays and persistent violations by their competitors.

## Separating Science from Policy and Politics

Our case studies—about derailing long-standing efforts to curb mercury pollution, blocking teenagers' access to the Plan B morning-after pill, neglecting ozone that threatens crops and forests, and ignoring the long-term health effects of Vioxx—illustrate the damaging effects of conflating the generation of scientific evidence, the exercise of policy discretion, and the introduction of special interest politics. Ironically, this melding of multiple factors into an indistinguishable morass was a by-product of the deregulatory call for rulemaking based on "sound science." Initially designed to forestall regulatory action until there was less scientific uncertainty, this mantra has been discredited by revelations that the man-made materials under consideration either posed a greater threat to public health and the environment than we initially thought (mercury, Vioxx, air pollution) or were quite safe (Plan B). In fact, judging solely by historical trends, we can be confident that with respect to industrial pollution, we have been right to exercise precaution and require abatement in the vast majority of cases and that, with respect to drugs, we cannot turn our backs on monitoring long-term effects as soon as they are initially approved for sale.

Our antidote to this unfortunate melding is to be honest about scientific uncertainty, encourage decision makers to acknowledge their use of policy discretion, and eliminate opportunities for the injection of bad politics into the mix. By bad politics, we mean decisions based on the stated preferences of a special interest group, without regard to the public interest of society as a whole. The injection of bad politics was a regular occurrence in our case studies during regulatory review at the White House. We would increase transparency at all stages of rulemaking, including the vetting of such proposals by the OMB and other White House offices, although we think a more effective solution would be to simply eliminate that final round of review, which provides too many opportunities for the White House to pressure an agency to change a regulation in order to please a special interest constituency.

*Pragmatic Regulatory Review*

We regard rulemaking as a pluralistic process that assembles all available evidence on the nature and scope of the threat and the advantages and disadvantages of the remedies available to prevent it in order to develop a pragmatic judgment regarding whether and how government should intervene. By pragmatic, we mean a decision that weighs all the evidence, considers the value judgments embedded in the statutes, confronts the implications of what we do not yet know, and makes a choice, with those in a position of authority standing ready to revisit the wisdom of the choice periodically. A pluralistic process means that every category of relevant expert is at the table, from the wide range of scientists who have struggled to understand the problem to the industry experts who will be required to engineer solutions to it.

Who could object to this approach? In fact, agencies follow such a process throughout the typical rulemaking, although too frequently they are not organized or articulate enough to explain what they are doing. At the end of those deliberations, which have become overly complicated, obscure, and long lasting, our system interjects a trump card—the performance of economic analysis to monetize everything from compliance costs to the value of a lost IQ point as a result of toxic chemical exposure. Cost-benefit analysis is likely to prevail as a decision-making methodology for the foreseeable future. But its own uncertainties—especially in the area of monetizing benefits—so limit its usefulness that agencies would be well advised to augment, rather than short-circuit, their own pragmatic processes.

### Tending the Civil Service

The biggest surprise of our research for this book was the intensity— indeed, the desperation—expressed by the blue ribbon Commission on Public Service with respect to the steady weakening of the federal bureaucracy. We knew the outline of regulatory failures that we described in chapter 1, and we understood from years of observation how Congress, the judiciary, and the White House had compounded those problems. We were not prepared for the statistics documenting the brain drain throughout the government, nor did we understand the money, time, and level of effort that must be devoted to correcting it.

We are not hopeful that these problems can be solved in the foreseeable future. We can imagine a slow revival in pride in serving the public and in the potential of government to make the quality of American life better in important ways. We can imagine young people being attracted to the civil service during a period when the private sector has lost millions of jobs. But we cannot feel confident that the battle to rationalize federal pay with comparable salaries in the private sector or, as vital, the need to reduce significantly the bloated ranks of middle management will become priorities for the White House or Congress. In the absence of those reforms, real change will be bounded, and our strong recommendations that civil service experts drive policy in the first instance will be much harder to achieve.

## Signs of Reform

Revival of the five agencies, when it comes, will be slow, halting, and difficult to recognize. All of the agencies, especially the EPA, are burdened by "midnight regulations"—last-minute decisions by the Bush II administration that would not have passed muster under President Obama. They cannot simply cancel these decisions but must reverse course using appropriate procedures. Midnight regulations are an unfortunate tradition in modern presidencies. To a large extent, they amount to conscious sabotage of the succeeding administration. This criticism is especially warranted in the case of the Bush II administration, which had a dismal track record of having its decisions reversed by the courts during its second term. In any event, one sign of revival will be the systematic reversal of such decisions and their replacement by policies shaped by the new president.

Another promising sign will be the agencies' formulation of concerted plans to change priorities and, if necessary, recommend amendments updating their authorizing statutes. Their acknowledgment of the need for change would represent a major step forward, although they will obviously depend on Congress's ability to act on these proposals.

Rehabilitation of enforcement programs, which were allowed to deteriorate to the point at which they lack credibility, would also provide encouragement to the agencies' supporters, not just in the public interest community but also among firms that shouldered the substantial financial burden of complying with regulatory requirements when they were first issued. We suspect these good corporate citizens are the majority, regardless of their silence as those programs withered.

## Conclusion

The other day we attended a conference that was designed to debate the wisdom of cost-benefit analysis and centralized White House review in the context of the regulatory failures we have described in these pages. Participants ran the gamut from conservative to progressive, from supporters of cost-benefit analysis and centralized review to fierce opponents of those approaches. During a session entitled "The State of the Agencies," Peter Barton Hutt, former Chief Counsel of the FDA (1971–75) and now senior counsel at Covington & Burling, a Washington, D.C., law firm that represents large drug manufacturers, recounted his experiences representing the FDA before the courts in those early years: "I would go in there and say 'My name is Peter Barton Hutt and I represent the agency that protects small children and pregnant women. Do you have any questions?' "

This obviously apocryphal anecdote got a laugh from the audience, several of whom were of an adequate age to remember that period of civil service esprit de corps verging on brashness. Those days will never come again. But if the agencies could recover even a fraction of that swagger, their road to recovery would surely be easier to navigate.

# Notes

## Preface

1. A Gallup Poll conducted in March 2008 found that 49 percent believed that "[p]rotection of the environment should be given priority, even at the risk of curbing economic growth," while 42 percent would reverse these priorities. Five percent would give these goals equal priority. Gallup Poll, March 6–9, 2008. On the other hand, 34 percent of the same respondents said that "[l]ife on earth will continue without major environmental disruptions only if we take additional, immediate, and drastic action concerning the environment," while 52 percent said we should take "some additional actions," and only 13 percent said we should continue to take the "same actions we have been taking on the environment." Poll results cited in notes 1–3 are at http://www.pollingreport.com/enviro.htm.

2. These results were reported by Ipsos Public Affairs in an Associated Press–Stanford University poll conducted on September 21–23, 2007.

3. A Harris poll conducted on October 16–23, 2007, found that 53 percent of all adults believed the United States has "too little" government regulation to protect the environment, while 21 percent said the country had "too much" regulation, and 21 percent thought the amount was "about right."

4. The origination of this quote, which is a Norquist trademark, is generally attributed to an article in the *Nation* magazine. Robert Dreyfuss, "Grover Norquist: 'Field Marshal' of the Bush Tax Plan," *Nation*, May 14, 2001, 11, 12.

## Chapter One

1. "Powell Endorses Obama for President," *Meet the Press*, NBC, October 19, 2008, http://www.msnbc.msn.com/id/27265369/ (former secretary of state General Colin Powell, in political roundtable with host Chuck Todd). Powell, who is African American, was chairman of the Joint Chiefs of Staff during the administration of President George H. W. Bush and served as secretary of state under President

George W. Bush. He crossed party lines to endorse Barack Obama's candidacy during the 2008 presidential election.

2. Barack Obama, "Obama Closing Argument Speech," *Chicago Sun-Times*, October 27, 2008, http://blogs.suntimes.com/sweet/2008/10/obama_closing_argument_speech_1.html (transcript of speech as delivered at the Canton Memorial Civic Center, Canton, Ohio, October 27, 2008).

3. National Commission on Product Safety, *Final Report Presented to the President and Congress* (Washington, DC: GPO, 1970), 9, 68.

4. *U.S. Code* 15 (2006), § 2051(b)(1)-(2). For analysis of the CPSC's difficulties in implementing these provisions, see Teresa M. Schwartz, "The Consumer Product Safety Commission: A Flawed Product of the Consumer Decade," *George Washington Law Review* 51 (1982): 32, 72; E. Marla Felcher, *The U.S. Consumer Product Safety Commission: The Paper Tiger of American Product Safety* (Washington, DC: Understanding Government, April 2002), http://understandinggov.org/reports/felcher.html.

5. *U.S. Code Annotated* 15 (West Supp. 2009), § 2064(c)(1).

6. *Consumer Prod. Safety Comm'n v. GTE Sylvania, Inc.*, 447 U.S. 102 (1980).

7. Robert S. Adler, "From 'Model Agency' to Basket Case—Can the Consumer Product Safety Commission Be Redeemed?" *Administrative Law Review* 41 (1989): 61, 109 (footnote omitted).

8. *Consumer Product Safety Amendments of 1981*, Public Law 97-35, § 1204, *U.S. Statutes at Large* 95 (1981): 703, 713, codified as amended at *U.S. Code Annotated* 15 (West Supp. 2009), § 2055(b)(5). The 1981 amendments also eliminated the public's right to petition the agency for safety standards and either receive an answer from the agency within 120 days or have the right to take it to court for a judicial review of its inaction. *U.S. Code* 15 (1976), § 2059 (original authority); and *U.S. Statutes at Large* 95 (1981): 703, 721 (repeal).

9. Congress Watch, *Hazardous Waits: CPSC Lets Crucial Time Pass before Warning Public about Dangerous Products* (Washington, DC: Public Citizen, 2008), 2, http://www.citizen.org/documents/HazardousWaits.pdf.

10. Louise Story and David Barboza, "Mattel Recalls 19 Million Toys Sent from China," *New York Times*, August 15, 2007, A1.

11. For an explanation of these problems, see John Dinsmore and Robert Lala, "Chinese Imports and Product Liability Coverage," *Insurance Journal*, September 24, 2007, http://www.insurancejournal.com/magazines/west/2007/09/24/features/85154.htm; Eric Lipton, "Safety Agency Faces Scrutiny Amid Changes," *New York Times*, September 2, 2007, § 1, 11; Jyoti Thottam, "The Growing Dangers of China Trade," *Time*, June 28, 2007, 28.

12. *Consumer Product Safety Improvement Act of 2008*, Public Law 110-314, *U.S. Statutes at Large* 122 (2008): 3016.

13. Lyndon B. Johnson, "Special Message to the Congress on Transportation—March 2, 1966," *Public Papers of the Presidents of the United States: Lyndon B. Johnson, 1966*, 1 (Washington, DC: GPO, 1966): 250, 256.

14. Brian O'Neill, interview by Barak Goodman and Marc Shaffer, "Rollover: The Hidden History of SUVs," *Frontline*, PBS, February 21, 2002, http://www.pbs .org/wgbh/pages/frontline/shows/rollover/.

15. Ralph Nader, *Unsafe at Any Speed*, 25th anniversary ed. (New York: Knightsbridge Publishing, 1991).

16. Jerry L. Mashaw and David L. Harfst, *The Struggle for Auto Safety* (Cambridge, MA: Harvard University Press, 1990), 4.

17. For statistical trends in traffic safety, see National Highway Traffic Safety Administration, *Fatality Analysis Reporting System (FARS) Encyclopedia*, http:// www-fars.nhtsa.dot.gov/Main/index.aspx.

18. William Haddon, Jr., Edward A. Suchman, and David Klein, *Accident Research: Methods and Approaches* (New York: Harper and Row, 1964).

19. *U.S. Code* 49 (2000), §§ 30111, 30120.

20. *Chrysler Corp. v. Dep't of Transp.*, 472 F.2d 659 (1972).

21. Mashaw and Harfst, *Struggle for Safety*, 91.

22. *Motor Vehicle and Schoolbus Safety Amendments of 1974*, Public Law 93-492, *U.S. Statutes at Large* 88 (1974): 1470.

23. Martin Goldfarb, interview in "Rollover: The Hidden History of SUVs."

24. *U.S. Code* 42 (2006), § 6201.

25. Danny Hakim, "A Regulator Takes Aim at Hazards of S.U.V.'s," *New York Times*, December 22, 2002, § 3, 31.

26. Hal R. Varian, "Economic Scene; Are Bigger Vehicles Safer? It Depends on Whether You're a Passenger or a Target," *New York Times*, December 18, 2003, C2.

27. For discussion of the connection, see Varian, "Economic Scene."

28. Senate Committee on Commerce, Science, and Transportation, *The TREAD Act Revisited: Hearing before the Subcommittee on Competition, Foreign Commerce, and Infrastructure*, 108th Cong., 2d sess., June 3 2004, http://www.nhtsa.dot .gov/nhtsa/announce/testimony/FINALTREADtestimony_06-03-200.html (statement of Jeffrey W. Runge, Administrator, National Highway Traffic Safety Administration).

29. Chronology, "Rollover: The Hidden History of SUVs."

30. U.S. Occupational Safety and Health Administration, "Conditions at Tyler Pipe: OSHA Inspection Report" (Washington, DC, 1999). A redacted version of the report appears on the Web site of the PBS news program *Frontline*, http://www .pbs.org/wgbh/pages/frontline/shows/workplace/mcwane/osha.html.

31. Kenneth D. Rosenman, Alice Kalush, Mary Jo Reilly, Joseph C. Gardiner, Matthew Reeves, and Zhewui Luo, "How Much Work-Related Injury and Illness Is Missed by the Current National Surveillance System?" *Journal of Occupational and Environmental Medicine* 48, no. 4 (2006): 357–65; J. Paul Leigh, James P. Marcin, and Red R. Miller, "An Estimate of the U.S. Government's Undercount of Nonfatal Occupational Injuries," *Journal of Occupational and Environmental Medicine* 46, no. 1 (2004): 10–18; Leslie I. Boden and David Ozonoff, "Capture-Recapture

Estimates of Nonfatal Workplace Injuries and Illnesses," *Annals of Epidemiology* 18, no. 6 (2008): 500–504.

32. Liberty Mutual Research Institute for Safety, *From Research to Reality:* 2007 *Annual Report of Scientific Activities* (Hopkinton, MA: Liberty Mutual, 2007), 5, http://www.libertymutualgroup.com/omapps/ContentServer?c=cms_document& pagename=LMGResearchInstitute%2Fcms_document%2FShowDoc&cid=1138 365868361.

33. *Occupational Safety and Health Act of 1970, U.S. Code* 29 (2006), § 655; "Occupational Safety and Health Standards," *Code of Federal Regulations*, title 29, § 1910 (2008).

34. For a description of these initiatives, see U.S. Government Accountability Office, *Workplace Safety and Health: Safety in the Meat and Poultry Industry, While Improving, Could Be Further Strengthened*, GAO-05-96 (Washington, DC: GPO, 2005), 13–15, http://www.gao.gov/new.items/d0596.pdf.

35. *Occupational Safety and Health Act of 1970, U.S. Code* 29 (2006), § 666(a), (b), (k).

36. Wayne B. Gray and John M. Mendeloff, "The Declining Effects of OSHA Inspections on Manufacturing Injuries: 1979-1998," *Industrial and Labor Relations Review* 57 (2005): 571–87.

37. *Indus. Union Dep't, AFL-CIO v. Am. Petroleum Inst.*, 448 U.S. 607, 615 (1980).

38. *Indus. Union Dep't*, 689 (Marshall, J., dissenting).

39. The PBS *Frontline* materials appear at http://www.pbs.org/wgbh/pages/ frontline/shows/workplace/mcwane/, and the CBC *Fifth Estate* materials appear at http://www.cbc.ca/fifth/pipes/index.html. See also David Barstow and Lowell Bergman, "At a Texas Foundry, an Indifference to Life," *New York Times*, January 8, 2003, A1; David Barstow and Lowell Bergman, "A Family's Fortune, a Legacy of Blood and Tears," *New York Times*, January 9, 2003, A1; David Barstow and Lowell Bergman, "Deaths on the Job, Slaps on the Wrist," *New York Times*, January 10, 2003, A1.

40. Arent Fox LLP, "The *New York Times* Series on OSHA: How Will It Affect Enforcement?" February 12, 2004, http://www.arentfox.com/publications/index .cfm?fa=legalUpdateDisp&content_id=1089.

41. Arent Fox LLP, "The *New York Times* Series on OSHA."

42. U.S. Government Accountability Office, *Workplace Safety and Health*, 1–3.

43. *Workplace Safety and Health*, 3–4.

44. FDA Science Board, *FDA Science and Mission at Risk: Report of the Subcommittee on Science and Technology* (Washington, DC: GPO, 2007), 1, http://www .fda.gov/ohrms/dockets/AC/07/briefing/2007-4329b_02_01_FDA%20Report% 20on%20Science%20and%20Technology.pdf.

45. House Committee on Energy and Commerce, *Science and Mission at Risk: FDA's Self-Assessment: Hearing before the Subcommittee on Oversight and Inves-*

*tigations*, 110th Cong., 2d sess., 2008, 1–2 (testimony of Peter Barton Hutt, Senior Counsel, Covington and Burling LLP). Hutt represents large drug companies and is widely considered the "dean" of the FDA bar.

46. See U.S. General Accounting Office, *FDA Drug Review: Postapproval Risks 1976-85*, GAO/PEMD-90-15 (Washington, DC: GPO, 1990), 3, http://archive.gao .gov/d24t8/141456.pdf (finding that 51.5 percent of the 198 drugs approved between 1976 and 1985 had serious postmarket risks). (The General Accounting Office changed its name to the Government Accountability Office in 2004.)

47. FDA Science Board, *FDA Science and Mission at Risk*, 2 (emphasis omitted).

48. Institute of Medicine, *The Future of Drug Safety: Promoting and Protecting the Health of the Public* (Washington, DC: National Academies Press, 2007).

49. Senate Committee on Finance, *FDA, Merck and Vioxx: Putting Patient Safety First?: Hearing before the Committee on Finance*, 108th Cong., 2d sess., 2004, 2 (statement of David J. Graham, Associate Director for Science and Medicine, Office of Drug Safety, U.S. Food and Drug Administration), http://finance.senate. gov/hearings/testimony/2004test/111804dgtest.pdf.

50. *Prescription Drug User Fee Amendments of 2007*, Public Law 110–85, *U.S. Statutes at Large* 121 (2007): 825.

51. We hasten to add that we do not intend this comparison to suggest that we think the meat and poultry inspection system is sound. The recall of 143 million tons of beef in February 2008, much of it sold to school lunch programs, suggests otherwise. Rather, we cannot imagine a reasonable justification for such disparities.

52. Trust for America's Health, *Keeping America's Food Safe: A Blueprint for Fixing the Food Safety System at the U.S. Department of Health and Human Services* (Washington, DC: Trust for America's Health, 2009), 1, http://www.rwjf.org/files/ research/20090325tfahfoodsafety.pdf.

53. Government Accountability Office, *Federal Oversight of Food Safety: FDA's Food Protection Plan Proposes Positive First Steps, but Capacity to Carry Them Out Is Critical*, GAO-08-435T (Washington, DC: GPO, 2008), http://www.gao.gov/new .items/d08435t.pdf.

54. *Ethyl Corp. v. EPA*, 541 F.2d 1, 6 (D.C. Cir. 1976).

55. William D. Ruckelshaus, "Stopping the Pendulum," *Environmental Forum*, November/December 1995, 25, 25–26.

56. *Clean Air Act, U.S. Code* 42 (2006), §§ 7401 et seq.; *Clean Water Act, U.S. Code* 33 (2006), §§ 1251 et seq.; *Safe Drinking Water Act, U.S. Code* 42 (2006), §§ 300f et seq.; *Federal Insecticide, Fungicide, and Rodenticide Act, U.S. Code* 7 (2006), §§ 136 et seq.; *Toxic Substances Control Act, U.S. Code* 15 (2006), §§ 2601 et seq.; *Resource Conservation and Recovery Act, U.S. Code* 42 (2006), §§ 6901 et seq.; *Comprehensive Environmental Response, Compensation, and Liability Act, U.S. Code* 42 (2006), §§ 9601 et seq.; and *Emergency Planning and Community Right-to-Know Act, U.S. Code* 42 (2006), §§ 11001 et seq.

57. Ruckelshaus, "Stopping the Pendulum," 25.

58. *Corrosion Proof Fittings v. EPA*, 947 F.2d 1201 (5th Cir. 1991).

59. National Research Council, Climate Research Board, *Carbon Dioxide and Climate: A Scientific Assessment*, (Washington, DC: National Academies Press, 1979), viii, http://www.nap.edu/catalog.php?record_id=12181.

60. Joint Science Academies, *Global Response to Climate Change* (June 7, 2005), http://nationalacademies.org/onpi/06072005.pdf. The signatories to this statement include the top scientists for the most elite scientific academies in Brazil, Canada, China, France, Germany, India, Italy, Japan, Russia, the United Kingdom, and the United States.

61. For an excellent description of this campaign, see Sheldon Rampton and John Stauber, *Trust Us, We're Experts! How Industry Manipulates Science and Gambles with Your Future* (New York: Penguin Putnam, 2001), 267–88.

62. Intergovernmental Panel on Climate Change (IPCC), *The IPCC 4th Assessment Report Is Coming Out: A Picture of Climate Change: The Current State of Understanding* (IPCC, 2007), http://www.ipcc.ch/pdf/press-ar4/ipcc-flyer-low.pdf.

63. IPCC, "IPCC Reports: Assessment Reports," http://www.ipcc.ch/ipccreports/assessments-reports.htm.

64. IPCC, *Climate Change 2007: Impacts, Adaptation and Vulnerability. Contribution of Working Group II to the Fourth Assessment Report of the Intergovernmental Panel on Climate Change*, ed. M. L. Parry, O. F. Canziani, J. P. Palutikof, P. J. van der Linden, and C. E. Hanson (New York: Cambridge University Press, 2007), http://www.ipcc.ch/ipccreports/ar4-wg2.htm.

65. *Clean Air Act, U.S. Code* 42 (2006), § 7602(g).

66. International Center for Technology Assessment et al., *Petition for Rulemaking and Collateral Relief Seeking the Regulation of Greenhouse Gas Emissions from New Motor Vehicles Under § 202 of the Clean Air Act*, special petition filed with the U.S. Environmental Protection Agency, October 20,1999, http://www.icta.org/doc/ghgpet2.pdf.

67. U.S. Environmental Protection Agency, Notice of Denial of Petition for Rulemaking, "Control of Emissions From New Highway Vehicles and Engines," *Federal Register* 68 (September 8, 2003): 52,922.

68. *Massachusetts v. EPA*, 549 U.S. 497 (2007).

**Chapter Two**

1. See, for example, Arthur Lupia and Mathew D. McCubbins, *The Democratic Dilemma: Can Citizens Learn What They Need to Know?* (New York: Cambridge University Press, 1998); Michael Schudson, *The Good Citizen: A History of American Civic Life* (New York: Free Press, 1998).

2. See, for example, Kenneth J. Meier and Laurence J. O'Toole, Jr., *Bureaucracy in a Democratic State: A Governance Perspective* (Baltimore: Johns Hopkins University Press, 2006), 6.

3. See, for example, David Epstein and Sharyn O'Halloran, *Delegating Powers: A Transaction Cost Politics Approach to Policy Making under Separate Powers* (New York: Cambridge University Press, 1999); D. Roderick Kiewiet and Mathew D. McCubbins, *The Logic of Delegation: Congressional Parties and the Appropriations Process* (Chicago: University of Chicago Press, 1991). Michael C. Jensen and William H. Meckling, "Theory of the Firm: Managerial Behavior, Agency Costs and Ownership Structure," *Journal of Financial Economics* 3 (1976): 305–60.

4. Lisa Schultz Bressman, "Procedures as Politics in Administrative Law," *Columbia Law Review* 107 (2007): 1749, 1768 (describing the phenomenon as "drift"); Michael E. Levine and Jennifer L. Forrence, "Regulatory Capture, Public Interest, and the Public Agenda: Toward a Synthesis," *Journal of Law, Economics and Organization* 6 (Special Issue 1990): 167–98 (describing the phenomenon as "slack").

5. *Administrative Procedure Act*, Public Law 79–404, *U.S. Statutes at Large* 60 (1946): 237, codified as amended at *U.S. Code* 5 (2006), § 500 et seq.

6. U.S. Constitution, art. 2, § 3.

7. See, for example, *Eastland v. United States Servicemen's Fund*, 421 U.S. 491, 504, n.15 (1975); *Barenblatt v. United States*, 360 U.S. 109, 111–12 (1959); *Watkins v. United States*, 354 U.S. 178, 187 (1957).

8. U.S. Constitution, art. 3, § 2.

9. See, for example, Steven Croley, "White House Review of Agency Rulemaking: An Empirical Investigation," *University of Chicago Law Review* 70 (2003): 821, 830; Lisa Schultz Bressman, "Procedures as Politics in Administrative Law," *Columbia Law Review* 107 (2007): 1749, 1768–69.

10. Peter Lindseth, "Agents without Principals? Delegation in an Age of Diffuse and Fragmented Governance" (University of Connecticut School of Law Working Paper 18, 2004), 2, http://lsr.nellco.org/uconn/ucwps/papers/18.

11. Edward L. Rubin, *Beyond Camelot: Rethinking Politics and Law for the Modern State* (Princeton, NJ: Princeton University Press, 2005), 48–56; Meier and O'Toole, *Bureaucracy in a Democratic State*, 122–23.

12. See, e.g., Anthony Downs, *An Economic Theory of Democracy* (New York: Harper and Row, 1957); William A. Niskanen, Jr., *Bureaucracy and Representative Government* (Chicago: Aldine-Atherton, 1971).

13. See, for example, George J. Stigler, "The Theory of Economic Regulation," *Bell Journal of Economics and Management Science* 2, no. 1 (Spring 1971): 3–21; Richard A. Posner, "Taxation by Regulation," *Bell Journal of Economics and Management Science* 2, no. 1 (Spring 1971): 22–50.

14. Steven P. Croley, *Regulation and Public Interests: The Possibility of Good Regulatory Government* (Princeton, NJ: Princeton University Press 2008), 10.

15. Scott R. Furlong, "Exploring Interest Group Participation in Executive Policymaking," in *The Interest Group Connection: Electioneering, Lobbying, and Policymaking in Washington*, 2d ed., ed. Paul S. Herrnson, Ronald G. Shaiko, and Clyde Wilcox (Washington, DC: CQ Press, 2005), 282, 290–91; Marianne Lavelle, "The Climate Change Lobby Explosion: Will Thousands of Lobbyists Imperil Action on Global Warming?" *Center for Public Integrity: Climate Change Lobby*, February 24, 2009, http://www.publicintegrity.org/investigations/climate_change/articles/entry/1171/.

16. Scott R. Furlong and Cornelius M. Kerwin, "Interest Group Participation in Rule Making: A Decade of Change," *Journal of Public Administration Research and Theory* 15 (2005): 353, 361; Furlong, "Exploring Interest Group Participation," 289.

17. Jason Webb Yackee and Susan Webb Yackee, "A Bias Towards Business? Assessing Interest Group Influence on the U.S. Bureaucracy," *Journal of Politics* 68 (2006): 128, 131–33. The four agencies were OSHA, the Employment Standards Administration, the Federal Railroad Administration, and the Federal Highway Administration. Yackee and Yackee, "A Bias Towards Business?" 131.

18. Marissa Martino Golden, "Interest Groups in the Rule-Making Process: Who Participates? Whose Voices Get Heard?" *Journal of Public Administration Research and Theory* 8 (1998): 245, 250–53. The three agencies were EPA, NHTSA, and the Department of Housing and Urban Development.

19. Three studies have found no association. Golden, "Interest Groups in the Rulemaking Process," 262; Wesley A. Magat, Alan J. Krupnick, and Winston Harrington, *Rules in the Making: A Statistical Analysis of Regulatory Agency Behavior* (Washington, DC: Resources for the Future, 1986), 143–45, 157; Maureen L. Cropper, William N. Evans, Stephen J. Berardi, Maria M. Ducla-Soares, and Paul R. Portney, "The Determinants of Pesticide Regulation: A Statistical Analysis of EPA Decision Making," *Journal of Political Economy* 100 (1992): 175, 194–95. Another study found statistical evidence that agencies altered final rules in a probusiness direction when there were a higher proportion of comments from business firms. Yackee and Yackee, "A Bias Towards Business?" 134–36.

20. Croley, *Regulation and Public Interests*, 3.

21. Levine and Forrence, "Regulatory Capture," 168.

22. Levine and Forrence, "Regulatory Capture," 178.

23. Levine and Forrence, "Regulatory Capture," 185–91.

24. Levine and Forrence, "Regulatory Capture," 190.

25. Meier and O'Toole, *Bureaucracy in a Democratic State*, 8 (footnote omitted).

26. Meier and O'Toole, *Bureaucracy in a Democratic State.*, 144. Meier and O'Toole survey this literature.

27. See, for example, James Q. Wilson, *Bureaucracy: What Government Agencies Do and Why They Do It* (New York: Basic Books, 1989); Amitai Etzioni, *Modern*

*Organizations* (Englewood Cliffs, NJ: Prentice-Hall, 1964); and Herbert Kaufman, *The Forest Ranger: A Study in Administrative Behavior* (Baltimore: Johns Hopkins Press, 1960).

28. See Gary L. Wamsley, "The Agency Perspective: Public Administrators as Agential Leaders," in *Refounding Public Administration*, ed. Gary L. Wamsley et al. (Newbury Park, CA: Sage, 1990), 114–62; see also Larry D. Terry, *Leadership of Public Bureaucracies: The Administrator as Conservator*, 2d ed. (Armonk, NY: M. E. Sharpe, 2003), 159–86.

29. *Clean Air Act, U.S. Code* 42 (2006), §§ 7401 et seq.

## Chapter Three

1. Robert Dreyfuss, "Grover Norquist: 'Field Marshal' of the Bush Tax Plan," *Nation*, May 14, 2001, 11, 12.

2. For an interesting analysis of the "manufactured reality" that the "federal government is broke" in the context of social welfare "safety net" programs for the poor, see Demetrios Caraley, "Dismantling the Federal Safety Net: Fictions versus Realities," *Political Science Quarterly* 111 (1996): 225, 241.

3. Vaudine England, "Why China's Milk Industry Went Sour," BBC News, September 29, 2008, http://news.bbc.co.uk/2/hi/asia-pacific/7635466.stm; Peter Ford, "Behind Bad Baby Milk, an Ethical Gap in China's Business," *Christian Science Monitor*, September 17, 2008, World, 1; Annys Shin, "Bailout May Delay Funds for New Law," *Washington Post*, September 25, 2008, D1.

4. Joseph E. Stiglitz and Linda J. Bilmes, "The $3 Trillion War," *Vanity Fair*, April 2008, http://www.vanityfair.com/politics/features/2008/04/stiglitz200804?printable=true&currentPage=all.

5. Stiglitz and Bilmes, "The $3 Trillion War."

6. Public Law 93–344, *U.S. Statutes at Large* 88 (1974): 297 (codified as amended in scattered sections of *U.S. Code* title 2).

7. For excellent descriptions of the process, see Sandy Streeter, Congressional Research Service, *The Congressional Appropriations Process: An Introduction*, RL 97-684 (Washington, DC: CRS, 2007), http://www.senate.gov/reference/resources/pdf/97-684.pdf, and U.S. General Accounting Office, *Budget Process: Evolution and Challenges*, GAO/T-AIMD-96-129 (Washington, DC: GPO, 1996).

8. Congress never completed budget resolutions in FY 1999, FY 2003, and FY 2005.

9. *Balanced Budget and Emergency Deficit Control Act of* 1985, Public Law 99–177, *U.S. Statutes at Large* 99 (1985): 1038 (codified in scattered sections of *U.S. Code* titles 2, 31, and 42). For an excellent description of those events, see Kate Stith, "Rewriting the Fiscal Constitution: The Case of Gramm-Rudman-Hollings," *California Law Review* 76 (1988): 593–668. The law was declared unconstitutional

by the Supreme Court because the statute gave the Comptroller General, head of what was then the General Accounting Office, the responsibility for enforcing its deficit-reduction provisions. This approach violated the constitutional principle of separation of powers by cutting the president out of the process. *Bowsher v. Synar*, 478 U.S. 714 (1986). Congress subsequently amended the process to cure the constitutional defect by giving the OMB this authority. *Balanced Budget and Emergency Deficit Control Reaffirmation Act of 1987*, Public Law 100–119, *U.S. Statutes at Large* 101 (1987): 754.

10. *Budget Enforcement Act of 1990*, Public Law 101–508, title XIII, *U.S. Statutes at Large* 104 (1990): 1388, 1388–573 (codified as amended in scattered sections of *U.S. Code* title 2); *Omnibus Budget Reconciliation Act of 1993*, Public Law 103–66, *U.S. Statutes at Large* 107 (1993): 312 (codified as amended in scattered sections of *U.S. Code* titles 7, 16, 19, 20, 26, 29, 30, and 47).

11. For a description of how the process works and how Congress has circumvented it, see Jason J. Fichtner, *Extending the Budget Enforcement Act: Revision of PAYGO Rules Necessary for Better Tax Policy*, special report prepared for the U.S. Congress Joint Economic Committee, May 2002, http://papers.ssrn.com/sol3/papers.cfm?abstract_id=665781.

12. For an explanation of this rationale, see Ellen Hays and Sandy Savis, *Congressional Budget Office Memorandum: Emergency Spending under the Budget Enforcement Act*, December 1998, http://www.cbo.gov/ftpdocs/10xx/doc1050/emspend.pdf.

13. For further information on these developments, see Robert Keith and Bill Heniff, Jr., Congressional Research Service, *PAYGO Rules for Budget Enforcement in the House and Senate*, RL-32835 (Washington, DC: CRS, May 3, 2005), http://www.llsdc.org/sourcebook/docs/CRS-RL32835.pdf.

14. For a description of this process, see Streeter, *The Congressional Appropriations Process*.

15. For a table showing the track record on these matters between 1977 and 2007, see Streeter, *The Congressional Appropriations Process*, 14.

16. Other committees get involved in crafting major environmental laws. For example, if legislation imposes taxes to pay for their programs, the Senate Finance Committee and the House Ways and Means Committee would have jurisdiction. Or if proposed amendments contain lawsuit provisions that would affect the federal courts, Senate and House Judiciary Committees could claim the right to consider the bills before they reach the House or Senate floor.

17. George Hager, "Senate–White House Deal Breaks Clean-Air Logjam," *CQ Weekly*, March 3, 1990, 652 ("marathon closed-door talks"); George Hager, "Clean Air: War About Over in Both House and Senate," *CQ Weekly*, April 7, 1990, 1057 ("decade in the making").

18. Hager, "Clean Air War," 1057.

19. Public Law 93–344, § 301(c), *U.S. Statutes at Large* 88 (1974): 297, 307.

20. Richard J. Lazarus, "Congressional Descent: The Demise of Deliberative Democracy in Environmental Law," *Georgetown Law Journal* 94 (2006): 619, 653.

21. 503 U.S. 429 (1992).

22. Historical budget data were collected from yearly *Budgets of the United States Government*. In each volume, the appendix lists the actual budget authority for individual agencies in the fiscal year two years prior. So, for example, to obtain the budget authority for CPSC in FY 2005, data were obtained from the appendix to the *Budget of the U.S. Government* for FY 2007. The *Budgets of the U.S. Government* for fiscal years 1996–2009 are available at http://www.gpoaccess.gov/usbudget/ browse.html. Monthly average Consumer Price Index (CPI) information from the Bureau of Labor Statistics was used to adjust for inflation. U.S. Department of Labor, Bureau of Labor Statistics, Consumer Price Index, ftp://ftp.bls.gov/pub/special .requests/cpi/cpiai.txt. CPI numbers from October through September were averaged to obtain an average CPI for each fiscal year from 1970 through 2007. The real budget for any given fiscal year was obtained by multiplying the nominal budget from the *Budget of the U.S. Government* by the ratio of the FY 2007 CPI to the CPI for the given year. For example, (Real 1970 Budget) = (Nominal 1970 budget) × (Average CPI for FY 2007)/(Average CPI for FY 1970).

23. U.S. Environmental Protection Agency, *Summary Report to the President: The Presidential Regulatory Reform Initiative* (Washington, DC: National Service Center for Environmental Publications, June 15, 1995), 2, http://nepis.epa.gov/Exe/ ZyPURL.cgi?Dockey=40000LMK.txt ("We have learned that by focusing on results, not on how results are achieved, we can tap the creativity of Americans to devise cleaner, cheaper, smarter ways of protecting the environment.").

24. See, for example, Susan E. Dudley, *Primer on Regulation*, Mercatus Policy Series, Policy Resource No. 1 (Arlington, VA: Mercatus Center at George Mason University, 2005), http://www.mercatus.org/uploadedFiles/Mercatus/Publications/ Primer%20on%20Regulation.pdf.

25. Randall Strahan, "Governing in the Post-Liberal Era: Gramm-Rudman-Hollings and the Politics of the Federal Deficit," *Harvard Journal on Legislation* 25 (1988): 593, 594, 609.

26. U.S. Senate Committee on the Budget, *Hearing on the President's Fiscal Year 2010 Budget Proposal*, 111th Cong., 1st Sess., March 10, 2009, Testimony of Peter R. Orszag, Director of the Office of Management and Budget, 15, http://budget .senate.gov/democratic/testimony/2009/Orszag_Testimony_March_10_2009%20 FINAL.pdf.

27. See Office of Management and Budget, "Assessing Program Performance," http://www.whitehouse.gov/omb/part/. The site also contains past reports.

28. Testimony of Peter Orszag, 15.

29. For proposals that would increase transparency, see U.S. Government Accountability Office, *Budget Process: Better Transparency, Controls, Triggers, and Default Mechanisms Would Help to Address our Large and Growing Long-term Fiscal*

*Challenge,* GAO-06-761T (Washington, DC: GPO, 2006), http://www.gao.gov/new
.items/d06761t.pdf.

30. U.S. Government Accountability Office, *Government Performance: Lessons
Learned for the Next Administration on Using Performance Information to Improve
Results,* GAO-08-1026T (Washington DC: GPO, 2006), 1, http://www.gao.gov/new
.items/d081026t.pdf.


## Chapter Four

1. Executive Order no. 12,291, *Code of Federal Regulations* title 3 (1982), 127.
The first Bush administration followed the Reagan approach. President Clinton
adopted a similar process, which President George W. Bush initially continued. Executive Order no. 12,866, *Code of Federal Regulations* title 3 (1993), 638. President
Bush later extended the requirement of assessment of costs and benefits to significant agency guidance documents. Executive Order no. 13,422, *Code of Federal
Regulations* title 3 (2008), 191. President Obama has announced his intention to revise Executive Order no. 12,866 and has revoked Executive Order no. 13,422, but as
this book goes to press, he appears likely to nominate Cass Sunstein, a fan of cost-
benefit analysis, to head the OMB office that implements these requirements. White
House, "President Obama Announces Another Key OMB Post," press release,
April 20, 2009, http://www.whitehouse.gov/the_press_office/President-Obama-
Announces-Another-Key-OMB-Post/.

2. For analysis of these problems, see Thomas O. McGarity and Ruth Ruttenberg, "Counting the Cost of Health, Safety, and Environmental Regulation," *Texas
Law Review* 80 (2002): 1997–2058. McGarity and Ruttenberg conclude that cost
estimates are generally not based on empirical analysis. See also Frank Ackerman
and Lisa Heinzerling, *Priceless: On Knowing the Price of Everything and the Value
of Nothing* (New York: New Press, 2004): 37–39. The second text is a good compilation of the critique of the cost-benefit issues we discuss here.

3. David M. Driesen, "Is Cost-Benefit Neutral?" *University of Colorado Law
Review* 77 (2006): 335, 355.

4. U.S. Government Accountability Office, *Rulemaking: OMB's Role in Reviews of Agencies' Draft Rules and the Transparency of Those Reviews,* GAO-03-
929 (Washington, DC: GPO, 2003), http://www.gao.gov/new.items/d03929.pdf.

5. Lisa Schultz Bressman and Michael P. Vandenbergh, "Inside the Administrative State: A Critical Look at the Practice of Presidential Control," *Michigan Law
Review* 105 (2006): 47, 50, 75.

6. Steven Croley, "White House Review of Agency Rulemaking: An Empirical
Investigation," *University of Chicago Law Review* 70 (2003): 821, 877.

7. Frank Ackerman, Lisa Heinzerling, and Rachel Massey, "Applying Cost-
Benefit to Past Decisions: Was Environmental Protection *Ever* a Good Idea?" *Administrative Law Review* 57 (2005): 155–92.

8. For a more detailed analysis of the statutes we cover here, see Sidney A. Shapiro and Robert L. Glicksman, *Risk Regulation at Risk: Restoring a Pragmatic Approach* (Stanford: Stanford University Press, 2003).

9. *U.S. Code* 42 (2006), § 7411(b)(1)(A).

10. *U.S. Code* 21 (2006), §§ 348(c)(3), 379e(b)(5)(B).

11. *U.S. Code* 29 (2006), § 652(8); *Indus. Union Dep't v. Am. Petroleum Inst.*, 448 U.S. 607, 642 (1980).

12. *U.S. Code* 42 (2006), §7409(b)(1). The Supreme Court reiterated that costs may not be considered in an 8-0 opinion authored by Justice Scalia, no fan of regulation. *Whitman v. Am. Trucking Ass'ns, Inc.*, 531 U.S. 457 (2001).

13. *U.S. Code* 29 (2006), §655(b)(5).

14. For a good description of these standards, see Robert V. Percival, Christopher H. Schroeder, Alan S. Miller, and James P. Leape, *Environmental Regulation: Law, Science, and Policy*, 4th ed. (New York: Aspen, 2003), 111–40.

15. Wendy E. Wagner, "The Triumph of Technology-Based Standards," *University of Illinois Law Review*, 2000, 83–113.

16. *Entergy Corp. v. Riverkeeper, Inc.*, 129 S. Ct. 1498 (2009).

17. *U.S. Code* 7 (2006), §§ 136(bb) (definition of adverse effects), 136a(a) (basic regulatory authority).

18. For an explanation of where this type of analysis fits into the larger public policy literature, see Sidney A. Shapiro and Christopher H. Schroeder, "Beyond Cost-Benefit Analysis: A Pragmatic Reorientation," *Harvard Environmental Law Review* 32 (2008): 433–502.

19. See, for example, recommendations made in Winston Harrington, Lisa Heinzerling, and Richard D. Morgenstern, "What We Learned," in *Reforming Regulatory Impact Analysis*, ed. Winston Harrington, Lisa Heinzerling, and Richard D. Morgenstern (Washington, DC: Resources for the Future, 2009), 215–38, http://www.rff.org/RFF/Documents/RFF.RIA.V4.low_res.pdf.

20. Laurence H. Tribe, "Trial by Mathematics: Precision and Ritual in the Legal Process," *Harvard Law Review* 84 (1971): 1329, 1361–62.

21. John F. Morrall III, "A Review of the Record," *Regulation* 10 (November/December 1986): 25, http://www.cato.org/pubs/regulation/regv10n6/v10n6-4.pdf.

22. Lisa Heinzerling, "Regulatory Costs of Mythic Proportions," *Yale Law Journal* 107 (1998): 1981–2070.

23. Tammy O. Tengs, Miriam E. Adams, Joseph S. Pliskin, Dana Gelb Safran, Joanna E. Siegel, Milton C. Weinstein, and John D. Graham, "Five Hundred Live-Saving Interventions and Their Cost-Effectiveness," *Risk Analysis* 15 (1995): 369–90; Tammy O. Tengs and John D. Graham, "The Opportunity Costs of Haphazard Social Investments in Life-Saving," in *Risks, Costs, and Lives Saved: Getting Better Results from Regulation*, ed. Robert W. Hahn (New York: Oxford University Press 1996), 167–82.

24. Lisa Heinzerling, "Five-Hundred Life-Saving Interventions and Their Misuse in the Debate over Regulatory Reform," *Risk: Health, Safety and Environment* 13 (2002): 151, 162.

25. Richard W. Parker, "Grading the Government," *University of Chicago Law Review* 70 (2003): 1345–486.

26. Robert W. Hahn, "Regulatory Reform: What Do the Government's Numbers Tell Us?" in *Risks, Costs, and Lives Saved,* 208–53.

27. Robert W. Crandall, Christopher DeMuth, Robert W. Hahn, Robert E. Litan, Pietro S. Nivola, and Paul R. Portney, *An Agenda for Federal Regulatory Reform* (Washington, DC: AEI Press, 1997), 5, http://aei-brookings.org/admin/authorpdfs/redirect-safely.php?fname=../pdffiles/agenda_for_reg_reform.pdf.

28. Parker, "Grading the Government."

29. National Highway Traffic Safety Administration, "Federal Motor Vehicle Safety Standard; Occupant Crash Protection," *Federal Register* 49 (1984): 28,962, 28,989–90.

30. Thomas O. McGarity and Sidney A. Shapiro, *Workers at Risk: The Failed Promise of the Occupational Safety and Health Administration* (Westport, CT: Praeger, 1993), 271.

31. Nicholas A. Ashford and Charles C. Caldart, *Technology, Law, and the Working Environment,* rev. ed. (Washington, DC: Island Press, 1996), 234–35; Roger G. Noll and James E. Krier, "Some Implications of Cognitive Psychology for Risk Regulation," *Journal of Legal Studies* 19 (1990): 747, 764.

32. Paul S. Carlin and Robert Sandy, "Estimating the Implicit Value of a Young Child's Life," *Southern Economic Journal* 58 (1991): 186–202.

33. Cass R. Sunstein, "The Arithmetic of Arsenic," *Georgetown Law Journal* 90 (2002): 2255, 2258.

34. George Tolley, Donald Kenkel, and Robert Fabian, "State-of-the-Art Health Values," in *Valuing Health for Policy: An Economic Approach,* ed. George Tolley, Donald Kenkel, and Robert Fabian (Chicago: University of Chicago Press, 1994), 323, 340–41; Ian Savage, "An Empirical Investigation into the Effect of Psychological Perceptions on the Willingness-to-Pay to Reduce Risk," *Journal of Risk and Uncertainty* 6 (1993): 75, 88.

35. Ackerman and Heinzerling, *Priceless,* 78–79.

36. *Entergy Corp. v. Riverkeeper, Inc.,* 129 S. Ct. 1498 (2009). For an analysis of the flaws in the EPA cost-benefit analysis, see Douglas A. Kysar, "Fish Tales," in *Reforming Regulatory Impact Analysis,* 190–214.

37. Office of Management and Budget, "Circular A-4: Regulatory Analysis," September 17, 2003, 33–34, http://www.whitehouse.gov/omb/circulars/a004/a-4.pdf.

38. Parker, "Grading the Government," 1374.

39. For a full discussion of the history of these provisions and the EPA's efforts to carry them out, see Rena I. Steinzor, *Mother Earth and Uncle Sam: How Pollution and Hollow Government Hurt Our Kids* (Austin, TX: University of Texas Press, 2008), 103–25; Sidney A. Shapiro and Christopher H. Schroeder, "Beyond Cost-Benefit Analysis: A Pragmatic Reorientation," *Harvard Environmental Law Review* 32 (2008): 433, 484–90. The statutory provisions are *U.S. Code* 42 (2006), § 7412(d), (n).

40. Office of Children's Health Protection, *America's Children and the Environment: Measures of Contaminants, Body Burdens, and Illnesses*, 2d ed. (Washington, DC: EPA, 2003), 59, http://www.epa.gov/envirohealth/children/publications/ace_2003.pdf, citing National Research Council, *Toxicological Effects of Methyl Mercury* (Washington, DC: National Academy Press, 2000): 9, 11.

41. Office of Air Quality Planning and Standards, U.S. EPA, *Regulatory Impact Analysis of the Final Clean Air Mercury Rule*, EPA-452/R-05-003 (Washington, DC: GPO, 2005), http://www.epa.gov/ttn/ecas/regdata/RIAs/mercury_ria_final.pdf.

42. *New Jersey v. EPA*, 517 F.3d 574, 582 (D.C. Cir. 2008).

43. Richard L. Revesz, "Environmental Regulation, Cost-Benefit Analysis, and the Discounting of Human Lives," *Columbia Law Review* 99 (1999): 941–1017.

44. Thomas O. McGarity, "Professor Sunstein's Fuzzy Math," *Georgetown Law Journal* 90 (2002): 2341, 2366.


## Chapter Five

1. Gail Russell Chaddock, "Congress Frets as Its Ratings Plummet," *Christian Science Monitor*, July 8, 2008, 3.

2. For these historical trends, see PollingReport.com, "Congress—Job Rating," http://www.pollingreport.com/CongJob.htm.

3. Chaddock, "Congress Frets," 3.

4. William J. Clinton, "State of the Union Address—January 23, 1996," *Public Papers of the Presidents of the United States: William J. Clinton, 1996*, 1 (Washington, DC: GPO, 1996): 79, 79.

5. Paul C. Light, *A Government Ill-Executed: The Decline of the Federal Service and How to Reverse It* (Cambridge, MA: Harvard University Press, 2008), 33.

6. Thomas E. Mann and Norman J. Ornstein, *The Broken Branch: How Congress Is Failing America and How to Get It Back on Track* (London: Oxford University Press, 2006).

7. One famous incident involved Senators John McCain and Charles Grassley, who erupted in a shouting match that ended in pushing and shoving until they were separated forcibly by colleagues at an informal meeting to discuss the fate of Vietnam prisoners of war. Michael Leahy, "McCain: A Question of Temperament," *Washington Post*, April 20, 2008, A1.

8. Bruce Burkhard, "Year in Review: Congress vs. Environment; Environmental Laws Suffer under GOP-Controlled Congress," *Cable News Network*, December 29, 1995, http://www.cnn.com/EARTH/9512/congress_enviro/. An audio recording of Congressman DeLay's comments is available through the online version of the article. The remarks were widely reported in the press and have been repeated in the media numerous times.

9. Nancy Gibbs and Michael Duffy, "Fall of the House of Newt: An Election Shock Ignites a Republican Revolt: Gingrich Is Only the First Victim in the Growing Fight for the Party's Future," *Time*, November 16, 1998, 38, 46.

10. The Pew Center for People and the Press reported poll results on November 1, 1998, showing that voters placed the Clinton/Lewinsky scandal "at the very bottom of the list" of issues that concerned them, while 35 percent opined that the congressional debate over impeachment was "significant." Pew Center for People and the Press, "Democrats Erase GOP Congressional Lead," November 1, 1998, http://people-press.org/report/76/democrats-erase-gop-congressional-lead.

11. Gibbs and Duffy, "Fall of the House of Newt," 44.

12. Richard Lacayo, Jay Branegan, James Carney, John F. Dickerson, J. F. O. McAllister, and Karen Tumulty, "Washington Burning: For Only the Second Time in History, the House Impeaches the President as Bombs Burst in Air and Partisanship Flares Out of Control," *Time*, December 28, 1998/January 4, 1999, 60, 61.

13. Lacayo, "Washington Burning," 62, 66.

14. David E. Price, "Congressman Reflects on Partisanship's Limits," *UVA Top News Daily*, August 19, 2004, http://www.virginia.edu/topnews/08_19_2004/davidprice.html.

15. Nelson W. Polsby, "The Institutionalization of the U.S. House of Representatives," *American Political Science Review* 62 (1968): 144, 144.

16. Polsby, "The Institutionalization of the U.S. House of Representatives," 145.

17. *Legislative Reorganization Act of 1970*, Public Law 91–510, *U.S. Statutes at Large* 84 (1970): 1140.

18. For an account of the 109th Congress's many problems, see Matt Taibbi, "The Worst Congress Ever: How Our National Legislature Has Become a Stable of Thieves and Perverts—in Five Easy Steps," *Rolling Stone*, November 2, 2006, 46–84.

19. Mann and Ornstein, *Broken Branch*, 170–75.

20. Scott Lilly, "When Congress Acts in the Dark of Night, Everyone Loses," *Roll Call*, December 6, 2004, 10, 13.

21. The campaign is named in honor of Ronald Reagan's popular press secretary, Jim Brady, who was gravely injured in the attempt to assassinate the president in March 1981.

22. Carl Hulse, "Democrats Try to Break Grip of the Senate's Flinty Dr. No," *New York Times,* July 28, 2008, A1. "I am not a go-along, get-along guy if I think it is the wrong way to go," Coburn told Hulse. "I am O.K. taking the consternation of my colleagues. I take my oath seriously."

23. Norman Ornstein, "Our Broken Senate," *American*, March/April 2008, http://www.american.com/archive/2008/march-april-magazine-contents/our-broken-senate.

24. Ornstein, "Our Broken Senate."

25. For an account of Foley's rise and fall, see Gail Sheehy and Judy Bachrach, "Don't Ask . . . Don't E-mail," *Vanity Fair*, January 2007, 100, http://www.vanityfair.com/politics/features/2007/01/foley200701.

26. CNN Poll, October 9, 2008, 12, http://i.a.cnn.net/cnn/2006/images/10/09/rel24a.pdf.

27. Mann and Ornstein, *Broken Branch*, 190–91.

28. Lyndsey Layton, "In Majority, Democrats Run Hill Much As GOP Did," *Washington Post*, February 18, 2007, A4.

29. Norman J. Ornstein and Thomas E. Mann, "When Congress Checks Out," *Foreign Affairs* 85, no. 6 (November/December 2006): 67, 68.

30. Ornstein and Mann, "When Congress Checks Out," 67.

31. Ornstein and Mann, "When Congress Checks Out," 79.

32. The two men led the Renewing Congress Project sponsored jointly by the American Enterprise and Brookings institutes. The project resulted in the publication of three books. See Thomas E. Mann and Norman J. Ornstein, *Renewing Congress: A First Report* (Washington, DC: American Enterprise Institute for Public Policy Research and the Brookings Institute, 1992); Thomas E. Mann and Norman J. Ornstein, *Renewing Congress: A Second Report* (Washington, DC: American Enterprise Institute for Public Policy Research and the Brookings Institute, 1993); Thomas E. Mann and Norman J. Ornstein eds., *Congress, the Press, and the Public* (Washington, DC: American Enterprise Institute for Public Policy Research and the Brookings Institute, 1994).

33. Peter Baker, "Tom Davis Gives Up," *New York Times Magazine*, October 5, 2008, 63, 64.

34. Public Law 96–510, *U.S. Statutes at Large* 94 (1980): 2767 (codified as amended at *U.S. Code* 42 [2000], §§ 9601–9675).

35. Professor Steinzor served as the senior staff person for the only municipal official on the commission, Mayor Susan Thornton of Littlefield, Colorado. For a more extensive account of what transpired, see Rena Steinzor, "The Reauthorization of Superfund: Can the Deal of the Century Be Saved?" *Environmental Law Reporter* 15 (1985): 10016; and Rena I. Steinzor, "The Reauthorization of Superfund: The Public Works Alternative," *Environmental Law Reporter* 25 (1995): 10,078.

36. Senate Subcommittee on Superfund and Environmental Health of the Senate Committee on Environment and Public Works, *Oversight Hearing on the Federal Superfund Program's Activities to Protect Public Health*, 110th Cong., 1st sess., 2007, 5, http://epw.senate.gov/public/index.cfm?FuseAction=Files.View&FileStore_id=2f7cffe9-81dc-4f52-b45d-7fd26f1f2bc6 (statement of Rena Steinzor, Professor, University of Maryland School of Law; Member Scholar and Board Member, Center for Progressive Reform).

37. The term "construction completion" refers to a stage in the cleanup of a site when any necessary physical construction and engineering work is complete, even if final cleanup goals have not been achieved. U.S. EPA, Office of Emergency and Remedial Response, *Close Out Procedures for National Priorities List Sites*, OSWER Directive 9320.2-09A-P (Washington, DC: EPA, 2000), 3-1, http://earth1

.epa.gov/superfund/programs/npl_hrs/closeout/pdf/guidance.pdf. According to the EPA, measuring success by simply looking at the ratio of deleted NPL sites to total sites on the NPL fails to "recognize the substantial construction and reduction of risk to human health and the environment that has occurred at NPL sites not yet eligible for deletion" (EPA, *Close Out Procedures for National Priorities List Sites*, 2000). So, in 1990, to "communicate more clearly to the public the status of cleanup progress" among NPL sites, EPA established the new category of "construction complete" as its main indicator of program success. "National Oil and Hazardous Substances Pollution Contingency Plan," *Federal Register* 55 (March 8, 1990): 8666, 8699 (codified at *Code of Federal Regulations*, title 40, pt. 300 [2008]).

38. Katherine N. Probst and David M. Konisky, *Superfund's Future: What Will It Cost?* (Washington, DC: Resources for the Future, 2001), 2–5, http://www.rff.org/RFF_Press/CustomBookPages/Pages/Superfunds-Future.aspx.

39. Katherine N. Probst, "Superfund at 25: What Remains to Be Done," *Resources*, Fall 2005, 20, 20, http://www.rff.org/News/Features/Documents/RFF-Resources-159-Superfund.pdf. Assuming that the EPA had received $1.3 billion in appropriations from FY 2000 to FY 2009, it would have received a total of $13 billion in funding. As compared with RFF's estimate of the total cost of the program, this leaves a funding gap of between $1.0 billion and $3.4 billion.

40. Rena Steinzor and Margaret Clune, *The Toll of Superfund Neglect: Toxic Waste Dumps and Communities at Risk* (Washington, DC: Center for American Progress and Center for Progressive Reform, 2006), 3, http://images1.american-progress.org/il80web20037/cap/superfund_neglect.pdf.

41. Mann and Ornstein, *Broken Branch*, 226.


**Chapter Six**


1. Richard E. Neustadt, *Presidential Power: The Politics of Leadership* (New York: John Wiley and Sons, 1960), 9 (emphasis in original).

2. David E. Lewis, *The Politics of Presidential Appointments: Political Control and Bureaucratic Performance* (Princeton: Princeton University Press, 2008), 89.

3. Jim Hoagland, "Dissing Government," *Washington Post*, November 30, 2003, B7.

4. Larry Hubbell, "Ronald Reagan as Presidential Symbol Maker: The Federal Bureaucrat as Loafer, Incompetent Buffoon, Good Ole Boy, and Tyrant," *American Review of Public Administration* 21, no. 3 (1991): 237, 244.

5. Hubbell, "Ronald Reagan as Presidential Symbol Maker," 246.

6. William J. Clinton, "Remarks at the Michigan State University Commencement Ceremony in East Lansing, Michigan—May 5, 1995," *Public Papers of the Presidents of the United States: William J. Clinton, 1995*, 1 (Washington, DC: GPO, 1995): 641, 645.

7. Thad E. Hall, "Live Bureaucrats and Dead Public Servants: How People in Government Are Discussed on the Floor of the House," *Public Administration Review* 62, no. 2 (2002): 242, 248.

8. Ronald Reagan, "Remarks at a White House Luncheon for the Chairman and Executive Committee of the Private Sector Survey on Cost Control in the Federal Government—March 10, 1982," *Public Papers of the Presidents of the United States: Ronald Reagan, 1982*, 1 (Washington, DC: GPO, 1982): 275.

9. William J. Clinton, "Remarks Announcing the National Performance Review—March 3, 1993," *Public Papers of the Presidents of the United States: William J. Clinton, 1993*, 1 (Washington, DC: GPO, 1993): 233.

10. Jo Becker and Barton Gellman, "Leaving No Tracks," *Washington Post*, June 27, 2007, A1.

11. Becker and Gellman, "Leaving No Tracks."

12. Hall, "Live Bureaucrats," 242, 246.

13. R. Sam Garrett, James A. Thurber, A. Lee Fritschler, and David H. Rosenbloom, "Assessing the Impact of Bureaucracy Bashing by Electoral Campaigns," *Public Administration Review* 66, no. 2 (2006): 228, 232.

14. Garrett et al., "Assessing the Impact of Bureaucracy Bashing by Electoral Campaigns," 234.

15. See, e.g., *Consumer Product Safety Act, U.S. Code* 15 (2006), §§ 2051–2084; *Clean Air Act, U.S. Code* 42 (2000), §§ 7401–7671; *Food, Drug, and Cosmetic Act, U.S. Code* 21 (2006), §§ 301–399; *Occupational Safety and Health Act, U.S. Code* 29 (2000), §§ 651–678; and the *Highway Safety Act, U.S. Code* 23 (2006), §§ 401–412.

16. Lisa Schultz Bressman and Michael P. Vandenbergh, "Inside the Administrative State: A Critical Look at the Practice of Presidential Control," *Michigan Law Review* 105 (2006): 47–99.

17. "The offices identified by EPA respondents were Chief of Staff, Legislative Affairs, Public Liaison, Intergovernmental Liaison, Press Secretary (including Communications), White House Counsel, Domestic Policy Counsel, National Economic Council, Political Affairs, Office of the Vice President (including the Council on Competitiveness in the Bush I administration), Office of Policy Development, Office of Management and Budget (other than OIRA), Council of Economic Advisors, Council on Environmental Quality, Office of the United States Trade Representative, Office of Science and Technology Policy, and the National Security Council." Bressman and Vandenbergh, *Inside the Administrative State*, 64, n.107.

18. Bressman and Vandenbergh, *Inside the Administrative State*, 70.

19. David Michaels, *Doubt Is Their Product: How Industry's Assault on Science Threatens Your Health* (Oxford: Oxford University Press, 2008); Thomas O. McGarity and Wendy E. Wagner, *Bending Science: How Special Interests Corrupt Public Health Research* (Cambridge, MA: Harvard University Press, 2008); Seth Shulman, *Undermining Science: Suppression and Distortion in the Bush Administration* (Berkeley: University of California Press, 2006); Wendy Wagner and Rena

Steinzor, eds., *Rescuing Science from Politics: Regulation and the Distortion of Scientific Research* (New York: Cambridge University Press, 2006); Chris Mooney, *The Republican War on Science* (Cambridge, MA: Basic Books, 2005); Linda Greer and Rena Steinzor, "Bad Science," *Environmental Forum* 19, no. 1 (January/February 2002): 28.

20. Union of Concerned Scientists, *Voices of Scientists at the EPA: Human Health and the Environment Depend on Independent Science* (Washington, DC: UCS, 2008), http://www.ucsusa.org/assets/documents/scientific_integrity/epa-survey-brochure.pdf.

21. Union of Concerned Scientists, *Voices of Scientists at FDA: Protecting Public Health Depends on Independent Science* (Washington, DC: UCS, 2008), http://www.ucsusa.org/assets/documents/scientific_integrity/fda-survey-brochure.pdf.

22. Union of Concerned Scientists, *Call to Action: Scientific Freedom and the Public Good* (2008), http://www.ucsusa.org/scientific_integrity/abuses_of_science/scientific-freedom-and-the.html.

23. Susan Wood was the Assistant FDA Commissioner for Women's Health. She resigned in protest after the initial Plan B decision. Michael Specter, "Political Science: The Bush Administration's War on the Laboratory," *New Yorker*, March 13, 2006, 58, 60.

24. *U.S. Code* 21 (2006), § 353(b)(3).

25. Gardiner Harris, "U.S. Rules Morning-After Pill Can't Be Sold Over the Counter," *New York Times*, May 7, 2004, A1.

26. Alastair J. J. Wood, Jeffrey M. Drazen, and Michael F. Greene, "Perspective: A Sad Day for Science at the FDA," *New England Journal of Medicine* 353 (2005): 1197, 1198.

27. U.S. Government Accountability Office, *Food and Drug Administration: Decision Process to Deny Initial Application for Over-the-Counter Marketing of the Emergency Contraceptive Drug Plan B Was Unusual*, GAO-06-109 (Washington, DC: GPO, November 2005), 5, http://www.gao.gov/new.items/d06109.pdf.

28. *Tummino v. Torti*, 603 F. Supp. 2d 519 (E.D.N.Y. 2009).

29. Specter, "The Bush Administration's War on the Laboratory," 61.

30. National Research Council, *Toxicological Effects of Methylmercury* (Washington, DC: National Academy Press, 2000), 9, http://books.nap.edu/openbook/0309071402/html/index.html.

31. Bill Kovacs, Vice President of Environment, Technology and Regulatory Affairs of U.S. Chamber of Commerce, U.S. Chamber of Commerce Radio Actuality, "Mercury Emissions," December 3, 2003, http://www.uschamber.com/press/actualities/2004/031203_mercury_emissions.htm.

32. *New Jersey v. EPA*, 517 F.3d 574, 582 (D.C. Cir. 2008).

33. *U.S. Code* 42 (2000), § 7412.

34. *U.S. Code* 42 (2000), § 7412(n)(1)(A); U.S. EPA, *Study of Hazardous Air Pollutant Emissions from Electric Utility Steam Generating Units—Final Report*

*to Congress*, EPA-453/R-98-004a (1998), http://www.epa.gov/ttn/caaa/t3/reports/eurtc1.pdf.

35. *U.S. Code* 42 (2000), § 7412(n)(1)(B); U.S. EPA, *Mercury Study Report to Congress*, EPA-452/R-97-003, 8 vols. (1997), http://www.epa.gov/hg/report.htm.

36. *U.S. Code* 42 (2000), § 7412(n)(1)(A).

37. U.S. EPA, "Regulatory Finding on the Emissions of Hazardous Air Pollutants from Electric Utility Steam Generating Units," *Federal Register* 65 (December 20, 2000): 79,825, 79,827.

38. Tom Hamburger and Alan C. Miller, "Mercury Emissions Rule Geared to Benefit Industry, Staffers Say; Buffeted by Complaints, EPA Administrator Michael Leavitt Calls for Additional Analysis," *Los Angeles Times*, March 16, 2004, A1.

39. U.S. EPA, "Standards of Performance for New and Existing Stationary Sources: Electric Utility Steam Generating Units," *Federal Register* 70 (May 18, 2005): 28,606—28,700 (to be codified at *Code of Federal Regulations* title 40, parts 60, 72, and 75); U.S. EPA, "Revision of December 2000 Regulatory Finding on the Emissions of Hazardous Air Pollutants from Electric Utility Steam Generating Units and the Removal of Coal- and Oil-Fired Electric Utility Steam Generating Units from the Section 112(c) List," *Federal Register* 70 (March 29, 2005): 15,994 (to be codified at *Code of Federal Regulations* title 40, pt. 63).

40. Kathryn R. Mahaffey, "Mercury Exposure: Medical and Public Health Issues," *Transactions of the American Clinical and Climatological Association* 116 (2005): 127, 146, citing U.S. Department of Health and Human Services, Centers for Disease Control, *Third National Report on Human Exposure to Environmental Chemicals* (July 2005), 45–51, http://www.cdc.gov/ExposureReport/pdf/thirdreport.pdf.

41. Leonardo Trasande, Philip Landrigan, and Clyde Schechter, "Public Health and Economic Consequences of Methyl Mercury Toxicity to the Developing Brain," *Environmental Health Perspectives* 113 (2005): 590, 593, http://www.ehponline.org/members/2005/7743/7743.pdf.

42. See, e.g., Executive Order No. 12,291, *Code of Federal Regulations*, title 3, § 127 (1982), reprinted in *U.S. Code* 5 (1988), § 601 (mandating analysis of the costs and benefits of regulations); Executive Order No. 12,866, *Federal Register* 58 (1993): 51,735 (Clinton version of the cost-benefit directive); Executive Order No. 13,422, *Federal Register* 72 (2007): 2763 (Bush II expansion of order to cover agency guidance documents).

43. *U.S. Code* 5 (2006), §§ 601 et seq.

44. *U.S. Code* 2 (2006), §§ 1501 et seq.

45. *U.S. Code* 44 (2000), §§ 3501 et seq.

46. *U.S. Code* 5 (2006), §§ 551 et seq.

47. Mark Seidenfeld, "A Table of Requirements for Federal Administrative Rulemaking," *Florida State University Law Review* 27 (2000): 533.

48. Peter Barton Hutt, "The State of Science at the Food and Drug Administration," *Administrative Law Review* 60 (2008): 431, 439–40 (footnotes omitted).

49. U.S. Government Accountability Office, *Clean Air Act: EPA Has Completed Most of the Actions Required by the 1990 Amendments, but Many Were Completed Late*, GAO-05-613 (Washington, DC: GPO, 2005), 3–4, http://www.gao.gov/new.items/d05613.pdf.

50. John Yoo, *The Powers of War and Peace: The Constitution and Foreign Affairs after 9/11* (Chicago: University of Chicago Press, 2005).

51. Elena Kagan, "Presidential Administration," *Harvard Law Review* 114 (2001): 2246; Steven G. Calabresi, "The Vesting Clauses as Power Grants," *Northwestern University Law Review* 88 (1994): 1377; Steven G. Calabresi and Saikrishna B. Prakash, "The President's Power to Execute the Laws," *Yale Law Journal* 104 (1994): 541; Steven G. Calabresi and Kevin H. Rhodes, "The Structural Constitution: Unitary Executive, Plural Judiciary," *Harvard Law Review* 105 (1992): 1153.

52. Peter L. Strauss, "Overseer, or the 'Decider'? The President in Administrative Law," *George Washington Law Review* 75 (2007): 696; Robert V. Percival, "Presidential Management of the Administrative State: The Not-So-Unitary Executive," *Duke Law Journal* 51 (2001): 963.

53. Becker and Gellman, "Leaving No Tracks."

## Chapter Seven

1. James Madison, "Federalist No. 10," *The Federalist Papers*, ed. Clinton Rossiter (New York: New American Library, 1961), 77.

2. 163 U.S. 537 (1896).

3. 347 U.S. 483 (1954).

4. *U.S. Code* 33 (2006), § 1365.

5. 448 U.S. 607 (1980).

6. 448 U.S. 690.

7. *AFL-CIO v. OSHA*, 965 F.2d 962 (11th Cir. 1992).

8. *Indus. Union Dep't v. Am. Petroleum Inst.*, 448 U.S. 607, 688 (1980).

9. *U.S. Code* 5 (2006), §553(b).

10. U.S. Constitution, art. 3, sec. 2.

11. *U.S. Code* 5 (2006), § 706(2)(A).

12. Sidney A. Shapiro and Richard E. Levy, "Judicial Incentives and Indeterminacy in Substantive Review of Agency Decisions," *Duke Law Journal* 44 (1995): 1051.

13. Karl N. Llewellyn, *The Common Law Tradition: Deciding Appeals* (Boston, MA: Little, Brown and Company, 1960), 214–15.

14. *U.S. Code* 5 (2006), § 702.

15. 504 U.S. 555, 560–61 (1992) (citing Supreme Court precedent).

16. Richard J. Pierce, Jr., Sidney A. Shapiro, and Paul R. Verkuil, *Administrative Law and Process*, 5th ed. (New York: Foundation Press, 2009), 169.

17. 513 F.3d 234 (D.C. Cir. 2008).

18. Antonin Scalia, "The Doctrine of Standing as an Essential Element of the Separation of Powers," *Suffolk University Law Review* 17 (1983): 881.

19. *Public Citizen*, 513 F.3d at 237 (quoting *Pub. Citizen, Inc. v. Nat'l Highway Traffic Safety Admin.*, 489 F.3d 1279, 1295 [D.C. Cir. 2007]).

20. See, e.g., *Massachusetts v. EPA*, 549 U.S. 497 (2007); *Friends of the Earth, Inc. v. Laidlaw Envtl. Servs., Inc.*, 528 U.S. 167 (2000); *Fed. Election Comm'n v. Akins*, 524 U.S. 11 (1998).

21. 467 U.S. 837, 842–43 (1984).

22. Miles and Sunstein, "Do Judges Make Regulatory Policy?" 825–26.

23. 489 F.3d 1364 (D.C. Cir. 2007).

24. *U.S. Code* 42 (2006), §§ 7412(c)(9)(B)(i), (d)(3).

25. Alan C. Miller and Tom Hamburger, "EPA Relied on Industry for Plywood Plant Pollution Rule," *Los Angeles Times*, May 21, 2004, A1.

26. *Natural Res. Def. Council v. EPA*, 489 F.3d at 1373.

27. Henry A. Waxman, Chairman, House Committee on Oversight and Government Reform, to Stephen L. Johnson, Administrator, U.S. Environmental Protection Agency, October 21, 2008, http://oversight.house.gov/documents/20081021110039.pdf.

28. *U.S. Code* 5 (2006), § 706(2)(A).

29. 401 U.S. 402, 416 (1971).

30. 463 U.S. 29, 43 (1983) (quoting *Burlington Truck Lines, Inc. v. United States*, 371 U.S. 156, 168 [1962]).

31. For a discussion of this era and the motivation of the judges, see Harold Leventhal, "Environmental Decisionmaking and the Role of the Courts," *University of Pennsylvania Law Review* 122 (1974): 509.

32. Douglas M. Costle, "Brave New Chemical: The Future Regulatory History of Phlogiston," *Administrative Law Review* 33 (1981): 195.

33. William H. Rodgers, Jr., "A Hard Look at *Vermont Yankee*: Environmental Law under Close Scrutiny," *Georgetown Law Journal* 67 (1979): 699; Mark Seidenfeld, "Demystifying Deossification: Rethinking Recent Proposals to Modify Judicial Review of Notice and Comment Rulemaking," *Texas Law Review* 75 (1997): 483.

34. Miles and Sunstein, "The Real World of Arbitrariness Review," 768.

**Chapter Eight**

1. See, e.g., U.S. EPA, Office of Research and Development and the Office of Environmental Information, *Draft Report on the Environment: Technical Document*, EPA 600–R–03–050 (Washington, DC: EPA, 2003), http://nepis.epa.gov/Exe/ZyPURL.cgi?Dockey=30005E2Z.txt; U.S. EPA, *EPA's Report on the Environment*,

EPA/600/R–07/045F (Washington, DC: EPA, 2008), http://nepis.epa.gov/Exe/ZyPURL.cgi?Dockey=P1002S1J.txt.

2. Steven F. Hayward, *Index of Leading Environmental Indicators* (San Francisco: Pacific Research Institute and American Enterprise Institute for Public Policy Research, 2008), http://liberty.pacificresearch.org/docLib/20080401_08_Enviro_Index.pdf. Hayward stars in a movie debunking the work of former Vice President Al Gore. See Steven F. Hayward, *An Inconvenient Truth . . . or Convenient Fiction?* (Great Falls, VA: Horizons Television, Inc., 2007), http://www.aconvenientfiction.com.

3. Public Law 103–62, *U.S. Statutes at Large* 107 (1993): 285, codified in scattered sections of *U.S. Code* titles 5 and 31; William J. Clinton, "Remarks on Signing the Government Performance and Results Act of 1993 and an Exchange with Reporters—August 3, 1993," *Public Papers of the Presidents of the United States: William J. Clinton,* 1993, 2 (Washington, DC: GPO, 1994): 1310–12.

4. *Federal Food, Drug, and Cosmetic Act,* Public Law 75–717, *U.S. Statutes at Large* 52 (1938): 1040, codified as amended at *U.S. Code* 21 (2006), § 301 et seq.

5. *Comprehensive Environmental Response, Compensation, and Liability Act of 1980,* Public Law 96–510, *U.S. Statutes at Large* 94 (1980): 2767, codified as amended at *U.S. Code* 42 (2006), § 9601 et seq.

6. *Emergency Planning and Community Right-to-Know Act of 1986,* Public Law 99–499, *U.S. Statutes at Large* 100 (1986): 1728, codified as amended at *U.S. Code* 42 (2006), § 11001 et seq.

7. Linda-Jo Schierow, Congressional Research Service, *Chemical Facility Security,* RL31530 (Washington, DC: CRS, 2006), http://www.fas.org/sgp/crs/homesec/RL31530.pdf.

8. *Consumer Product Safety Improvement Act of 2008,* Public Law 110–314, §225, *U.S. Statutes at Large* 122 (2008): 3016, 3070.

9. John W. Kingdon, *Agendas, Alternatives, and Public Policies,* 2d ed. (New York: Addison-Wesley Educational Publishers, Inc., 1995).

10. Kingdon, *Agendas, Alternatives, and Public Policies,* 87.

11. Kingdon, *Agendas, Alternatives, and Public Policies,* 90, 102.

12. Kingdon, *Agendas, Alternatives, and Public Policies,* 87.

13. Kingdon, *Agendas, Alternatives, and Public Policies,* 98–100.

14. Government Accountability Office, *Environmental Indicators: Better Coordination Is Needed to Develop Environmental Indicator Sets that Inform Decisions,* GAO–05–52 (Washington, DC: GPO, 2004), 5, 8, http://www.gao.gov/new.items/d0552.pdf.

15. Howard R. Ernst, *Chesapeake Bay Blues: Science, Politics, and the Struggle to Save the Bay* (Lanham, MD: Rowman and Littlefield Publishers, 2003); Tom Horton, *Turning the Tide: Saving the Chesapeake Bay,* rev. ed. (Washington, DC: Island Press, 2003).

16. For an explanation of some of the changes that might be necessary, see William L. Andreen and Shana Campbell Jones, "The Clean Water Act: A Blue-

print for Reform" (White Paper 802, Center for Progressive Reform, Edgewater, MD, 2008), http://www.progressivereform.org/articles/CW_Blueprint_802.pdf.

17. Government Accountability Office, *Chesapeake Bay Program: Improved Strategies Are Needed to Better Assess, Report, and Manage Restoration Progress,* GAO–06–96 (Washington, DC: GPO, 2005), 17, 35, http://www.gao.gov/new.items/d0696.pdf.

18. Chesapeake Bay Program, *A Report to the Citizens of the Bay Region: Chesapeake Bay Health and Restoration Assessment* (Washington, DC: EPA, 2007), 6, http://www.chesapeakebay.net/content/publications/cbp_26038.pdf.

19. *Government Performance and Results Act of 1993,* Public Law 103–62, § 2, *U.S. Statutes at Large* 107 (1983): 285, 285.

20. *U.S. Code* 5 (2006), § 306.

21. *U.S. Code* 31 (2006), §§ 1115–1116.

22. Public Law 102–571, *U.S. Statutes at Large* 106 (1992): 4491 (codified as amended in scattered sections of *U.S. Code* title 21). Congress extended PDUFA in the *Food and Drug Administration Modernization Act of 1997,* Public Law 105–115, § 103, *U.S. Statutes at Large* 111 (1997): 2296, 2299–304 (codified as amended at *U.S. Code* 21 [2006], § 379h), and again in the *Prescription Drug User Fee Amendments of 2002, Public Health Security and Bioterrorism Preparedness and Response Act of 2002,* Public Law 107–188, §§ 501–509, 521–523, 531–532, *U.S. Statutes at Large* 116 (2002): 594, 687–97 (codified as amended in scattered sections of *U.S. Code* titles 21, 42, and 47).

23. U.S. General Accounting Office, *Food and Drug Administration: Effect of User Fees on Drug Approval Times, Withdrawals, and Other Agency Activities,* GAO–02–958 (Washington, DC: GPO, 2002), 17–18, http://www.gao.gov/new.items/d02958.pdf.

24. U.S. FDA, *Strategic Action Plan: Protecting and Advancing America's Health* (Washington, DC: FDA, 2003), http://www.fda.gov/oc/mcclellan/FDAStrategic-Plan.pdf.

25. U.S. FDA, *Strategic Action Plan,* 12.

26. U.S. EPA, 2006–2011 *EPA Strategic Plan: Charting Our Course* (Washington, DC: EPA, 2006), http://www.epa.gov/ocfo/plan/2006/entire_report.pdf.

27. U.S. EPA, *Performance and Accountability Report, Fiscal Year 2007: Environmental and Financial Progress,* EPA-190-R-07-001 (Washington, DC: EPA, 2007), http://www.epa.gov/ocfo/par/2007par/par07report.pdf.

28. U.S. EPA, 2006–2011 *Strategic Plan,* 67.

29. U.S. EPA, 2006–2011 *Strategic Plan,* 67. A "removal action" is a short-term, relatively inexpensive cleanup. See *U.S. Code* 42 (2006), § 9601(23) ("The term includes . . . security fencing or other measures to limit access, provision of alternative water supplies, temporary evacuation . . . and any emergency assistance which may be provided . . . .").

30. *Merriam-Webster's Collegiate Dictionary,* 11th ed., s.v. "Metric."

31. *Merriam-Webster's Collegiate Dictionary*, s.v. "Standard."

32. See *U.S. Code* 21 (2006), § 355 (requiring the FDA to approve new drugs); §§ 351–352 (providing authority for the FDA to monitor adulterated and misbranded drugs and devices).

33. See *U.S. Code* 42 (2000), § 7408 (requiring the EPA to publish a list of air pollutants); § 7409 (requiring the EPA to establish primary and secondary ambient air quality standards).

34. U.S. Senate Committee on Governmental Affairs, *Report to Provide for the Establishment, Testing, and Evaluation of Strategic Planning and Performance Measurement in the Federal Government, and for Other Purposes: Additional Views of Senator Pryor*, 103d Cong., 1st sess., 1993, S. Rep. 103-58, http://www.whitehouse.gov/omb/mgmt-gpra/gprptm.html#h44.

35. U.S. EPA, *Unfinished Business: A Comparative Assessment of Environmental Problems*, EPA-230-2-87-025A (Washington, DC: EPA, 1987), http://nepis.epa.gov/Exe/ZyPURL.cgi?Dockey=2000BZOP.txt.

36. Science Advisory Board, U.S. EPA, *Reducing Risk: Setting Priorities and Strategies for Environmental Protection*, SAB-EC-90-021 (Washington, DC: EPA, 1990), http://nepis.epa.gov/Exe/ZyPURL.cgi?Dockey=2000PNG1.txt.

37. EPA, Office of Water, *National Water Quality Inventory: Report to Congress: 2002 Reporting Cycle*, EPA-841-R-07-001 (Washington, DC: EPA, 2007), http://www.epa.gov/305b/2002report/report2002305b.pdf. The inventory reports are required by § 305(b) of the Clean Water Act, which is codified at *U.S. Code* 33 (2006), § 1315.

38. General Accounting Office, *Water Quality: Inconsistent State Approaches Complicate Nation's Efforts to Identify Its Most Polluted Waters*, GAO–02–186 (Washington, DC: GPO, 2002), 3, http://www.gao.gov/new.items/d02186.pdf.

39. Senator Roth, lead sponsor of the legislation, said in his floor statement, "The Federal Government today is primarily process-oriented. Its focus is on following detailed procedural rules within rigidly structured programs. . . . [Under GPRA, agencies will] publish annual performance reports showing the actual outcomes." *Congressional Record* 139 (July 30, 1993): S17,973.

40. James Q. Wilson, *Bureaucracy: What Government Agencies Do and Why They Do It* (New York: Basic Books, 1989), 373–74.

41. Clinton, "Remarks on Signing," 1310–11.

42. U.S. General Accounting Office, *Results-Oriented Government: GPRA Has Established a Solid Foundation for Achieving Greater Results*, GAO–04–594T (Washington, DC: GPO, 2004), 9, http://www.gao.gov/new.items/d04594t.pdf ; U.S. General Accounting Office, *Managing for Results: Agencies' Annual Performance Plans Can Help Address Strategic Planning Challenges*, GAO/GGD–98–44 (Washington, DC: GPO, 1998), 7, http://www.gao.gov/archive/1998/gg98044.pdf; U.S. General Accounting Office, *Managing for Results: Regulatory Agencies Identified Significant Barriers to Focusing on Results*, GAO/GGD–97–83 (Washington, DC:

GPO, 1997), 1, http://www.gao.gov/archive/1997/gg97083.pdf ; U.S. General Accounting Office, *Managing for Results: Analytic Challenges in Measuring Performance*, GAO/HEHS/GGD-97-138 (Washington, DC: GPO, 1997), 1, http://www.gao.gov/archive/1997/h297138.pdf ; U.S. General Accounting Office, *Performance Budgeting: Past Initiatives Offer Insights for GPRA Implementation*, GAO/AIMD-97-46 (Washington, DC: GPO, 1997), 2, http://www.gao.gov/archive/1997/ai97046.pdf; U.S. General Accounting Office, *GPRA: Managerial Accountability and Flexibility Pilot Did Not Work As Intended*, GAO/GGD-97-36 (Washington, DC: GPO, 1997), 3, http://www.gao.gov/archive/1997/gg97036.pdf ; U.S. General Accounting Office, *Executive Guide: Effectively Implementing the Government Performance and Results Act*, GAO/GGD-96-118 (Washington, DC: GPO, 1996), 1, http://www.gao.gov/archive/1996/gg96118.pdf.

43. For an explanation of the term "regulatory underkill," and instances in which it occurred, see William W. Buzbee, Robert L. Glicksman, Sidney A. Shapiro, and Karen Sokol, *Regulatory Underkill: The Bush Administration's Insidious Dismantling of Health and Environmental Protections* (White Paper 503, Center for Progressive Regulation, Washington, DC, 2005), http://www.progressivereform.org/articles/Underkill_503.pdf.

## Chapter Nine

1. Francis E. Rourke, "American Bureaucracy in a Changing Political Setting," *Journal of Public Administration, Research, and Theory* 1 (1991): 111. Professor Rourke retired from Johns Hopkins University in 1993 and died in 2005.

2. Michael Sanera, "Implementing the Mandate," in *Mandate for Leadership II: Continuing the Conservative Revolution*, ed. Stuart M. Butler, Michael Sanera, and W. Bruce Weinrod (Washington, DC: Heritage Foundation, 1984), 457, 514–15, quoted in James P. Pfiffner, "Political Appointees and Career Executives: The Democracy-Bureaucracy Nexus in the Third Century," *Public Administration Review* 47 (1987): 57, 59.

3. Paul A. Volcker, National Commission on the Public Service, *Urgent Business for America: Revitalizing the Federal Government for the 21st Century* (Washington, DC: Brookings Institution, 2003), http://www.brookings.edu/~/media/Files/rc/reports/2003/01governance/01governance.pdf.

4. David E. Lewis, *The Politics of Presidential Appointments: Political Control and Bureaucratic Performance* (Princeton, NJ: Princeton University Press, 2008), 12; B. Guy Peters, "Searching for a Role: The Civil Service in American Democracy," *International Political Science Review* 14 (1993): 373, 373–74; U.S. Constitution, art. 2, sec. 2, cl. 2.

5. *Civil Service (Pendleton) Act*, Chapter 27, *U.S. Statutes at Large* 22 (1883): 403.

6. *Act to Prevent Pernicious Political Activities (Hatch Act)*, Chapter 410, sec. 9(a), *U.S. Statutes at Large* 53 (1939): 1147, 1148, codified as amended at *U.S. Code* 5 (2006), § 7323.

7. Francis E. Rourke, "Responsiveness and Neutral Competence in American Bureaucracy," *Public Administration Review* 52 (1992): 539, 541.

8. Hugh Heclo, "The In-and-Outer System: A Critical Assessment," *Political Science Quarterly* 103 (1988): 37, 39.

9. *U.S. Code* 15 (2006), § 2058.

10. *Code of Federal Regulations* title 16, §. 1500.18 (2009).

11. *Code of Federal Regulations* title 16, §. 1500.18 (2009).

12. "China's Toxic Toymaker," *Economist*, August 18, 2007, 58.

13. Kenneth A. Bamberger and Andrew T. Guzman, "Keeping Imports Safe: A Proposal for Discriminatory Regulation of International Trade," *California Law Review* 96 (2008): 1405.

14. The explanation of beryllium's regulatory history and toxic characteristics contained in this section relies upon an excellent book by Professor David Michaels, an epidemiologist who served as the Department of Energy's Assistant Secretary for Environment, Safety and Health from 1998 through January 2001. David Michaels, *Doubt Is Their Product: How Industry's Assault on Science Threatens Your Health* (New York: Oxford University Press, 2008), 124–41.

15. The information on the internal treatment of the beryllium guidance within OSHA is drawn from R. Jeffrey Smith, "Under Bush, OSHA Mired in Inaction," *Washington Post*, December 29, 2008, A1.

16. U.S. Department of Labor, OSHA, "Preventing Adverse Health Effects from Exposure to Beryllium in Dental Laboratories," Hazard Information Bulletin HIB 02-04-19, May 14, 2002, http://www.osha.gov/dts/hib/hib_data/hib020419.html.

17. *U.S. Code* 29 (2006), §666(b), (k) (emphasis added).

18. *U.S. Code* 29 (2006), § 666(a), (e).

19. David Barstow and Lowell Bergman, "With Little Fanfare, a New Effort to Prosecute Employers that Flout Safety Laws," *New York Times*, May 2, 2005, A17. The story reported that OSHA and the EPA had set up a new, integrated task force to prosecute safety and environmental violations and high-priority targets. See also U.S. Government Accountability Office, *Workplace Safety and Health: OSHA Can Strengthen Enforcement through Improved Program Management*, GAO-03-45 (Washington, DC: GPO, 2002), 4–7, http://www.gao.gov/new.items/d0345.pdf.

20. *U.S. Code* 42 (2006), §7408.

21. *U.S. Code* 42 (2006), §7409.

22. *U.S. Code* 42 (2006), §7412(d)(4).

23. *Whitman v. Am. Trucking Ass'ns, Inc.*, 531 U.S. 457 (2001).

24. For a compilation of the key documents telling this story, see a docket compiled by the Democratic staff of the House Committee on Oversight and Government Reform. "White House Overruled EPA Administrator on Ozone Regulation" (May 20, 2008), http://oversight.house.gov/story.asp?id=1958.

25. *U.S. Code* 42 (2006), § 7409(d)(2)(A).

26. House Committee on Oversight and Government Reform, *Hearing on EPA's New Ozone Standards*, 110th Cong., 2d sess., 2008, 4, http://oversight.house .gov/documents/20080520141503.pdf (written testimony of Rogene F. Henderson; emphasis omitted).

27. Stephen Johnson, "Transcript of Press Conference Call Regarding National Ozone Standards—Final Rule Announcement," Washington, DC, March 12, 2008, http://yosemite.epa.gov/opa/admpress.nsf/dff15a5d01abdfb1852573590040b7f7/ cfbccfab3e93282f8525740a0073a9ba!OpenDocument.

28. Johnson, "Transcript of Press Conference Call" (emphasis added).

29. National Commission on the Public Service, *Urgent Business*, iii.

30. National Commission on the Public Service, *Urgent Business*, 1.

31. National Commission on the Public Service, *Urgent Business*, 2.

32. Partnership for Public Service, "Issue Brief: Brain Drain 2008," May 5, 2008, http://www.ourpublicservice.org/OPS/publications/viewcontentdetails.php?id=126.

33. National Commission on the Public Service, *Urgent Business*, 8.

34. National Commission on the Public Service, *Urgent Business*, 9.

35. U.S. Government Accountability Office, *Human Capital: Trends in Executive and Judicial Pay Suggest a Reexamination of the Total Compensation Package*, GAO–06–1116T (Washington, DC: GPO, 2006), http://www.gao.gov/new.items/ d061116t.pdf.

36. Partnership for Public Service, *Roadmap to Reform: A Management Framework for the Next Administration*, (Washington, DC: Partnership for Public Service, 2008), 5, http://www.ourpublicservice.org/OPS/publications/viewcontentdetails .php?id=129.

37. Partnership for Public Service, *Roadmap to Reform*.

38. Paul C. Light, *Thickening Government: Federal Hierarchy and the Diffusion of Accountability* (Washington, DC: Brookings Institution, 1995).

39. Light, *Thickening Government*, 62–63.

40. The messages are collected at the House Committee on Oversight and Government Reform's Web site. See "White House Overruled EPA Administrator on Ozone Regulation," May 20, 2008, http://oversight.house.gov/story.asp?ID=1958.

41. Barack Obama, "Closing Argument Speech, Transcript as Delivered at the Canton Memorial Civic Center, Canton, Ohio," *Chicago Sun-Times*, October 27, 2008, http://blogs.suntimes.com/sweet/2008/10/obama_closing_argument_speech _1.html.

42. Barack Obama, "Remarks from Campaign Trail at Henderson, Nevada," *CNN Transcripts*, November 1, 2008, http://transcripts.cnn.com/TRANSCRIPTS/ 0811/01/cnr.02.html.

43. National Commission on Public Service, *Urgent Business*, 19.

44. National Commission on Public Service, *Urgent Business*, 20.

45. See Letter from Jeffrey Rosen, White House General Counsel, to Representative Henry Waxman, Chairman of the House Oversight and Government Reform

Committee, June 18, 2008, http://oversight.house.gov/documents/20080620114746
.pdf.

46. *U.S. Code* 5 (2006), § 552(b)(5).

47. H.R. Rep. No. 89-1497 (1966), reprinted in 1966 U.S.C.C.A.N. 2418, 2427–28.

48. *United States v. Nixon*, 418 U.S. 683, 708 (1974), discusses executive privilege
in the context of communications with the president.

49. *Nat'l Wildlife Fed'n v. United States Forest Serv.*, 861 F.2d 1114, 1116–17 (9th
Cir. 1988); *Petroleum Info. Corp. v. United States Dep't of the Interior*, 976 F.2d 1429,
1435 (D.C. Cir. 1992).

50. National Commission on Public Service, *Urgent Business*, 25.

51. National Commission on Public Service, *Urgent Business*, 30–31.

52. National Commission on Public Service, *Urgent Business*, 27.

53. National Commission on Public Service, *Urgent Business*, 20.


**Chapter Ten**


1. John W. Kingdon, *Agendas, Alternatives, and Public Policies*, 2d ed. (New
York: Addison-Wesley Educational Publishers, Inc., 1995).

2. Public Law 103–62, *U.S. Statutes at Large* 107 (1993): 285, codified in scattered
sections of *U.S. Code* titles 5 and 31.

# Index